Deconstructing Images of "The Turkish Woman"

Deconstructing Images of "The Turkish Woman"

edited by
Zehra F. Arat

MACMILLAN

First published 1998 by
MACMILLAN PRESS LTD
Houndmills, Basingstoke, Hampshire RG21 6XS
and London
Companies and representatives
throughout the world

ISBN 0–333–73112–3

A catalogue record for this book is available
from the British Library.

10   9   8   7   6   5   4   3   2   1
07 06 05 04 03 02 01 00 99 98

Printed in the United States of America by
Haddon Craftsmen
Bloomsburg, PA

Contents

List of Figures and Tables

FIGURES

TABLES

Acknowledgments

All books have a history and accumulate gratitude during the course of that history. As is common with edited volumes that have numerous and overseas contributors, this one has a rather long history that generated considerable debt to many people.

The inspiration of the book was a panel that I organized with Sibel Erol for the 1991 annual meeting of the Middle East Studies Association (MESA). The panel that we called "The Image and Reality of Modern Turkish Women" was interdisciplinary and included four papers that offered economic, political and literary analyses of the representation of contemporary Turkish women. The level of interest that the papers and their discussions generated at the MESA meeting and the inquiries we received about the papers afterwards convinced us that the topic deserved more attention and a larger study. Thus, Sibel and I decided to launch a book project, and in the summer of 1993 we issued an announcement and called for papers. We deliberately avoided commissioning papers; instead of limiting the invitation to the scholars whom we already knew, we preferred to reach as many potential contributors as possible. Moreover, the purpose of the book was broadly defined in the announcement as identifying the images attributed to Turkish women and the analysis of the continuity and change in women's representation since the late Ottoman period. Our intention, in pursuing this strategy, was to obtain proposals that would reflect the diversity of approaches and topics concerning the study of Turkish women.

Many people volunteered both information and time and contributed to the circulation of the announcement. Nilüfer Çağatay, by dictating half of her address book on the phone, enabled me to directly contact many colleagues in Turkey. Yıldız Ecevit organized a meeting, and Feride Acar opened her house for it. That meeting, which generated discussions as rich and delightful as the tea and pastries served, gave me the opportunity to meet a distinguished group of scholars in Ankara, explain the purpose of the project, and receive stimulating feedback. The colleagues at that meeting, including Aynur Demirdirek, Ayşe Saktenber, and Oya Çulpan, along with Hayat Kabasakal, Nermin Abadan-Unat, Şemsa Özar, Ferhunde Özbay, and Oya Tokgöz, also provided encouragement and informed other potential contributors about the project. An anonymous supporter placed the announcement on the internet. Consequently, nearly forty exciting proposals were submitted. I am grateful to all those who gave us the opportunity to select from such a large number of interesting writings and especially to the authors who generously shared their works and ideas. It is needless to state that even the submissions that are not included in the book made a valuable contribution to it by expanding our vision and thus enriching the entire process.

Among all who made this book possible, I would like to highlight the role played by Sibel Erol. As the person who shared the editorial responsibilities with me for the first two years, she played a crucial part in conceptualizing and even naming the book, selecting the papers, and providing guidance for the first revisions. Due to her other pressing responsibilities she could not continue to participate in this project, and I had to carry on without the benefit of her insight and invaluable input. I only hope that the final output is as strong and satisfactory as we originally envisioned and that she will be pleased and proud.

I received considerable succor also from my colleagues at Purchase College. Peter Schwab and the members of my feminist research group (the BBs) that includes Deborah Amory, Karen Baird, Kim Christensen, and Judith Kornberg have been always encouraging with their moral support. The questions and comments of the BBs on various parts and versions of the manuscript were enlightening and critical especially in improving my introductory essay.

The book owes plenty also to our two anonymous reviewers. Their approval and positive remarks reassured the publisher, but more importantly, their constructive criticisms ameliorated the manuscript. I also appreciate the dedicated team at St. Martin's Press: Karen Wolny, our editor, for her confidence in this book; Alan Bradshaw, Kate Lovelady, and Rick Delaney for their careful copyediting; and Ruth Mannes for skipping lunch and spending hours in converting computer files from various systems into one that I could manage. In the later stages of editing the manuscript, the work of my undergraduate assistant, Farah Bazai, was essential for maintaining the timetable. Moreover, her curiosity, enthusiasm, and commitment made the routine bearable, the delays only temporal, and the frustration laughable.

Finally, there is the family; my husband Serdar and my son Hasan Can, who not only went through the ups and downs with me but also helped me in numerous ways. The best feeling is that I can count on their continuous support; even though my youngest assistant, while producing photocopies, complained by saying "Mom, I hope this will be your last manuscript," I know he will be there for me to help with the next one.

Zehra F. Arat

INTRODUCTION: POLITICS OF REPRESENTATION AND IDENTITY

Zehra F. Arat

> *A Female Teacher Candidate—What should the Turkish woman be like?*
>
> *M. K. Atatürk—The Turkish woman should be the most enlightened, most virtuous, and most reserved woman of the world. . . . The duty of the Turkish woman is raising generations that are capable of preserving and protecting the Turk with his mentality, strength and determination. The woman who is the source and social foundation of the nation can fulfill her duty only if she is virtuous. . . . Let's remember the famous verse by [the poet] Fikret: "Naturally declines the mankind, if the woman is destitute."*
>
> —Teachers Training School for Girls, İzmir, 1925[1]

"THE TURKISH WOMAN" is a cultural reference that has been engendered to describe the "ideal" as well as the "pitiful," and the analysis of this construct constitutes the focus of this book. The excerpt that begins this essay is from a dialogue between Mustafa Kemal Atatürk, the founder of the Republic of Turkey, and a female teacher-candidate, and a rare example of an overt expression of the effort to articulate the "desirable" characteristics of "the Turkish woman." The example is significant not only because it displays the attempt to push women into an idealized prototype but also because it shows the willingness of women (at least some of them) to accept and participate in the construction of their gender. It also reflects prevalent power relations; being aware of their subordinate condition, women look up to and seek guidance from men, especially from those whose power is enhanced by political authority. But, most importantly, the excerpt indicates that the construction of "the ideal Turkish woman" was an essential component of the Republican elite's "nation-building" project.

However, we should not assume that Turkish women, even at times of extraordinary national unity, have always agreed to this construction. Not only is it true that "where there is power, there is resistance,"[2] but people always strive to define their identities, both individually and collectively, even though their claims or resistance may not always appear in the form of organized actions or social movements. Likewise, Turkish women's search for identity and their expression of demands and contention have taken different forms. They are usually characterized as complacent or resilient, but defiance has not been a stranger to them either; they have resisted being forced into assigned roles and being compressed into the all-homogenizing category of "the Turkish woman."

Referring to the totality of the adult female population in the singular as "woman" has been a common and, by the same token, a disturbing practice. While the similar usage of "man" has an elevating implication for the male population—after all, it is often employed to mean "humankind"—the references to women in the singular almost always negates women, disregards their diversity and individuality, and imposes uniformity. In fact, collapsing multiples into a prototypical singular is often consciously pursued by the privileged for the purpose of justifying and reinforcing their domination.

As a legacy of colonialism and a result of Western hegemony, both men and women of the "Third World" are "reactively homogenized" by the West.[3] Racial and ethnic minorities in the West are subject to the same treatment. The divisions and differences among them are recognized by creating new categories of the singular that are distinguished from each other by their "definitive" adjectives, as in the examples of "the black man" and "the immigrant woman." Even some "Western" feminists fall into this trap and find themselves at odds with Third World feminists who criticize them for holding "a homogenous notion of the oppression of women as a group" and for producing "the image of an 'average third world woman.'"[4] Mohanty argues that by assuming "this average third world woman leads an essentially truncated life based on her feminine gender (read: sexually constrained) and her being 'third world' (read: ignorant, poor, uneducated, tradition-bound, domestic, family oriented, victimized, etcetera)," Western feminists not only privilege themselves but also advance colonial discourses and foster male oppression.[5] However, while being criticized for employing the indiscriminant "Third World woman" reference, even these "privileged" women cannot escape the same fate of being treated as a monolithic subject by men, either. Even when the language choice reflects plurality, the underlying sentiment remains a homogenizing one; for example, it is not uncommon to see an individual woman's comments taken as the "women's view."

This distortion of reality and its degrading impact on women (or various ethnic groups) has been criticized in postcolonial literature and feminist writings as a symptom and tool of imperialistic and patriarchal systems. However, neither the differences among groups that collapse into these broad ideological clusters nor the way their discourses on women feed each other have been adequately scrutinized. Also not problematized are the gender implications of molding the plural into one in *cultural reconstruction projects* undertaken by the nationalist or modernizing elite in their deliberate efforts to define the "ideal" and to push the target population to reshape itself.

This volume examines the cultural construct of "the Turkish woman" in order to scrutinize the imperialistic, nationalistic, and other influential currents behind it. Thus, rather than taking on the task of showing the diversity of Turkish women or the different challenges they face, which has been attempted in other volumes,[6] this collection focuses on *the representation of women*. The purpose is not only to reveal the multiplicity of images used in constructing "the Turkish woman," but also to identify the agents of construction, to distinguish the ideological goals that they intend, or unintentionally serve, and to show how seemingly contradictory and competing projects build upon and reinforce each other. This study also attempts to position women in these processes of construction—how women perceive, enter into, and react to the prevalent discourses of their time.

Our contention is that by juxtaposing the diverse images that have resurfaced in different discourses and been resurrected at different time periods, we can expose their constructed nature and tacit goals. Moreover, only through the deconstruction of these images can we challenge two common, ironically opposite but equally simplistic views of contemporary Turkish women: one that sees them as a secluded and inert mass oppressed by the harsh patriarchal rules of Islam; and the other that perceives them as liberated by and living within Mustafa Kemal Atatürk's secular state.

A concern with the illustration of the revival and reproduction of images requires us to contextualize discourses chronologically. Hence the essays are organized under three politically distinct periods: (1) The Late Ottoman Era (the late nineteenth and early twentieth centuries), (2) The Early Republican Era (from 1920 to 1960), and (3) The Era of Political Mobilization and Diversity (from 1960 to the present). This longitudinal design, however, was not developed as a comparative historiography or a genealogy of particular discourses on Turkish women. Rather than being concerned with defining the specific characteristics of each period and contrasting them, this volume employs an interdisciplinary approach to explore the continuities and connections in addressing "the woman question" within the context of changing political and cultural paradigms.

With that purpose in mind, the contributing authors were not asked to adopt a particular theory or approach beyond following the unifying theme of the book, that is, the multiplicities and continuities in the representation of Turkish women. In fact, since the objective is to reveal the multiplicity of images, and since we all inevitably produce our own depictions when undertaking the tasks of defining, describing, interpreting, and analyzing others' representations, each contribution is expected to express the perception and interpretation of its author.

Following an interdisciplinary approach and informed by the diverse background of the authors (in terms of their disciplines, approaches within each discipline, demographic characteristics, and personal experiences), this volume draws on and contributes to the important research and theorizing that has taken place within various fields of study (anthropology and ethnography, history, literary analysis, political science, sociology, etcetera), but especially within Women's Studies. Enriched by the different methodologies employed by the contributors, this collection extends beyond textual analysis; by introducing data from statistical sources, field research, and face-to-face interviews, it addresses the nitty-gritty of everyday life and its contradictions. Thus, in addition to contributing to bodies of knowledge and methodologies within specific fields, the articles together present a case study focusing on Turkish women; they analyze a range of discourses concerning "the Turkish woman" and deconstruct these varied representations.

It is important to clarify what we mean by "deconstruction" since the term reminds one of "deconstructionism," which is associated with Jacques Derrida.[7] Different form Derrida's deconstructionism, in this project, "deconstruction" is used as *an* opposite of construction, to refer to the process of breaking down the singular to reveal not only the diversity of the "subject" population but also the variety of images that have been used to describe it. By "deconstructing" how Turkish women have been represented, we will expose the ideological and cultural constructions of "the Turkish woman" by the dominant political forces, external critics, and domestic opposition groups that have also presented these constructions as natural and real. These presentations and images are at times so powerful that women agree to and participate in their construction; believing that it is for their own good, they often aspire to the presented "ideal."

Arguing that women and their lives are culturally and historically constructed, however, does not assume that women are merely passive victims in these processes of construction. On the contrary, they are involved as active agents. They not only participate in constructing and sustaining their subordinate entity and roles, but they also establish various forms and fronts of resistance, even if they are not always conscious and purposeful agents in either of these processes.

Emphasizing women's agency, our project of deconstruction also rejects the Lacanian treatment of the subject as a mere construction that lacks internal coherence, autonomy and self-knowledge. Identities are usually culturally assigned, and they may debilitate the individuals who hold them. Despite their restrictive impact, however, even culturally assigned identities may serve as points of departure and opportunities for change. This point raises the issue of power: Since culture is produced and reproduced by the collective, the power positions in these processes of cultural construction are diffused and blurred. Analyzing power, Foucault emphasizes its dispersed condition:

Power is employed and exercised through a net-like organization. And not only do individuals circulate between its threads; they are always in the position of simultaneously undergoing and exercising this power. They are not only its inert or consenting target; they are always also the elements of its articulation. In other words, individuals are the vehicles of power, not its points of application.[8]

Understanding and accepting that power is everywhere, that it is not unidirectional or monopolized, however, does not mean that its diffusion is even. Power is located within and across particular social structures that contain specific loci of concentration and are often superimposed. We can observe this most clearly in countries where development and modernization have been pursued as government policies and the power of the state has been omnipresent.

POLITICAL CHANGE, MODERNIZATION REFORMS, AND WOMEN'S ROLE

Culture is usually treated as a closed and coherent system that changes very slowly. Especially when it is analyzed in dichotomous categories of "traditional" and "modern," the "traditional" is treated as almost static and apt to change mainly as a result of "cultural contact" with outsiders. Once Europe became "modern" and asserted its hegemony over other regions, it fixed both the parameters and paradigms of modernity. Modernity became synonymous with European ways, and modernization became the goal for the colonized and the subdued. In fact, emulation of the Western technology and culture began to be seen as necessary to achieve the economic development that would enable a country to resist the Western economic and political domination.

In line with this popular notion of culture and modernity, "Turkish culture" under Ottoman rule has been characterized as a "traditional Islamic culture" that experienced very little change for centuries. What change did occur has typically been attributed to Western contact, and the culture was believed to have been transformed into a new entity after the establishment of the Republic of Turkey in 1923. This belief, of course, has also been the official line of the Republican regime, and a widely accepted characterization (both popular and academic) of social change in Turkey.

This volume challenges these received notions by tracing debates on social change and women's activism back to the Ottoman Empire. Moreover, it shows how various modernization discourses—which themselves rely upon static models of culture and history, as well as gender—have borrowed from each other. Following a discussion of gender politics of the three periods in Turkish history and the ways each chapter addresses them, I will return to these issues in the conclusion of this introduction.

The Late Ottoman Era
(The Late Nineteenth and Early Twentieth Centuries)

It is a widely shared view that the period following Sultan Abdülmecid's proclamation of a reform charter, known as *Tanzimat*, in 1839, marks the beginning of the process of "purposive modernization" by the Ottoman state. All aspects of this modernization project were not welcomed by all segments of the population, and ironically, the opportunities that it created allowed the public to question and discuss its implications. Within this modernization controversy, women's social condition and role became an issue. Even before some "progressive" men of *belles lettres* and essayists such as Namık Kemal (1840-1888) and Şemseddin Sami (1850-1904) addressed the need for women's education, in order to improve both the quality and quantity of labor in various areas, the state introduced educational programs and opened new schools for girls. In 1842, a midwifery program was introduced at the medical school. Secondary schools for girls were started in 1858. In 1860, a reformist statesman, Mithat *Paşa*, in order to meet the clothing needs of the army, established an industrial workshop in Ruscuk that was later developed into a school. It was the first of what later came to be known as girls' schools of arts and crafts. Also as a part of this education campaign a teachers training college for women, Darülmuallimat, was established in İstanbul in 1870.

In addition to education, this reform era witnessed heated discussions of other issues pertaining to women such as the illegitimacy or immorality of polygamy, the propriety of women's concealing, etcetera.

The constitutional reform of 1876 further facilitated debates on modernization, the role of religion, and "the woman question." Consequently, some limited changes toward narrowing the domain of religious law took place (for example, women gained inheritance rights comparable to their male siblings). But it was the 1908 revolution that established the constitutional monarchy (in the real sense of the term) that affected women's lives most. The somewhat liberal aura that emerged after the revolution allowed women to enter into public life as professionals, writers, and activists.

Women organized various associations with objectives ranging from performing general charity work to educating and training women for work, to helping defend the country by supporting soldiers in the fronts, to promoting women's rights.[9] These women were typically from urban, upperclass backgrounds; as one of them frankly stated, they were a minority of educated women detached from the needs of the majority of women in the society.[10] Nevertheless, they introduced women's perspectives on issues, participated in public debates, and initiated a new discourse that was probably instrumental in passing new legislation somewhat favorable to women (for example, the 1917 family law that restricted polygamy by requiring the consent of the first wife).

The last two decades of the empire, however, were also the years of turbulence. Changes in political and social life and Westernization were taking place at a time when the empire's conflicts with the West were real and European occupation was more than an idle threat. The interplay of these forces and their discordant urges were influential in shaping public debates.

Palmira Brummett's chapter examines the satirical revolutionary press of İstanbul after the Constitutional Revolution of 1908, between 1908 and 1911, by focusing on the cartoon images of women. Distinguishing a series of these female images as "mother," "nation," "citizen," and "subversive," Brummett analyzes the functions each served in interpreting the situation of the country. The cartoon images reflect a blend of cultural traditions, both in form and content, as she argues that they were not only influenced by both European styles and the traditional figures of Turkish shadow puppet theater, but that their content was also determined by threats of European imperialism as well as by folk humor. Although Brummett sorts the numerous female depictions in Ottoman revolutionary cartoons into distinct categories that range from patriotic to subversive, the depictions all seem to collapse into an image of women as weak and vulnerable and, therefore, needing to be protected or controlled. This may be most obvious in those cartoons that link the honor of the female to the honor of the nation—the captive woman image represents the invasion/violation of the country. The cartoons that present the land/country in the form of a promiscuous Westernized woman who is flirting with men of various European nationalities carry a subtle warning about the perils of rapid Westernization for the country in general, as well as its effect on women in particular.

In fact, the pace of change and the level of imitation of the West were troubling to many at the time. Reformists in particular were concerned with striking a balance between Islam and modernization as reforms and reformist proposals encountered resistance and criticisms.[11] Not surprisingly, "the woman question" was central to the debate. As women became more visible in public after the 1908 revolution, critics became more vocal in opposing the reforms for being sacrilegious. In order to appease the opposition, some reformists assumed the task of showing the compatibility of Islam and women's participation in public life and affairs. Halit Hamit, who argued in favor of women's suffrage and even proposed extending women's rights to include the right to run for public office, wrote a book entitled *Feminism and Islam, or Complete Equality for the World of Womanhood* (İslamiyette Feminizm yahut Âlem-i Nisvanda Musavat-ı Tamme).[12] Alternatively, those who embraced the cosmopolitan notions of Western Enlightenment and Humanism (for example, Abdullah Cevdet, Tevfik Fikret, and Salahaddin Asım) identified religion as the main obstacle to the development of rationalism and the progress of women. Perceiving the West as the home of Positivism, some of them rejected the idea of selective borrowing from the West and referred to Western civilization as "a totality which must be accepted with its roses and thorns."[13] Women writers, such as the novelist Fatma Aliye (1864-1924), also argued for women's rights, condemned polygamy, and criticized the advocates of the latter for misinterpreting Islam.[14]

Women's history is a nascent field, and Ottoman women's lives and contributions are still in the process of being discovered. For decades, Turkish women were made to believe that they had been granted some rights by the Republican regime without struggling for them. Leaving the old Arabic scripts behind in 1928 and teaching the young only the new Turkish script based on the Latin alphabet kept the following generations completely detached from their past. This important policy, referred to as the Language Reform, contributed to the widespread acceptance of Republican interpretations of history that treated the War of Independence (1919-1922) and the subsequent establishment of the Turkish Republic in 1923 as the beginning of a new Turkish society and negated the progress and achievements of its Ottoman past. Recently, however, Turkish scholars have developed an active interest in Ottoman historiography, and feminist scholarship in this area has been yielding data that amounts to rewriting history, both literally and figuratively.

Aynur Demirdirek's chapter, based on her larger project that attempts to recover the writings of Ottoman women, shows that there was a viable "feminist" movement—or at least feminist aspirations shared among urban Ottoman women—in the late nineteenth and early twentieth centuries. Several women's journals were published in major Ottoman cities (the oldest known appeared in 1886), and women writers addressed women's issues, along with other problems of the country. Articles and letters from the readers of these journals indicate that Muslim women of the empire debated the issue of women's rights and discussed their compatibility with Islam; addressed the inequalities within the Muslim family; and demanded women's education, incorporation into the work force, protection in marriage, and participation in public affairs. Some women criticized women's organizations that were engaged in raising funds for the military, and they argued for channeling the efforts to help women and girls instead. Evidently following the foreign press and aware of women's movements in Europe, some identified with more encompassing concepts of sisterhood and feminism. As a response to a well-known male novelist's argument about the "alien nature of feminism," Nimet Cemil wrote an article, in 1921, entitled "Feminism Again, Feminism Always!":

. . . Yakup Kadri *Bey* takes the absence of a word that would be equivalent to feminism in our language as evidence of the absence of

feminism [in our lives]. He should excuse us for rejecting this statement. Because there are some very important things that every nation
has, but again many nations lack the words or even translations to
name them (telegraph, automobile, ship . . .). Therefore, we feel no
need for [employing] words like *nisâsilik* or *nisâiyyun* [as alternative
translations]. We prefer to use the word feminism just like that. Let's
have another foreign word in our language, what is the harm? However, it is impossible to deny the existence of feminism. [See Demirdirek's chapter in this volume.]

Ottoman women, of course, were not alone in describing and
depicting their lives. In addition to state officials and intellectual men
who took various positions about the role and future of Ottoman
women, foreigners produced their own imagery and prescriptions.

Thanks to travelers' notes and translations of supposedly original
"Oriental" fiction and history texts, Europeans produced a discourse
now commonly referred to as "orientalist." Orientalists depicted
women of the East, including Ottoman women of various ethnic
origins, as idle prisoners of harems grooming themselves and waiting
to be called by their masters to satisfy their endless and inconceivable
sexual desires. In his analysis of the erotic texts of the orientalists,
İrvin Schick treats the erotic as the manifestation of a political
discourse of spatiality. Arguing that "gender and especially sexuality
are fundamental (imputed) attributes of socially constructed space,"
he refers to Europeans' sexualized images of the *other* as "key markers
of place" that served as "determinants of identity and alterity." Schick
agrees with earlier critiques of Orientalism and shows that erotic
literature and its claims to be the "representation of reality" not only
eroticized the East and its people but also enabled gendering and
helped forge a powerful colonial discourse. More importantly, however, he notes that sexuality in orientalist discourse had a function
beyond creating and justifying "a male/active colonizer penetrating a
female/passive territory," but it allowed Europe to form its own
identity and define its place in the world. Thus, several often contradictory images were attributed to Ottoman women: "repulsive and
alluring, crude and refined, disgustingly filthy and obsessed with
bathing, unspeakably ugly and fabulously beautiful, ragged and elegant, shapeless and perfectly proportioned, clumsy as a duck and

graceful as a gazelle, languorous and a beast of burden, a wily manipulator and a helpless prisoner, a scheming evil-doer and innocent as a child." Schick points out that the multiplicity and inconsistency of the depictions, coexisting with claims such as Oriental women's "physical and moral uniformity" produces simply "one single type," are consistent with the alteritist discourse because each characterization contributed to "the process of Europe's self-definition through othering" and, consequently, to the colonial project.

Curious readers may ask how this discourse affected its subject, since the consumption of the material produced by European travelers, translators, and artists could not be limited to the West, and "the product" eventually traveled back to the society of its "origin." This cyclical process of production, consumption, and reproduction of orientalist discourses, repeated both in the West and in "the Orient," is beyond the purpose of Schick's discussion of orientalist erotica.[15] However, Pelin Başcı addresses this issue by examining how Western missionaries' imagery of the "Oriental woman" entered Turkey at a particular juncture in history and affected the discourse on women's emancipation.

Başcı's study of the missionary texts that were produced at the turn of the century is revealing not only in terms of how the American missionaries constructed and circulated images of women in Turkey, but it also shows how they related themselves to the "other" women. While arguing that female missionaries viewed women of the Ottoman Empire as the ultimate objects of a cultural, religious, and mental transformation, Başcı exposes their perceptions' tacit linkage to the orientalist discourse; missionaries were not only familiar with and influenced by orientalist works, but they also contributed to that discourse by creating and circulating similar images. According to Başcı, by presenting the "Ottoman woman" as the ultimate victim and evidence of "backwardness" and assigning themselves the role of her savior, women missionaries were able to justify their own recent emancipation and increasingly public role. The complex relationship between the stated goals and the unspoken (even subconscious) intentions of these women, and their equally confused attitude toward their "subject" women, display the intricacies of the subaltern condition in its various forms and layers. Başcı also explores the relationship between missionaries' views and the definition of the "modern Turkish woman." Using the case of Halide Edib Adıvar (a prominent novelist, feminist, nationalist, educated at Üsküdar American missionary school in İstanbul), Başcı shows that missionaries used the images of their students to promote their own cause, shaped the self-image and gender identity of their graduates, and ultimately, with the help of these new elite women as intermediaries, contributed to the production of the Kemalist discourse on women.[16]

Early Republican Era (1920–1960)

Although the Republic of Turkey was proclaimed on October 29, 1923, the leadership that founded the new Turkish state had established its political power earlier. By rejecting the terms of agreement imposed on the Ottoman Empire by the victors of World War I and launching the "War of Independence" against the British, French, Italians, and Greeks in 1919, Mustafa Kemal Atatürk and his associates presented themselves as an Anatolian alternative to the government of the Ottoman dynasty in İstanbul. In 1920, the Grand National Assembly was created as the "legitimate" legislative body, and with the abolishment of the Sultanate in 1922 Ottoman dynastic rule and the empire were officially ended.

Thus, the three decades between 1920 and 1950 are commonly referred to as the "Kemalist" rule or era, since the ideological principles established by Mustafa Kemal Atatürk were sustained by the governments of his party enjoying uncontested power in a single-party regime, even after his death in 1938. Without much historical distortion, we can extend the Kemalist period to cover the 1950s, since despite the initiation of multi-party elections in 1946, and the transition of administration from Atatürk's Republican People's Party to the Democratic Party in 1950, the underlying principles of the Kemalist regime prevailed. Arguably, some compromises, especially in regard to the Kemalist principles of secularism and statism, were devised by the Democratic Party. Nevertheless, they could not reverse the general path of social change set in motion during the Atatürk years. More significantly (for our purposes), the policies of the new administration included no provisions that would imply a shift in the approach of the state toward gender issues.

Among the Ottoman male reformers and proponents of women's rights, Ziya Gökalp, a Durkheimian sociologist, stands out as one who rejected the synonymic treatment of Westernization and modernization. According to him, the "modern" was inherent in Turkish civilization, and women were its guards. Contemporary analysts agree that Gökalp, with his unique theory of Turkish civilization and nationalism, became a major influence on the Republican leaders and provided the starting point for Kemalist ideology, despite the fact that he died only a year after the formation of the Turkish Republic.[17] Thus, his ideas on civilization, religion, and family were crucial to building a unified and secular "Turkish nation-state" based on an identity as distinct as possible from the Islamic character of the multiethnic, multinational Ottoman Empire.

K. E. Fleming analyzes Ziya Gökalp's contribution to this project of "nation-building." She argues that Gökalp rejected Western modernity as a model for the Turkish nation and proposed the revival of the nation's ancient past, both "real" and constructed. The emancipation of women, as well as the progress of the nation, depended not on the imitation of the West, but on a return to this original Turkish civilization, in which "women were equal to men." Gökalp attributed the deterioration of the culture, as well as the decline in women's status, to the foreign influence: "Under the influence of the Iranian and Greek civilizations, women have become enslaved and have sunk to a low legal status." Thus, the cause of nationalism was connected to feminism. Also, by depicting women as the guarantors of the lost "Turkish past," Gökalp treated the emancipation of women and a "restoration" of gender equality as essential to the revival of authentic Turkish civilization and the development of the "Turk" as opposed to the *Osmanlı* (Ottoman). As Fleming points out in her chapter, Gökalp also made strong and radical claims about his contemporary nationalists: "Turkish nationalists are both popular and feminist, not only because these two principles are values in our age, but also because democracy and feminism were two bases of ancient Turkish life."

However, while Gökalp's influence can be observed in Republican government policies and in the official discourse that connected women's mobilization to national development,[18] the feminist aspirations of his teachings were not completely fulfilled. Moreover, despite Gökalp's efforts to separate "modern civilization" from "Western civilization," treating the two as one was common among Kemalists. The West was defined as the "civilized," and the transformation of Turkish society according to the Western model was targeted as a national goal, one articulated as "ascending Turkey to the level of civilized societies." Women were assigned an important part in this modernization project, and their progress was interpreted as an important measure of success in achieving modernity.

Trusting its transformative capacity, education was made the cornerstone of the Kemalist modernization/Westernization project. Committed to offering a comprehensive public education system, a principle of free education was adopted at all levels, and primary school education was made mandatory for both sexes in 1923. In addition, measures were taken to improve the quality of education, and the number of schools, teachers, and students dramatically increased.

Another target of legislative and administrative reforms was the structure of the family. In 1926, the Grand National Assembly adopted the Swiss Civil Code as the basis of its Civil Law. This law, which included the Family Law, abolished polygamy; prevented child marriages by imposing a minimum age for marriage; recognized women as legal equals of men in certain areas (for example, as witnesses in courts and in inheriting and maintaining property); and granted women the right to choose their spouses, initiate divorce, and maintain their maternal rights after a divorce.

Moreover, the physical segregation of the sexes was seen as a distorted Islamic practice and rejected as being backward. Increasing women's presence and visibility in the public sphere was sought both as a way of overcoming backward practices and also to show how "modern" the new Turkey had become. Arguably to serve the same purposes, women were granted political rights in the 1930s—the right to vote and to run in municipal elections in 1930, and in national elections in 1934.

The Kemalist discourse on women and the gender policy of the regime constitute the focus of the chapters by Ayşe Durakbaşa and myself. We both analyze the aspirations and impacts of the Kemalist reforms, particularly in relation to their moral and ideological imperatives.

Durakbaşa argues that the Kemalist reforms constructed a modern femininity that was in line with the overall pragmatism of Kemalist ideology. Consequently, a combination of conflicting roles and images was presented to women as the model to follow: an educated professional woman at work, a socially active woman engaged in organizing clubs and associations, a properly trained mother and wife, a feminine woman dressed in gowns and dancing at balls. Durakbaşa also notes that while women were encouraged to enter and participate in the public sphere of life, they were restricted by some moral and behavioral codes that were meant to preserve the "respectability" and "honor" of their families. Defining the gender approach of the regime as a synthesis of a puritan morality based on an Islamic principle of female modesty and a modernization goal framed by the ethics of nationalism and professionalism, Durakbaşa's chapter serves as a reassessment of the "state feminism" of the Kemalist regime. In addition to identifying the images engendered by the regime, Durakbaşa explores the meaning and significance of the images to the creation of a new Turkish identity and nationalism.

As powerful agents of socialization, schools were, of course, instrumental in molding the new generations according to Kemalist ideology. Examining the educational system of the Turkish Republic in its formative years, during the 1920s and 1930s, my chapter attempts to identify the underlying goals of the education policy, which emphasized schooling of girls, and to show how ideological moral and behavioral codes were transmitted in school curricula and regulations. To this end, I juxtapose my analysis of the secondary school curricula and government documents with the assessments of women who went through the system and became the first generation of educated daughters of the Republic. The analysis of documents shows that, despite the emphasis on women's education, the system maintained a gender bias by assigning primacy to the education of males, reinforcing traditional gender roles in the curricula and in vocational specialization, and attempting to restrict female students' mobility and femininity. Arguing that the regime saw "motherhood" as the primary task of women, I find the gendered curricula and the emphasis on vocational training in home economics, fashion, midwifery, and nursing as consistent with its ideology. The interviews with the women in the study also reveal that government policies were in line with "progressive" parents' values and expectations, and the restrictive and disciplinary rules implemented in schools were largely internalized by students. Interestingly, however proud of the discipline and high quality of education they received, the women in the study overlook the "biases" that I see, and they reject the notion that any gender discrimination or inequality existed in schools during the "Atatürk years" of the Republic.

Thus, the study illustrates how "reality" can be perceived and presented differently and how perceptions can be influenced by a powerful official ideology. Nevertheless, it should be noted that the perceptions of these women were based on their experiences, their experiences (which might have included indoctrination) marked their "reality," and, most importantly, it was that reality that they transmitted to the next generations.

The Era of Political Mobilization and Diversity (from 1960 to the Present)

The 1960 coup d'etat marks the beginning of a new era in Turkish history and politics, even though it may not strike us as a significant milestone in women's history. The constitutional reforms and political restructuring that followed the coup, however, had both immediate and long-term implications for women's lives and political struggles. The introduction of individual rights and recognition of labor rights in the 1961 constitution ushered in an era of freedom that allowed the emergence of various ideological groups. Although constitutional recognition did not guarantee the full exercise of freedoms—two military interventions, in 1971 and 1980, and frequent resort to martial law and other emergency measures by civilian governments curtailed them substantially—it allowed challenging voices and relatively open debate and competition among them. In that sense, the post-1960 period can be recognized as one that witnessed the inauguration of political pluralism, an era in which the state's ability to maintain a monolithic ideology and monopoly over political mobilization was seriously shaken and eclipsed by the emergence of new and ideologically distinct opposition groups. Although none of these political groups focused on women's issues and rights, they played the important role of politicizing women, since they recruited and mobilized women for other purposes and causes.

Political parties multiplied both in number and in the ideological platforms they presented. They established women's auxiliaries and used them to expand their electoral bases as well as for fundraising activities. Left-wing organizations appealed mostly to the younger generation of women, especially to university students. Like mainstream parties and organizations, however, they also marginalized women and women's issues.[19] Nevertheless, despite their disregard for gender equality, as they postponed the emancipation of women or subsumed it within some other "primary" goal, the emergence of new groups and the increased political competitiveness caused women's political participation and activism to increase.

The experience they gained in various organizations during the 1960s and 1970s prepared women to organize around their immediate concerns in the 1980s. Arguably, their earlier disappointments with these organizations also led them to seek new venues and formulations. Ironically, the contradictory impacts of the military takeover in 1980 and its repressive policies also stimulated women's activism. On the one hand, the ban on political parties, the restrictions imposed on labor unions, and the repression of organizations that espoused class politics compressed the political spectrum and limited the opportunities within old political organizations. Having those doors closed, however, also enabled women to free themselves from the boundaries of previously subscribed ideologies. Thus, the 1980s were demarcated by the emergence of a new feminism and new autonomous women's movements in Turkey.

In our analyses of this era, women's participation in the economy and what constitutes women's work are the concern of the first two chapters. Integration of women into the "productive" work force— implying a movement from the "private" to the "public" domain and promising economic independence—usually has been considered a prerequisite of women's liberation. Işık Urla Zeytinoğlu assesses the extent to which this employment condition has been "proximated" by Turkish women. She notes that the bulk of female "productive labor" has been in the agricultural sector, where women work as unpaid (and unrecognized?) laborers on family farms. Her analysis of women's participation in the nonagricultural formal economy yields mixed findings. While the overall participation of women in salaried and waged employment appears to be generally low, she also finds the sectoral and occupational distribution of female labor uneven. Women tend to be proportionally better represented in professional positions than in other areas (for example, in waged labor), but even in the professional sector women tend to specialize in areas that are considered more "feminine" (such as health care and teaching). Zeytinoğlu argues that the obstacles to women's participation in the formal economy and engagement in gainful employment, as well as women's difficulty in entering certain occupations and sectors, arise from both cultural norms that oppose women taking jobs outside the home and from legal restrictions. By perceiving women as fragile, naturally caring and nurturing, and preoccupied with neatness and cleanness, they push women either away from employment or into more "suitable" occupations.

Based on field research conducted in two Turkish villages in 1986, Emine Onaran İncirlioğlu's ethnographic study focuses on the gender division of labor within the rural sector. In addition to exploring the extent to which such a division of labor exists, she examines the value assigned to men's and women's tasks by villagers, the extent of women's control over their work, and women's perceptions of their own work and ability. Also discussed are the relevance and significance of these factors in constructing and maintaining the gender hierarchy. İncirlioğlu argues against the stereotyping of village women as burdened with "backbreaking labor"; ignorant of social, economic, and political issues; and passive about their conditions. Pointing to some "a-typical" (according to prevailing social scientific paradigms) behaviors and roles played by the village women that she studied, İncirlioğlu challenges representations in ethnographic studies that exclude "anomalies" in favor of "patterns" and neat models.

Hayat Kabasakal focuses on professional women who have made it to "the top." She notes that not unlike women in other countries around the world, women in Turkey are also underrepresented in managerial and administrative posts. Indeed, the disadvantageous position of women becomes more obvious at the higher echelons of administrative hierarchies. Yet, the very existence of women in top executive positions in spite of the social, cultural, and institutional constraints and obstacles raises a curious question: What are the common characteristics of these women? Kabasakal presents a profile of women who have climbed up the corporate ladder that is not completely surprising but is somewhat disturbing from a feminist perspective. Women who have reached the top are from families with a high socioeconomic status, married to men from the same strata, and they are highly educated and ambitious. The research reveals that these women try to keep a feminine but not overtly sexual look in the workplace and demonstrate a strong desire and ability to maintain invisibility. By avoiding the limelight they seem to be attempting to carve a space for themselves within the administrative hierarchy without appearing too aggressive and challenging (to men). Moreover, probably as a part of the same cautious strategy, they refuse to identify with the rising women's movements and with feminism.

While a group of privileged women in power has been unable to relate to women's issues and has shown a conscious effort to refrain from even the appearance of being engaged in a feminist struggle, some others, especially starting in the 1980s, prioritized and politi-cized women's position in social institutions. Among these recently emerged women's groups is what Aynur İlyasoğlu refers to as "the elite Islamist women." The activism of Islamist women who are university students or graduates has revived the debate on the nature of moder-nity and modernization, as well as the roles of religion and women in the modernization process. While Islamist parties and the male leadership of Islamist groups attempt to confine women to the home and recognize them only as wives and daughters, İlyasoğlu states that self-identified Islamist women reject these restrictions and struggle to redefine women's social roles in Islam. Focusing on the practice of the new veiling, *tesettür*, that is followed by some educated Turkish women who are engaged in gainful employment outside the home, İlyasoğlu discusses the relation of a woman's attire and body to her social role. Showing how educated Islamist women use the new veiling as a tool to define and redefine a feminine identity, İlyasoğlu questions the validity of sociological paradigms that focus on dichotomous classifi-cations such as modern versus traditional or public versus private. Her argument holds that the new veiling practice is not a way of returning to the "traditional,"[20] but a device that allows the diffusion of the private with the public and that generates a "self-modernizing" process engineered by Islamist women themselves. İlyasoğlu's inter-views and her reading of fiction and essays by Islamist women reveal that "elite" Islamist women assign a primacy to family and emphasize motherhood, but they refuse to be identified *only* in such terms.

Interestingly, just like the Kemalist women whom they vehemently criticize, Islamist women also seek fulfillment by contributing to society at large and define their work as professionals in the altruistic terms of "serving others."

The significance of domestic life for Turkish women is problematized also by Carel Bertram. Through the textual analysis of short stories by four well-known contemporary women writers—Füruzan, Nazlı Eray, Sevgi Soysal, and Zeynep Karabey—Bertram examines how the house became a gendered, social construct that is perceived as highly and peculiarly relevant to women. By using the Islamic concept of *fitne-i âlem* (literally, a beauty who sets the whole wold in commotion, but it also points to the disruptive potential of female sexuality that should be contained), Bertram suggests a process by which "the modern Turkish woman," as exemplified by the protagonists in these stories, became the icon, the prisoner, and the guardian of domestic space. She argues that housework, or woman's work, becomes a metaphor in these stories for a more existential chaos-containment that if unleashed would change the meaning of the house and threaten the social order. She also argues that the female self-consciousness that was once unified by the concept of *fitne* has begun to unravel, and women have begun to defy or subvert the old role expectations. Although each protagonist follows a different strategy for change, the site of this unraveling of self-consciousness is invariably the home, and thus the meaning of social order is contested *in the home*. Although the women in the stories are unsuccessful in their attempts, Bertram shows how their strategies can help us identify the direction of change taking place in Turkish houses.

In addition to pointing to an area of women's discontent and protest, Bertram's chapter raises a number of questions. Even if their rebellions fail to fill the void in these women's lives, can we say they are inconsequential? Can individual rebellions by the subaltern have a cumulative effect? Or do they need to raise collective consciousness and organize group action for any sustainable transformation to occur? Which women would participate and benefit from such activities? What alternative approaches and structures would they offer? Arzu Öztürkmen and Yeşim Arat provide some clues to these latter questions in their studies of two different forms of feminism that emerged in the 1980s.

Through a content analysis of several issues of the magazine *Kadınca,* meaning "womanly" in Turkish, Öztürkmen examines the place and role of the magazine within prevailing feminist movements and discourses. She argues that *Kadınca* first appeared in December 1978 as a conventional women's magazine, but later took a turn that has distinguished it from similar publications; by emphasizing the individuality of women and their existence independent of their families, the magazine has tried to promote a certain "female consciousness." With its flashy advertisements of household appliances and cosmetics, it has often been criticized by other feminist groups. However, Öztürkmen argues that by employing a rhetoric different than those of academic and activist feminists, *Kadınca* has been important in asserting and maintaining the issue of women's rights for nonpoliticized women.

Yeşim Arat's chapter involves another current of feminism that emerged in the 1980s and its efforts at institution building. Focusing on battered women's shelters, specifically the "Purple Roof Women's Shelter," Y. Arat examines Turkish feminists' struggle to work within a patriarchal system by employing alternative organizational structures and collective leadership. Her review of the conditions and events that led women to build shelters and the peculiar rules suggested by municipal governments—such as seeking the husband's permission before admitting a battered woman to the shelter—reflect how wide the gulf is between feminist goals and male politicians' approaches to women's problems. The internal conflicts of Purple Roof, on the other hand, are also illustrative of the difficulties of pursuing feminist ideals of sisterhood, solidarity, and participant democracy within an organization that must operate within the larger framework of a materialist culture, capitalist economy, and male-dominated and essentially undemocratic political system.

CONTINUITIES IN DOMINATION AND STRUGGLES

Considered as a whole, the essays in this volume offer important evidence that modernization projects and nation-building efforts by the Ottoman and Republican reformists were conducted through the symbolic manipulation of women's issues and representations.

Improving women's lot was treated as the focal point of community interests by all competing ideological groups: advocates of Western modernization, Western missionaries, defenders of Islam, promoters of Ottoman patriotism, preachers of Turkish nationalism, and socialist reformists and revolutionaries. Moreover, they all manipulated the same images and metaphors in the presentation of their own ideology. Consequently, these same images have served as the site of important political struggles for a century.

Despite the Republican leaders' efforts to present the new regime as a complete break from a "backward" or "compromising" Ottoman past, the chapters in this volume by Demirdirek, Brummett, and Başcı reveal how the framework of the Republican debate had already been set by the Ottoman state and its reformist subjects. Arguments regarding the rights that women had gained under the Republic were incipient in debates that predated the Republic, and, more importantly, these debates included women's voices. Even if some groups vanished and their programs were discontinued, central metaphors survived and were subsequently redeployed. The various depictions of Ottoman women by Ottoman male cartoonists that Brummett brings to our attention, for example, bear more than a simple similarity to the approach of the Republican regime, which was also riddled with contradiction, as Durakbaşa demonstrates. While women were expected to be modern—that is, Westernized—in their looks and outlooks, they were also criticized if they appeared to be *too* European in the way they dressed or behaved. The Ottoman cartoon images of women—depicted as either physically or spiritually weak (subversive) and thus in need of protection or restraining—could very well have been produced by the Kemalist governments or by their Islamist opponents.

The Republican regime wanted to mobilize women, but only under state leadership and only to the point that was permissible by men. Women were called to national duty and action and allowed to enter the public domain, but without the autonomy and power enjoyed by men. The Civil Law of 1926, which is often praised for establishing parity and taken as the evidence of the feminist inclinations of the Kemalist regime, improved women's position in the family to some extent but also assured the continuation of women's dependency on men; the husband remained the legally recognized head of the household and the wife had to seek his permission to work outside the home and earn money.[21] Many women who were involved in the Kemalist movement and were once allies of the Republican male leadership—such as Nezihe Muhittin, who founded the Association for Protection of Ottoman Turkish Women in 1913, the Women's People's Party in 1923, and the Women's League of Turkey after the party was abolished within the same year—later lost favor with the regime, and their political demands were continuously ignored. In addition to pressuring women to abolish the Women's People's Party in 1923,[22] the League's attempt to nominate its own parliamentary (male) candidates for the 1927 elections was blocked,[23] and women's demand for membership to the ruling Republican People's Party was denied in the early 1930s.[24]

Modernizing "the Turkish Woman" and Politicizing the Private

Approaching issues from their own vantage point, what was challenged by all ideological groups of the nineteenth and twentieth centuries was women's "backwardness," not male dominance (with the exception of some women groups). By criticizing Turkish women's "enslaved" conditions, orientalists justified Western colonial expansion, Western missionary women privileged themselves and reinforced Western cultural hegemony, and Ottoman and Turkish reformists tried to create a trained labor force and enlightened wives.[25] Nevertheless, speaking of domestic life, family, and household politics as public issues marked by gender, they all effectively *politicized the private* and thus contributed to the development of a new paradigm of modernity that was completely different from that of Western liberal discourse, yet not necessarily inconsistent with the Western approach to development (in other countries) or contradictory to the interests of Western hegemony and capitalism. In fact, the Orientalist roots of this new paradigm were central to the development of modernization theory in the West, which emerged in the 1950s and prescribed a capitalist economy, integration of markets through free trade, and the introduction of Western education and cultural products (such as movies) to the "emerging new states" of the post-colonial era.[26]

The political ethos of Western liberalism, as best illustrated in John Locke's writings, is based on the separation of the public and the private (a dichotomy that has been both reified and critiqued by feminist theorists). Indeed, according to the liberal tradition, the private domain in the West, by definition, is meant to be kept far from the reach of public authority as embodied by the state; it is excluded, to a great extent, from policy debates and formulations. In approaching the East and Ottoman society, however, Western critics identified polygamy, women's seclusion, and other aspects of domestic life as pressing areas for change. Similarly, the transformation of the private domain under the guidance of a modern state was targeted by Ottoman and Kemalist reformists and statesmen. Their modernization projects—introducing and increasing state control over marriage, divorce, inheritance, etcetera—problematized precisely that which was private. In this sense, Ottoman and Kemalist reformists, especially Mustafa Kemal Atatürk, established themselves as forerunners of modernization theorists.

Atatürk envisioned the centralization of power and the penetration of the state into other institutions and every corner of the country both as the means and measure of modernization and "nation-state" building more than three decades before modernization theorists in the United States launched their "academic" projects (under the auspicious of the Social Science Research Council Committee on Comparative Politics).[27] Moreover, by emphasizing the nuclear family; reinforcing ties within that institution through monogamy; curtailing the power of traditional sources of authority, and especially religion, by dismantling its central institutions (that is, undermining *sheriat* in legal structures and legislation, abolishing sultanate and caliphate, closing down *tarikats* and *vakıfs*); and following Western ways as the norms of modernity, Atatürk presented a model that could serve as a blueprint for implementing the prescriptions of modernization theory.

Economic development, a central issue for both Kemalists and modernization theorists, is defined by both groups in terms of industrialization. The statism of the Kemalist development model may appear to conflict with modernization theory's commitment to free enterprise and capitalism. Contrary to common perceptions and presentations of modernization theorists, however, the statism followed in Turkey and many other developing countries is a development strategy that was dictated by the condition of low capital accumulation; it tends to subsidize and supplement private enterprise, not to repress or compete with it.[28]

Concerned with increasing production and productivity, both Kemalism and modernization theory see cultural transformation as not only valuable and desirable in itself but also as essential to achieving economic development. Perceiving women as an under-utilized labor force and acknowledging their potential, both seek to increase women's contributions to the economy. However, this effort does not change the overall gendered and dualistic approach prevalent in both discourses. The public domain continues to be seen as man's domain and it is defined in masculine terms. Women, on the other hand, with their lives anchored in the family, continue to be seen in terms of reproductive functions such as childbearing, child care, and home economics. Indeed, the theme of motherhood as an essential function and important "duty" of women repeatedly surfaces in Atatürk's speeches.[29]

Moreover, Kemalist modernization kept intact the culture that perceived women as the symbol of honor—of family and nation. The *namus* (honor) of a family depends on, and thus can be damaged by, the behavior of women (especially by her sexual conduct and virginity), but it has to be protected by men, who are in charge of the family. Thus, the notion of *namus* not only restricts women's sexuality, behavior, and opportunities (such as in employment), but it also arms men with an extraordinary weapon. In addition to putting psychological pressure on women, men of the family—husbands, fathers, uncles, brothers, etcetera—can invoke *namus* to justify violence against women and girls. Regardless of the pattern of violence, we can argue that, with Kemalism and modernization, the preoccupation with *namus,* which had been prevalent in Mediterranean culture and was reinforced by the Islamic notion of *fitne,* must have been increased as a result of the desegregation of the sexes and women's participation in public life.[30] As we see in Durakbaşa's chapter, such concerns were frequently raised by young women, their parents, statesmen, and journalists of the early Republican era.

Nevertheless, neither the totalizing logic of Kemalist reforms that fused secularization and Westernization with modernity, nor the modernization theorists' dichotomization of culture as "traditional" or "modern," can explain the emergence and nature of religious movements in "modern" societies. They both fail to see that what is branded as "traditional" can be relevant to "modern" problems and embraced by people both in a reactionary mode and in order to harness or create an alternative modernity. Ironically, this strategy, reviving the old to adopt to or cope with the new, was also once followed by Kemalists, who, vacillating between modernization/Westernization and the articulation of a distinct "Turkish nation," resorted to a "secular tradition" described and authenticized by Ziya Gökalp. Now in contemporary Turkey educated women living in the metropolises of İstanbul and Ankara turn to Islam not to reverse the modernization process but to eliminate the exigencies of modern life while retaining and maximizing the opportunities such as education and professional employment that it creates (see İlyasoğlu herein).

Women's Approaches and Movements

While they all had the same concerns about the conditions of Ottoman Muslim women and urged women to be more involved in public life, the contributors to Ottoman women's journals set different priorities and presented different justifications for their demands. Among the activist Ottoman women, some embraced the Muslim identity and attempted to reform the family using the religious framework. Others subscribed to secularism and questioned the legitimacy of male privileges and domination.[31]

Today, the rising popularity of Islam and the new veiling—practiced by educated Islamist women and thus brought to the institutions that are the edifice of Kemalist modernity (such as universities and government offices)—are criticized for being anti-modern and reactionary by women who were the first beneficiaries of Kemalist reforms and education (see Z. Arat in this volume). In addition to their adherence to the principle of secularism, these women critics express only gratitude and devotion to both Atatürk and his reforms. Considering themselves privileged and owing that privilege to the opportunities created by the Kemalist modernization project, they have been fully dedicated to the nationalist cause and have not questioned the gender inequalities in the new Civil Code, school system, or other reforms. Proud of their progress, they have been largely content and complacent. Privileged women who demanded more substantial changes and equality in political life constituted only a small minority, and they could be easily coopted or subdued by the Kemalist regime. In an atmosphere that emphasized national unity and expected everyone to sacrifice self-interest for the development of the country, economic rights of women could not even be an issue. Thus, the struggle for women's economic and social independence has been postponed.

Today, a younger generation of women who acquired power as corporate executives, concerned about preserving their privileged positions, also act content and refrain from controversies (see Kabasakal herein). Such privileged and powerful women, including the former Prime Minister Tansu Çiller, may be products of Kemalist reforms and subscribers of Kemalist ideology, but they should not be mistaken for Kemalist feminists. Explicitly rejecting feminism and activism, their ability to fight for the protection of cherished benefits and rights, which came under attack with the rise of Islamists and the Welfare Party, is questionable. Their indirect contribution to women's cause (appearing as role models for girls) calls for further research.[32] However, within the rank and file of Kemalists are feminists such as Nermin Abadan-Unat who choose activism. Kemalist feminists, taking the legalist approach, emphasize the protection and expansion of what is already granted in Kemalist reforms and struggle against the Islamists who constitute for them the threat of revoking women's gains.[33] They collaborate with other feminists and have played a significant role in the establishment of women's centers within university structures. Other feminist groups that emerged in the 1980s insist on their autonomy from the state and, in addition to full legal equality, they demand parity in the household and cultural and behavioral change in men that would free women from domestic violence and sexual harassment.

By the 1990s, all women's movements, however different—Islamist, Kemalist, Socialist, Liberal or Radical feminist, etcetera—not only demanded women's right to work, but also emphasized the need to gain and sustain an independent identity. The emergence of new feminist groups and the changes in women's agendas may be interpreted as a reaction to the limitations, unfulfilled promises, or the marginalizing effect of Kemalist reforms.[34] Another contributing factor lies in the economy. The Republican regime's emphasis on industrialization and the concentration of industrial investments in urban centers has squeezed the agricultural sector. Economic policies that stressed rapid economic growth, as opposed to balanced economic development, created a structure that has been characterized by social and regional inequalities and income disparities. The social cleavages and the economic gulf between people and regions have increased in the 1980s and 1990s as a result of the emphasis on the export-led industrialization and the implementation of the IMF-prescribed austerity measures. The encumbering impact of these policies and the globalization of markets have been felt by women of all classes, even if experienced differently. As the market's encroachment on private life has increased, a second source of income has become a necessity for families struggling for survival or coping with escalating consumerism.

While acknowledging the significance of these grave conditions in fueling women's movements in Turkey, however, we can also look beyond the marginalizing impact of crises. Alberto Melucci offers a view of social movements that emphasizes their creative potential: "The movements are not the residual of development or manifestations of discontent on the part of marginal categories. They are not only the product of the crisis, the last expressions of a society which is dying. On the contrary, they are signs of what is being born."[35]

This view seems to be particularly relevant to Turkish women's movements. Both in the Ottoman Empire and the Turkish Republic, participants in women's movements might have been marginalized as women, but they have not been recruited from peripheral or poor segments of society. The Ottoman women's literary movement at the turn of the century included women who constituted an "elite" by all definitions of the term. So too were the women who were politically active—attempting to form a Women's party and establish women's organizations—during the early years of the Republic.[36]

The recent women's movements draw a larger perimeter of participants but still reflect similar demographic characteristics. Öztürkmen (in this volume) indicates that Kadınca writers and readers come from urban middle-class backgrounds. Similarly, members of the feminist movements that emerged in the 1980s appear to be from the educated and upper strata of the urban sector. Their activities are limited to big cities, taking place mainly in İstanbul and Ankara. Even if the resonance of some of these feminist activities and events may travel to other cities, small towns, and villages, the ability of women to connect and communicate with each other is questionable. Similarly, Islamist activist women also belong to a privileged urban population, and the irrelevance of their cause and approach is already articulated at least by one village woman, who ridiculed a government official's wife's attempt to recruit village women to the Islamist movement:

> Every now and then she gathers them together at the village mosque, talks to them, but in two hours, women completely forget about all she says; then she gathers them again.... We milk cows, there is farm work, the dung to collect, the bread to bake, and carpets.... There is a lot of work in the village; no one has time to follow her. The same thing has been going on for five years now.... So, she could not gather anyone under her protection. [See İncirlioğlu's chapter in this volume.]

In fact, if the view expressed above is shared by other village women, Islamist women are less likely to find allies in the rural sector than in the cities.

Indeed, the strong, articulate, and politically aware village women introduced by İncirlioğlu make us question whether a person has to march under the banner of feminism in order to raise women's issues, to struggle for women's rights, or to advance the feminist cause. While most of the work comprising this book explicates the continuity of themes in constructing women, many of them (for example, Demirdirek, İlyasoğlu, Öztürkmen, Y. Arat, Bertram, İncirlioğlu) also show that women can act autonomously to challenge their cultural shaping and ordering. The subject's ability to avoid "conformity to dominant cultural norms and rules" and to escape acting "within the patterns that power inscribes" is stressed by Dirks, Eley, and Ortner:

> ... such an actor is not only possible but "normal," for the simple reason that neither "culture" itself nor the regimes of power that are imbricated in cultural logics and experiences can ever be wholly consistent and determining. "Identities" may be seen as (variably successful) *attempts* to create and maintain coherence out of inconsistent cultural stuff and inconsistent life experience, but every actor always carries around enough disparate and contradictory strands of

knowledge and passion so as always to be in a potentially critical position. Thus the practices of everyday life may be seen as replete with petty rebellions and inchoate discontent.... Even if the subject cannot always be recuperated as a purposeful agent, neither can it any longer be seen as only the effect of subjection.[37]

The longitudinal review of Turkish women's experience presented here demonstrates not only internal inconsistencies of culture and the competition among conflicting discourses, but also how, despite their apparent antagonisms, these multiple discourses enable, accommodate, and complement each other. This almost subversive relationship can be best observed in the contemporary Islamist women's challenge to the conditions set by the secularist reforms of Kemalism. In addition to sharing the altruistic rhetoric of Kemalist women, the "elite" Islamist women use the opportunities created by the Kemalist modernization project to advance their own goals and even refer to some women leaders of that project, albeit without acknowledging their connection to Kemalism, as their role models (see İlyasoğlu in this volume).

As Peter Dews aptly observes, "social systems are both imposed by force from above—they embody relations of *power*—and are adhered or rejected from below."[38] Informed by the examples from the Turkish case, we can add that neither does the adherence to power have to be absolute nor the opposition complete; one does not need to assume or reject the system in its totality. A residual acceptance of what the system offers and the reorientation of prevailing structures and discourses seem to be the strategy followed by Turkish women in the Ottoman Empire and Turkish Republic. Their ways may very well epitomize how the emergence of alternatives becomes possible in all power structures.

Notes

Author's note: I am grateful for the enriching conversations and debates that I enjoyed with Deborah Amory, Karen Baird, Kim Christensen, Sibel Erol, and Liena Gurevich over the years. They addressed many issues discussed here and helped clarify my thoughts. Moreover, Amory's and Baird's invaluable and detailed comments on the draft of the introduction, along with suggestions provided by Carel Bertram and İrvin Schick, allowed me to improve the presentation of ideas in its revised version.

1. *Atatürk'ün Söylev ve Demeçleri,* 1989. Volume II, p. 242; translation mine.

2. Foucault, 1978, Volume I, p. 95.

3. Criticizing "the so-called radical teaching of literary criticism and literature in the United States and perhaps also in Britain," Gayatri Spivak writes that the "dominant *radical* reader in the Anglo-U.S. reactively homogenizes the Third World and sees it only in the context of nationalism and ethnicity." See Spivak, 1988:246.

4. Mohanty, 1991:56.

5. Mohanty, 1991:56.

6. Abadan-Unat, 1986; Özbay, 1990; Ş. Tekeli, 1994a; White, 1994; *Turkey: Women in Development,* 1993.

7. Derrida's deconstructionism involves unfolding metaphors to reveal their underlying logic, which consists of simple binary oppositions (for example, subject/object, men/women, etcetera,) that stand in a hierarchal relation to each other as the superior and subordinate. In this approach, *all differences* are not only reduced to binary formulations but are also believed to reflect domination.

8. Foucault, 1994:214.

9. Çakır, 1991:139-157.

10. Nezihe Muhittin (1889-1958), a feminist intellectual who was active under both the Ottoman and Republican rules, addressed this gap in her book, *Türk Kadını* (The Turkish Woman), published in 1931. See Baykan, 1994:101-116.

11. Göle, 1991:24-47. See also the English version, Göle, 1996:30-44.

12. Göle, 1991:28.

13. Abdullah Cevdet as quoted in Göle, 1996:37; Göle, 1991:26.

14. Jayawardena, 1988:29; Göle, 1996:33.

15. For an example of a recent reproduction of orientalist perception of the harem by a Turkish "scholar," see Croutier, 1989. Without questioning the credibility of the orientalist sources, in fact by using them as the historical record, the author caters to the fantasy of her Western readers.

16. Indeed, Halide Edib was a founding member of the Society for the Elevation of Women in 1909. She was a speaker at the famous "Sultan Ahmet Rally" organized to protest the invasion of İstanbul by the British and its allies after the First World War. She and her husband were close associates of Mustafa Kemal during the War of Independence; they left İstanbul and joined him in his resistance movement in Ankara.

17. T. Parla, 1985.

18. Gökalp's assertions about pre-Islamic Turkish societies, that they were based on gender equality, were renewed by Afet İnan, the adoptive daughter of Mustafa Kemal Atatürk, who was charged by Atatürk to undertake the task of tracing the origins of Turks and their contribution to Anatolian civilizations. See Kandiyoti, 1991c:22-47.

19. Berktay, 1990.

20. Similarly, in her study of the practice in Morocco, Leila Hessini argues that women practice the new veiling not to follow tradition, but out of conviction. See Hessini, 1994.

21. Z. Arat, 1994a.

22. Z. Toprak, 1988.

23. Sirman, 1989:13.

24. Ş. Tekeli, 1982:215.

25. See Jayawardena, 1988; Kandiyoti, 1991b:10.

26. For the best example of an application of this approach to Turkey and other Middle Eastern countries, see D. Lerner, 1958.

27. For an analysis of the gendered nature of the modernization theory and the work of the SSRC Committee, see Scott, 1995.

28. Z. Arat, 1991:33-41.

29. See *Atatürk'ün Söylev ve Demeçleri*. For some translated excerpts, see Z. Arat, 1994a; for a collection of references to women and motherhood made by "progressive" and reformist men, including Atatürk, see Cunbur, 1988.

30. Consequently, in addition to the family members, teachers, and principals, even supervisors at work appointed themselves guardians of especially young women's behavior and sexuality. See my article on women's education here. My interviews revealed that controls similar to the ones at schools were used in the workplace. For example, bank managers and principals

could specify how much makeup and what color lipstick a staff member could wear.

31. See Demirdirek in this volume; Baykan, 1994; Çakır, 1991.
32. Yeşim Arat, in a recent article (forthcoming in *Women and Politics*), discusses Tansu Çiller's background and gender approach. Placing Çiller into the Kemalist elite category, Arat argues that Çiller has been detached from women's problems and approached women as a distinct constituency only during the 1995 elections. In her final analysis, however, Arat states that Çiller affected Turkish politics by introducing a "feminine" style and serving as a role model for other women and girls. I am grateful to the author for rushing me a draft of this article.
33. N. Arat, 1991:11-20.
34. Sirman, 1989; Y. Arat, 1994.
35. As quoted in Jelin, 1990:5.
36. See Baykan, 1994; Z. Toprak, 1988:30-31.
37. Dirks, Eley, and Ortner, 1994:18.
38. Dews, 1988:110-111.

PART I

THE LATE OTTOMAN ERA

DRESSING FOR REVOLUTION: MOTHER, NATION, CITIZEN, AND SUBVERSIVE IN THE OTTOMAN SATIRICAL PRESS, 1908–1911

Palmira Brummett

CARTOONS, two-dimensional images cut in wood, stone, or metal, are, by their very nature, designed to confound the dimensions of time, space, language, and perceived reality.[1] The effect of a cartoon is dependent both upon its invoking a perceived "reality" and upon its subsequently breaking the boundaries of that perception. That is, cartoons are expected to alter reality, radically or subtly, in ways that are both familiar and startling. To do so, cartoons employ tropes (in narrative and image) of character, dress, aspect, setting, and situation that are themselves caricatures. Thus, the cartoon is essentially deconstructive; it mocks the attempt to bound signifier and signified.

The purpose of this chapter is to examine the cartoon images of women found in a very specific genre of literature, published in one specific city, at a particular, highly charged moment in Ottoman history. The genre is the periodical press, specifically the satiric gazette (*mizah mecmuası*). The city is İstanbul: Ottoman capital, endowed by the wealth of multiple imperial patrons, residence of one of the last monarchs in an Ottoman line that had ruled there for over four and one-half centuries. The historical moment is one in which the Ottoman revolution of 1908 had forced the sultan, Abd ül-Hamid II, to accept a constitutional regime, had exposed the empire to attack by foreign powers, and, more significantly for our purposes, had freed the press from a long period of stringent censorship.[2] This chapter, then, examines cartoons published at a time when Ottoman state and society were rapidly evolving, seriously stressed by political, social, and economic changes, and particularly vulnerable. It was a unique period in the history of the press; neither before nor after 1908-1910 was the Ottoman press so dynamic and so unrestrained.

More specifically, this chapter focuses on images of women in Ottoman revolutionary satire. Most Ottoman cartoon figures were male. But female figures were made representative in revolutionary cartoons in certain significant and characteristic ways; women came to stand for the Ottoman nation itself, its vulnerability, and for an amorphous citizenry responding in responsible or irresponsible ways to European imperialism. These specific images of women were employed in the process of trying to reenvision Ottoman state and society.

For that reenvisioning, satire was a particularly apt vehicle because it was a skeptical genre, defending neither the old nor the new order. Satire expressed the anxieties of a people undergoing rapid political and social transformation. The Ottoman press employed many forms of satire: in essays, dialogues, poems, editorials, plays, stories, and even phony letters and ads. But the cartoon, because its message was primarily visual, was the most telling and immediate form. Many cartoon images were designed to be intelligible without captions and could thus be "read" by the illiterate. Cartoons combined the symbols of the literate and illiterate classes into a visual "print" culture that could be consumed without reading. Thus, cartoons could be a very accessible type of satire.[3]

The small number of cartoons shown here suggest characteristic ways in which women figured in the Ottoman cartoon space.[4] I have classified these images under a set of sometimes overlapping categories: mother, nation, citizen, subversive. My classification is a reflection of the ways in which women were made representative in cartoons rather than a prior paradigm into which I am attempting to fit the images.[5] Each cartoon woman shown here has similar counterparts in other gazettes; each draws on the symbolic repertoire available to the editors and cartoonists of İstanbul in the revolutionary period. These categories of representing women emerged out of a context in which the empire was perceived to be seriously threatened by foreign powers. In the Ottoman cartoon space, those threats and the potential for the Ottoman state to respond to them were embodied in images of women, who symbolized the nation and its "citizens": their honor, their weakness, their need for protection, or their valor in the face of adversity. Cartoon women were caricatures of specific notions of femininity (serene, beautiful, sexual, motherly, fashionable). Symbols of the nation (sometimes mother, more often beloved), they were objects of love, desire, and protection.[6]

The drawing of women figures in the Ottoman cartoon space is particularly pertinent to understanding the cultural schizophrenia of the empire: its imagining of a new (and an old) nation; its construction of revolutionary Ottoman identities; and its attempt to challenge, resist, and internalize the possibilities of European hegemony. While male figures could also be used for these purposes, the female figure was employed in ways the male figure was not, or could not, be used. The male, for example, could not be a mother of the nation, an image that quickly generated a whole different set of emotions than the image of a father might. Woman, in the cartoon space, sometimes maternal, sometime sexually charged, became the quintessential symbol of the nation itself and of its vulnerability. Threatened or enticed by foreign powers, she required devotion, loyalty, and restraint.

The images of women treated here are not female self-reflections. The press was essentially a male-centered and male-driven operation. Although there was an Ottoman women's press (designed for a female audience and employing female editors and writers) as early as the nineteenth century, the editors, writers, cartoonists, and content of the Ottoman press at the turn of the twentieth century were predominantly male. The target audience for the satirical press was also predominantly male. There were, clearly, female readers, as indicated by forms of address employed in editorials, women's sections, ads targeting women, illustrations showing women readers, and the evidence of female readers in letters columns and lists of contest participants. Nonetheless, all of the images of women treated in this article were apparently produced by men. I am not arguing that there is some simple or single male ideology constructed in Ottoman cartoons of women. The agents of revolutionary satire represented a broad spectrum of political and social ideology. They could be enthusiastic about or hostile to the new regime; they could support or reject the Europeanization of women's dress, manners, and education. Their cartoon women employed a broad, if finite, range of diverse symbols to suggest the nature of the female and her relationships to the male and to the nation. Still, understanding the nature of Ottoman cartoon images of women, as images of the female body produced by men for other men to look at, is critical to understanding how the critique of European imperialism was linked to the female form and to imagining the emotions these images hoped to evoke or embody.

Also critical to understanding these images is the fact that they were produced in what I would call a colonial context. Although the empire had not been subjected to military conquest and direct foreign rule, its economic and cultural systems had been "colonized"—that is, infiltrated and dominated by European interests and styles.[7] This kind of colonization dramatically affected the options for self-identification found in the Ottoman satirical press and became a major theme in Ottoman cartoons. Thus, analyses of constructions of women in the Ottoman Empire would benefit from contemporaneous comparisons to similar constructions in formally colonized territories like South Asia and Mexico.[8] The immediate effect of such comparisons is a recognition that the political, economic, and cultural power of Europeans and European states was much more than an external threat or influence; it was a major conditioning factor in the Ottomans' revolutionary constructions of their social order.[9] As such, it is also a major factor in the construction of the Ottoman cartoon space and of the female (and male) inhabitants of that space.

CARTOON, COSTUME, AND COLONIAL CONTEXT

Ottoman cartoons pose their women to evoke powerful images. These women take on certain roles: nation, citizen, mother, subversive. As an allegorical figure of the nation, the cartoon woman stands for the empire as a whole—its survival, victories, and defeats. As citizen, the cartoon woman symbolizes the collective identity either of all Ottomans, all female Ottomans, or some subgroup thereof. As mother, she symbolizes the nurturing or reproductive powers of the nation, its honor and need for protection. As subversive, she symbolizes the weakness of the Ottoman nation or its citizens, their susceptibility to Western imperialism; she is the threat from within. These four roles and identities are not mutually exclusive. Thus, cartoons diapose caricatures of women in expected or proper costume (suggesting female types) to caricature of women in composite costume (suggesting apparently contradictory identities). Each female figure is first enscribed in a certain setting. Then clothing, props, and accessories are layered upon her like a set of transparencies. She can wear the transparency labeled "citizen" and the transparency labeled "subversive" at the same time.

Cartoon females were either mythic (by which I mean they were allegorical, representing concepts like freedom, the nation, or the heroic past) or they suggested real Ottoman women (members of the Ottoman public or subsets thereof, rather than specific named individuals). The latter were types such as mothers, servants, or housewives. *Türkiye* (as the motherland), an idealized mythic symbol of the nation, was often shown, after the revolution, as trading one predatory male, sultanic despotism, for another, European imperialism.[10] The non-mythic cartoon females were shown caught in a similar dilemma between the lure of fashionable European womanhood and an imagined past ideal of the "traditional" Ottoman woman, demure and dressed in "traditional" costume.

Women became sacred cows in the Ottoman cartoon space. Signifying much more than herself, a woman-figure could represent the empire itself, or its wealth, glory, survival, and honor. Historically, women and cows have both been treated as booty. In artistic imagery, both have been symbols of the wealth of nations.[11] Taking this notion literally, one cartoon in *Kalem* (Pen) showed the empire as a cow besieged by greedy European imperialists attempting to steal her milk. This image was a direct borrowing from European iconography: a well-known engraving depicting the wealthy Netherlands as a huge cow set upon by neighbors (like England and Spain) who were intent upon exploiting her.[12] The Ottoman version showed the empire as a huge cow surrounded by little men (representing the various states of Europe) armed with milk pails.[13] An Ottoman soldier stepped forward to warn the interlopers swarming over her that they could no longer enjoy the stolen goods. The nation, in effect, would no longer submit to European exploitation.

Figure 1.1

This same configuration, the gargantuan nation beset by foreign men whose thieving would no longer be tolerated, is duplicated in a cartoon (Figure 1.1) in *Lak Lak* (Stork). This time, however, it is a woman, rather than a cow, who symbolizes the empire. Her name is *Meşrutiyet* (Constitutionalism). She is the mythic female image of the nation, bound in chains but towering over the tiny men (European states) who gaze up at her. Though chained in the shackles of *cehalet* (ignorance) and *imtiyazat* (capitulations), she is smiling because, as she announces to her would-be enslavers, she will no longer tolerate the bonds that have been imposed upon her.[14] Here, the cartoon female becomes an Ottoman sacred cow: something special, something not to be violated, an embodiment of the nation triumphant in female form.

This image divides the cartoon frame between the Ottoman enemies and the Ottoman self, represented by Meşrutiyet. She dominates the space. Her erstwhile captors, the European imperialists, are insignificant in size; they cannot control her even though she still bears the chains that they and the past regime have forged. She is dressed in a caricature of "traditional" costume that is not necessarily a mirror image of actual traditional dress, but a trope for "nationality," a device to suggest identity. This dress is meant to reinforce her identity and to separate her irrevocably from her one-time European oppressors. Each of them (Austria, England, France, Russia, etcetera) is drawn and dressed in such a way as to suggest his national character.

European states, unlike the Ottoman nation, were almost always gendered male in Ottoman cartoons. France, as an imperial power, was drawn as a short, unseemly male. The exception was when France stood for the revolutionary ideals of liberté, égalité, fraternité; then it was invariably drawn as the nubile and beautiful Marianne. England was John Bull or the English king. Austria and Russia were embodied either in the persons of their monarchs, or as wolves or bears, or as generic soldiers in "national" costume. They bore the facial and dress markers of their national identities: noses, mustaches, kilts, uniforms, flags, helmets. This male gendering was accompanied by the attribution of aggressive traits; the European states were greedy, militaristic, threatening, swaggering, lustful. They were often shown swallowing, cutting up, or seducing the Ottoman nation.[15] They were cast in a fairly limited number of roles, usually as imperialists dressed either in military uniform or business costume.

Such dressing of cartoon figures was no accident. All cultures mark meaning with items of clothing. In cartoon culture this marking of ideology through dress becomes more urgent because the cartoon image must often relay its message without benefit of caption, epithet, or narration. The image must speak for itself, and this speaking requires a simplification of dress codes, one in which a hat, a style of drapery, or a veil says all (about identity, about ideology, about orientation). Thus clothes, in cartoons, are exaggerations, caricatures. Yet the dress markers of cartoon culture are enscribed in a specific time, place, and audience. Their apparent simplicity clothes a complex set of emotions, cultural expectations, and political manipulations.

Dress markers were manipulated on Ottoman cartoon women to create a series of identifications: for women, for men, and for the nation.[16] Images of women, in particular, were used to embody the Ottoman nation (or its component parts), a nation which was incompletely imagined.[17] This female nation could be perceived as suffering from assaults that might prove fatal, or as reasserting past glories and refashioning herself in a new and heroic mode. Often, in order to emphasize the possibilities just mentioned, she was dressed in classical robes or in exaggerated "traditional" costume to differentiate her from Europeans or Europeanized women. Cartoon Ottoman women, identified by the clothing they wore, prompted their audience to shame, to patriotism, to the envisioning of a glorious new society or the dismal specter of the empire's honor (military, economic, and sexual) sacrificed on the altar of European imperialism.[18] Dress markers were used to point out and exaggerate ethnicity and, conversely, to suggest the ways in which ethnic and national identities were being mixed, compromised, or challenged.[19]

European women in Ottoman cartoons tended to be archetypes; they were ordinarily young and very fashionably dressed, often shown socializing with men. Their function, apparently, was to provide an ideal (admirable or contemptible) to which Ottoman women were either contrasted or approximated. Europeanized Ottoman women (those who adopted European-style fashions, language, education, manners, or entertainments) were often typed as subversives in the Ottoman cartoon space. Their dress, along with that of their chic male counterparts, suggested collusion with the imperialist enemy and, additionally, a subversion of traditional mores. Western styles were not always criticized in Ottoman cartoons, especially since European fashion was common among the upper classes in İstanbul by the time of the revolution.[20] Some cartoons equated the imitation of Western culture and the consumption of Western goods with progressive attitudes and material prosperity. But exaggerated European dress, like exaggerated traditional dress, produced readily identifiable types in the Ottoman cartoon space. Clothing Ottoman women in Paris fashion was a ready-made vehicle for suggesting the imbalance of power between the Ottoman state and its European competitors. Europe dictated fashions, the empire consumed them. The Ottoman female body, in European *haute* (or not so *haute*) *couture,* signified extrava-gance, unwarranted consumption, compromised morals, and even subversive intent against the nation.[21] The figure of *Meşrutiyet,* Figure 1.1, dressed conspicuously in harem pants (*şalvar*), head scarf, and pointed shoes, stood in direct contrast to Westernized females dressed in the symbols of European domination.

In this context, in which the empire was envisioned as surrounded by threatening male imperialists, allegorical images of the nation equated women with territory or property. In these women, the honor of the nation was embodied; and because the bodies were female, the military and sexual honor of the nation was confounded. The imagery in cartoons that contained female signifiers of the nation could be much more explicitly sexual than in Figure 1.1. One of the most expressive of these cartoons about the compromising of Ottoman political, cultural, and sexual honor was a cartoon that showed the Ottoman regime as a slave merchant, offering his female wares (dressed in traditional costume) to the appraising eye of the Austrian king, who has usurped the sultan's throne.[22] In such cases, the female figures may still be allegorical but they no longer have mythic proportions. They are drawn in realistic proportion to their potential male seducers. Two cartoons of this type showed Ottoman women embodying specific regions of the empire: Crete, Bosnia, and Herze-govina. In each case, the women were young and alluring "pieces" of the nation. The male figures in these cartoons signified European nations poised to seduce or carry off the objects of their desire, the Ottoman women.

The first example has some similarities to the *Lak Lak* cartoon in Figure 1.1., but in Figure 1.2, Crete, a demure young woman in traditional dress, is surrounded by her *düvel-i hamiye* (protector nations), England, Austria, and a third figure, possibly France. But here they are larger than she.[23] Arm-in-arm, they are marching her off. Standing before them, but not confronting them directly, is a noble-looking Ottoman soldier. Here, the nation is vulnerable. She is in need of protection, but there is a competition between contending males over who will serve that protective function, the Ottoman Empire (here called *Türkiye*), or the imperial powers of Europe. Crete at this time was still depicted as Ottoman "property," and "her" abduction

Figure 1.2

was, in effect, a rape.[24] The Ottoman soldier could not stop her "protectors" and, therefore, could not preserve the nation's honor.[25]

There is, however, another way to read this cartoon. Rather than being abducted, Crete might be running off with her virile companions, all dressed in military costume. In either reading, the Ottoman male is emasculated, his honor compromised. In this latter scenario the female is at once nation, citizen, and subversive. Crete becomes the symbol of violated Ottoman territorial integrity. But because that territory is embodied in human form, Crete also stands for the Ottoman citizen, tempted to violate the sovereignty of the nation by engaging in separatist national projects. Finally, the cartoon Crete is subversive. She provides the opportunity for foreign states to penetrate and disarticulate the empire. She is a member of the nation who is willing to compromise its integrity for a better offer. Once she is gone, the nation is diminished. Nonetheless, I think it would be a mistake to suggest that this cartoon shows some kind of empowerment of the female Crete. Although she may be flirting with her new protectors, the tacit assumption is that she must have a male protector. There is no question of autonomy. Even though she walks arm-in-arm with the European powers, she is surrounded, and they are, in effect, captors.[26]

A similar cartoon shows Austria as a dirty old man in uniform, attempting to seduce the nubile young Bosnia and Herzegovina, who are dressed in traditional clothing (*şalvar*, fezzes, sashes, and pointed shoes). The young women are standing in a courtyard within the large protective gates of a domestic compound, but the gates are open.[27] Austria beckons to them, saying, "Please, Mademoiselles, I've been waiting for you too long!"[28] Again, the females signify a part of the nation that has become detached, thus shaming the (here absent) Ottoman men. Here too, the women take on the roles of nation, citizen, and subversive; they have not decisively rejected the advances of the Austrian, even though they are demurely hanging back. As with Crete, the perceived threat to Ottoman territory and honor was very real, since Austria did indeed annex Bosnia and Herzegovina in the immediate aftermath of the 1908 revolution. In both these seduction scenes, women have the power to honor or shame the nation. They signify the nation itself, the nation's property (its citizens), and an internal force that by its very nature can subvert and dishonor the nation.

A third example of the cartoon threatened female contains a similar scenario but with a different outcome. In this frame (Figure 1.3), the woman in need of protection is *Hürriyet* (freedom).[29] She is a figure of the beloved: slight and pretty, cowering under the strong, sheltering arm of the noble Ottoman soldier.[30] A Marianne-like figure, she is dressed in a combination of classical robes and a cap reminiscent of French revolutionary headgear. The soldier is a St. George figure, holding off the menacing dragon with his sword, the army. "Do not fear, my Dear, I'm here and my sword is sharp," he assures her. In this case, the threat to freedom is not external but internal. The dragon is labeled *irtica* (forces of reaction), suggesting the threat that, under the new revolutionary order, had replaced despotism. Here the Ottoman male preserves his honor; he will triumph through force of arms and presumably win the

L'ARMÉE — N'aie pas peur, je suis là.   ‏اوردو ــ (حریته) قورقه یاوروم، بن بالکدیم، قلیجم کسکیندر.‏

Figure 1.3

undying love and gratitude of *Hürriyet*. Still, the dragon is two-headed and not yet slain, suggesting that real threats still remain to the empire's new-found freedom. *Hürriyet* is drawn small and youthful to represent her "newness" and fragility; her size exaggerates that of both the male figure and the dragon and emphasizes her need for protection. This nubile form of *Hürriyet* is a common form of the Marianne figure, a younger counterpart to the buxom or bare-breasted Marianne found in French revolutionary satire. Her cap symbolizes a linking of the Ottoman to the French Revolution.[31] But the approximation of this woman

Figure 1.4

image to that of Marianne also suggests that Ottoman political reality has already been inevitably subverted, even in the cartoon space, by European hegemony. At a very precarious point in the revolution's history (November 1908, before the new government had been installed) only a Western style of freedom, preserved by force, could protect the "new" nation from chaos.

The cartoon nation, gendered female, can be strong or vulnerable, as shown above. While some cartoons suggest she is inviolable, others suggest she has already been violated. These options of strength, of vulnerability, of loyalty at risk are woven into images of the female as nation. The cartoon female as nation-symbol has the potential to be either patriot or subversive depending on how she is framed in the cartoon space: her dress, her manner, her action, her associates.

The cartoon citizen, like the figures of the nation, can also be either patriot or subversive. These options are suggested in two cartoons showing the Ottomans in colonial context. They concern the Ottoman boycott of Austrian goods that was launched when Austria annexed Bosnia and Herzegovina in 1908. The first example (Figure 1.4) is the allegorical image of woman as nation and as citizen. Here she appears as a mother rather than a beloved. She is serene, beautiful yet strong, not like the Marianne figure in Figure 1.3 who cowers while her male "George" tries to kill the dragon. Türkiye, here, has supporters bearing her along, rather than protectors. In this cartoon (one segment of a large frame showing the boycott and a triumphant procession in which Türkiye is the central figure) the proud Ottomans and their allies are the heroic figures resisting the evil interloper, Austria.[32]

The female Ottoman nation is the centerpiece of the frame. She is peaceful but will not submit to the violence of the boycott, just as our earlier figure of Türkiye would not submit to the violence of the capitulations. Next to her is Marianne as France personified, but this time Marianne is also an older, motherly figure. They are mother nations, alongside Britain (in uniform) and Russia (in peasant costume) as father nations. Türkiye has donned the identities of mother, nation, and citizen. Her simple and conservative dress, with hair, neck, and arms covered, suggests her dignity and the honor and respect due her. In her lap she bears the slogan "Liberty, Peace, Progress." Above all, she is a patriot, signifying the endurance and stability of the nation, which will survive and adapt to the onslaught of European imperialism. She accepts Europeans who will support her and rejects those who threaten her. This cartoon is somewhat unusual in that its producers are willing to make a distinction (which many Ottoman revolutionary cartoons would reject) between good and bad European imperialists. In most cartoons, Britain and France, like Austria, are cast in the role of grasping imperial powers.

A contrasting image is that of the Ottoman woman (not the allegorical Türkiye) responding to the boycott. Such an image is found in the gazette *Dalkavuk* (Toady/Buffoon).[33] Unlike the serene mother nation, the woman in this cartoon is a wife, accompanying her husband. Rejecting the temptation to consumerism, she passes by the Pera shopkeeper offering Western goods. She is not the nation; instead, she is the citizen patriot *par excellance,* putting aside her own wishes to serve the interests of the country. As long as the boycott continues, the pleading shopkeeper cannot expect her patronage. She has resisted the temptation to become (or to continue being) the subverted citizen, consumer of imported goods, the symbol of European dominance. The citizen patriot wears traditional costume or she wears "modern" (that is, Europeanized) costume that is understated, not flashy, sexy, or exaggerated. In her role of patriot she is an almost-man or rather, getting as close to a man as possible, a subordinate partner.

The female citizen boycotter is a patriot under male guidance. As a bearer of children, however, the citizen can be a patriot in her own right. In the role of mother, as with the allegorical figure of Türkiye, the citizen patriot takes on a most powerful and compelling form. A classic example of this role is depicted in a cartoon called "The New Generation" (Figure 1.5).[34] In this frame, three female citizens, typed by their exaggerated traditional dress, are kibitzing during a visit. One woman, apparently the hostess, is rocking her baby, who is dressed in a crescent-decorated fez and holding a rifle. One of the visitors hails her, "May God spare you sister, is it a girl or a boy?" She replies, "A soldier, by God!" Here, the mother is the nurturer of a new generation of soldiers who will defend the honor of the nation through military power. She is a patriot through procreation. Like the allegorical image of Türkiye at the boycott, and unlike most Ottoman cartoons, this cartoon suggests some hope for the future of the empire. Yet its message is ironic. Not only does the revolution require that its female citizens bear soldiers, not children, but the baby is de-gendered. Although there is no overt reference to colonial context in this cartoon, it is the threat of European imperialism that, in this period, genders the new generation not as male or female, but as soldier, defender of the motherland.

Nation and citizen both come in mother forms. But there is another type of mother figure in the Ottoman cartoon space. She is found primarily in social satire: the nagging, enduring, compassionate, hard-working, extravagant, or long-suffering woman. She is an older woman ("postsexual," as in historian Leslie Peirce's model of Ottoman harem women, "menopausal" according to current literary convention).[35] There is a whole series of post-sexual woman figures, with antecedents in the *Arabian Nights* and Asian epic literature, in Ottoman satire: *Cadaloz* (Old Nag), *Büyük Hanım* (Granny), and the mascots for the

Figure 1.5

journals *Diken* (Thorn) and *Geveze* (Gabber or Noisy One). Such everywoman figures tend to be mothers, who are constrained neither by modesty nor by sexual contexts from speaking their minds where the organization of politics or society is concerned. These women are beyond seduction. They are outspoken citizens. The use of these figures suggests that voice, in the public arena, was more readily granted to or expected from those women who had reached a certain age.

FASHION AND SUBVERSION

When, however, nation and citizen are represented as subject to temptation, their paradoxical position is most often suggested by dress markers. Dress markers indicate that the sacred cow may be stolen away, that the citizen patriot may be tempted, or polluted, or may voluntarily surrender herself to the enemy. When she dons the dress markers of the enemy—Parisian fashion—then she becomes something abnormal and unsettling. Women wearing Paris fashion are equated, for example, with cholera. When Crete, Bosnia, and Herzegovina are depicted as women dressed in traditional costume, it is not clear whether they are subversive or not; they may simply signify the

Figure 1.6

victimization of the nation. When a cartoon woman is dressed in European fashion, the "fact" that she is a subversive may still be unclear; but she is not a victim, because her role is decidedly active. Such women choose to participate in the Europeanization of the empire. They are consumers, and the fact of that consumption, as signified by their dress, suggests that they are complicit in the cultural and economic undermining of the nation.

Paris fashion became an easy way to suggest luxury, frivolity, and a dearth of patriotic spirit; this engendering of suspicion through dress

Figure 1.7

was applied to men as well as women. Dressing in Western fashion is associated, in cartoons, with immorality or unrestrained sexuality.[36] Ottoman males are shown as Europeanized dandies. Ottoman bureaucrats are shown consorting with fashionable European females in order to suggest that their actions compromise Ottoman integrity. A cartoon by Sedad Nuri, who was unrelenting in his satirization of Europeanized Ottomans, shows such a subversion motif by depicting a generic "Young Turk" in France (Figure 1.6).[37] The cartoon is captioned, "At Marienbad, Triple Alliance." It shows a member of the Ottoman government walking with two fashionable and curvaceous Frenchwomen. His hands rest casually on the young women's hips. This frame illustrates the generic foreign woman: young, sexual, subverting the empire from without. The Young Turk is her co-conspirator; he too subverts the empire by placing his own gratification first and the interests of the state second. Indeed, this cartoon is a counterpart to the one of Crete; foreign men seduce the female nation in one cartoon, and foreign women seduce the Ottoman man in the other.

Fashion satire as a satire of subversion, however, achieved its most extravagant forms with the dressing of the Ottoman female. "Paris fashion" was the easiest way to type the collaborator (witting or unwitting); it became the dress marker of choice to symbolize the fears of the empire: looking foolish, economic exploitation, conquest, and the corruption of moral norms. The most obvious collaborator was the Ottoman woman consuming Western fashions.

An allegorical example, using both male and female figures, of this relationship of conspicuous consumption is found in a cartoon in *Davul* (Drum) that diaposes the fashionable, Westernized İstanbul elites to a poor Anatolian beggar (Figure 1.7).[38] The cartoon is entitled, "Returning from the Benefit Ball for Those Striken by Drought and Famine in Anatolia." It shows a beggar approaching a prosperous couple who are leaving the ball; the man is in a tuxedo, the woman is in a low-cut European gown. "Be compassionate," says the beggar, "In the country my child is dying of hunger." The smiling woman ignores the petitioner, while her escort snarls, "What an ingrate you are! We were just now working for your benefit." Here, the beggar becomes the symbol of the nation. The starving Anatolians are a metaphor for the empire, reduced to beggary by oppression and by the extravagance and consumerism of its elites. The European threat is not the threat of conquest symbolized by European males in uniform, rather it is the more insidious threat of economic and cultural imperialism symbolized by Western fashions in dress and entertainment.[39] The affluent Ottoman couple are citizen subversives, their identity revealed by their dress. But the male is the spokesman. The female has been approximated as closely as possible to the female European subversive, only her setting and peasant countryman testify to her Ottoman identity. He is approximated to the European exploiter, taking on the foreigner's dress and his disregard for the Ottoman people. This couple is the polar opposite of the cartoon couple, noted above, who are boycotting the Pera shopkeeper. In both cartoons, the woman is subordinate to her male partner. But in the earlier cartoon, the woman, as citizen patriot, actively resists the temptation to consume European goods. She signifies a sense of unity with her fellow boycotters and countrymen. In the latter image, the female figure, as citizen subversive, is not only at ease with her consumption of European dress, but she is silently complicit in her partner's rejection of a countryman's appeal. This is not only a satire of class, but a satire that shows that the Europeanized Ottoman has lost his/her proper sense of identity.

CONCLUSION

Women's roles and identities, then, are drawn within a set of contextual frames that shape the possibilities, in cartoons, for real or imagined women. These frames are a function of the events of the day, the audience, the limits of the cartoon medium, and the symbolic repertoire available to editors and cartoonists in the revolutionary period. The colonial context, the empire's subordination or threat of subordination to Europe, was never far from the surface in the Ottoman cartoon space. And because the cartoon audience was predominantly male, women's bodies became the most significant implements for expressing the empire's options of triumph or humiliation. Furthermore, cartoons of women confounded the dichotomy of public and private spheres. These spheres could not be rigidly bounded because cartoons made all space (male or female) public, from the boudoir to the coffeehouse to the bazaar. As a figure of the nation, the cartoon female was approximated to the male figures of foreign nations. Thus, cartoons violated or acknowledged the porous nature of the boundaries between public and private.[40]

So in the Ottoman cartoon space, women, like the empire itself, take on a complex set of evolving identities. Character types, mythic or manikin, are stretched and altered in the interstitial spaces between cartoonists' art, social expectation, and audience reception. And, in the end (although our own attention belies an end to the communicative power of these cartoons), Ottoman satire's treatment of women defies easy classification. The satirical press was unsure that the state would survive the radical transformation from empire to nation. Nowhere could this anxiety be more effectively expressed than on the female body. It should not, then, surprise us that citizen and subversive are confounded. In colonial context, even the nation herself, and her daughters, became suspect. Although the 1908 revolution was relatively bloodless, it occurred during a period of radical reconfiguration of Ottoman cultural reality. In such circumstances, cartoons make explicit what we already know, that the behaviors of humans are easier to predict than are the ways in which they imagine themselves.

Notes

Author's note: My own work here is part of a larger monographic project in progress on the Ottoman press, entitled *Image and Imperialism in the Ottoman Revolutionary Press,* that focuses on the satirization of European political and cultural imperialism, and for which I have surveyed over sixty-nine gazettes of the revolutionary period. I wish to thank Joe Rader, director, and Hua Li at the University of Tennessee Archive for their production of the digitally scanned cartoons employed in this chapter. Note that dating for all periodicals is Ottoman financial year (*malî*) dating.

1. The cartoons treated here are, by definition, satirical: the genre of satire provides them with their confounding power. Although, as in other genres of literature and art, the degree to which these dimensions are confounded varies from one type of cartoon to another, I would argue that such confounding is a part of the essence of the cartoon.

2. Censorship during Abd ül-Hamid's reign was never complete; many contrived to circumvent it. But it did severely limit the quality and quantity of press output. In the first year after the revolution, over two hundred new gazettes were published in

İstanbul alone, more than the total published during the sultan's reign from 1876 to the revolution.

3.   This type of print culture cannot, then, be considered merely a reflection of elite culture, even though the gazette (and hence the narrative in which the cartoon was embedded) was often aimed at a highly sophisticated audience. Its "vulgar" modes of narrative and visual satire, like the ubiquitous shadow puppet theater dialogues, were shared across all strata of Ottoman society. The polarization of literate vs. illiterate society and the typing of print culture as elitist obscures the porous nature of the boundaries between elite and "popular" in the press. Nor is there a firm line between literate and illiterate audiences, especially in a society in which newspapers were routinely read aloud in coffeehouses and elsewhere.

4.   Cartoons in this era ranged from the highly sophisticated to the very primitive, and it would take many more cartoons than are shown here to form a representative sample. As a genre, Ottoman cartooning presents an elaborate mix of cultural influences, both domestic and foreign—from direct pirating of the English satiric gazette, *Punch,* to the direct transfer of traditional oral theater into visual images. It is important to note that there was no sense of clear ownership or copyright as such. Most cartoons were anonymous; and cartoons were reprinted from one gazette to another.

5.   The cartoon samples here were chosen for their representative nature and varied visual style, and because the four gazettes from which they were extracted were available for digital scanning. Little systematic work has been done on the Ottoman press; recently, a very useful survey has been published by Çeviker, 1986-1991, covering the period from the *Tanzimat* to 1923, which includes multiple illustrations and brief treatments on individual gazettes, publishers, and cartoonists.

6.   On these same symbols in Iranian nationalist literature, see Najmabadi, 1993. Conversely, on the imagining of the European female "nation" in Iranian literature, see Tavakoli-Targhi, 1994.

7.   For an intriguing approach, premised on India, to notions of nations, women, and colonial contexts, see Chatterjee, 1993:116-157. Chatterjee's work also includes a critique of the

boundary-breaking study on nation and identity by Anderson, 1983.

8. One good example is Rajan, 1993:6. Rajan, in this work on Indian women, has suggested that postcolonial nations, as a result of their shared experience of colonialism, can be marked by: ". . . the central role of the state; inequalities in social structures; the contrary pulls of nationalism and regionalism (or centralization and federalization); and the conflicts between tradition and modernity ." These four characteristics certainly fit post-Ottoman Turkey, even though it is not a post-colonial state in the classic sense of that term. I would, however, argue that Rajan's characterization is too rough as a general classification (especially since she seems to mean something very specific when she speaks of inequalities of social structure).

9. Anderson's images, for example, of colonized nations in Southeast Asia are often quite comparable to those of the evolving Ottoman nation (1983:140).

10. This was the polarized dilemma of the revolutionary Ottoman state as illustrated in cartoons in *İncili Çavuş,* 12:4, 16 Eylül 1324/29 September 1908, showing the Ottoman nation as a man drowning in *istibdad* (despotism) while being attacked by European states; and in *Kalem,* 104:7, 2 Kanun-ı evvel 1326/15 December 1910, showing Iran as a man who, "while bathing in the constitutional waters," had his clothes (territories) stolen by Russia and England. Iran was ordinarily gendered as male when personified in Ottoman cartoons.

11. In Ottoman cartoons, when animal herds are shown, they are ordinarily sheep rather than cows. In epic Turkish literature, such as *The Book of Dede Korkut,* a people's wealth lies in its horse herds; when the villains want to humiliate their male rivals, they steal their horses and women. This idea was echoed in Machiavelli's *The Prince,* when he advised the monarch that people (meaning men) could be governed if the prince did not interfere unduly with their property or with their women. So, when I call Ottoman cartoon women sacred cows, I am not borrowing a traditional image from Ottoman iconography. Rather, I am combining the notion of cows as wealth from Africa, India, or other parts of Europe and equating it with another idea of a sacred cow—that is, something mystical, something that is

not to be touched, something to which the honor of the people, and the nation, is inviolably attached.

12. It was not unusual for Ottoman cartoons to imitate conventions of European satire. Some Ottoman gazettes also published cartoons from the English, French, German, and Italian presses.

13. *Kalem,* 45:1, 9 Temmuz 1325/22 July 1909.

14. *Lak Lak,* 12:1, 24 Eylül 1325/7 October 1909.

15. Here again, the Ottoman nation could be gendered male (or neuter, a thing) and be the object of European (male) state aggression, as in a cartoon in *Dalkavuk* 1:5, 30 Ağustos 1324/12 September 1908, showing foreign doctors cutting up a male patient representing the empire. But these cartoons tended more toward humor and less toward compulsion than those with a female embodiment of the nation. They were not directly sexual. The nation, as a female, could also be shown as the object of the attentions or threats of Ottoman men, as in a cartoon similar in situation to the one in *Dalkavuk* (a patient surrounded by those ministering to him/her), which showed the Ottoman constitution as a sick woman (a mother-figure) surrounded by members of the Ottoman government whose ministrations have already worsened her condition (*Kalem* 76:5, 18 Şubat 1325/2 March 1910).

16. The pioneering study of fashion satire in the Ottoman press has been done by Şeni (1990), who traces the representation of women in late-nineteenth-century Ottoman satire and analyzes the motifs of fashion, the comparisons between Eastern and Western women through fashion, and thematic treatments of sexuality and feminism.

17. The Ottoman nation was often gendered female even though *vatan* (homeland) is characteristically translated as "fatherland" in the historiography on nationalism. *Vatan* is often interpreted as the equivalent of the French *patrie* (fatherland) but it often has a female connotation, at least in the Ottoman cartoon space. The female nation had different names, suggesting the geographic whole (Türkiye), regional parts (Crete), or symbolic aspects of the nation or government; see, for example, *Hürriyet* (Freedom) as an idealized and beautiful fairy, in *Falaka,* 8:1, approximately 20 Eylül 1327/3 October 1911.

18. For treatments of images of women and fashion in Western settings, see Powell and Childs, 1990; and Ribeiro, 1986.

19. It is important to note here that Ottoman revolutionary cartoons, although they could clearly indicate ethnicity or ethnic types, did not seem overly preoccupied with making ethnic or religious distinctions for characters within the empire; rather, they were preoccupied with suggesting the ethnic types, and hence the divisions, between Ottomans and non-Ottomans (especially Europeans).

20. Micklewright, 1986.

21. Mazumdar, 1994, speaking about turn-of-the-century Bengali literature, has noted the effect of opposing the "material" West to the "spiritual" East on cultural constructions of women: ". . . and over the course of the nineteenth and early twentieth century, the upper-caste Hindu Indian woman became the repository of this national spiritual essence; a 'goddess' who must remain untainted by 'westernization' and its implied pollu-tion" (p. 257). Ottoman cartoon women did not ordinarily embody the spiritual, but they were often used to draw dichoto-mies between the "goddess" of the nation and Western "pollu-tion."

22. *Kalem*, 23:8-9, 22 Kanun-ı sani 1324/5 February 1909.

23. *Kalem,* 52:8, 27 Ağustos 1325/10 September 1909. Crete had not been under real Ottoman control for some time; it was finally annexed by Greece in 1912.

24. Much has been written on colonial rape imagery. Of particular interest here is Sharpe, 1993:137-162. What Sharpe notes for the *Jewel in the Crown* can also be applied to the Ottoman cartoon on Crete: ". . . when deployed as a concept-metaphor for imperial-ism, 'rape' does not designate the penetration and control of the female colonial body; rather it designates the emasculation of the male one" (p. 155).

25. A similar cartoon in *Nekregu ile Pişekar,* 3:1, 3 Haziran 1325/16 June 1909, has a happier outcome. It shows an Ottoman soldier rescuing Crete. She is, however, half naked, perhaps suggesting that she has already been compromised.

26. In fact, the nation as a female in need of protection was a much more common scenario than that shown in Figure 1.1, in which

the female figure of the nation is shown triumphing over her male persecutors.

27. Their positioning, poised in the gateway, also suggests a violation of the boundary between the public and domestic spheres. Austria is a stranger encouraging them to leave the "sacred" precincts of their domicile or to violate the "sacred" trust of loyalty to the nation. Such positioning is common in the cartoon space, where much of the action takes place in the streets. Cartoons demonstrate that boundaries between male and female spheres are and have always been very porous, at least in the imagination.

28. *Kalem,* 10:7, 23 Teşrin-i evvel 1324/6 November 1908. A similar cartoon, *Kalem,* 22:4, 15 Kanun-ı sani 1324/28 January 1909, shows Bosnia and Herzegovina as counterparts to Alsace and Lorraine, all female bodies representing contested territory.

29. *Kalem,* 11:1, 30 Teşrin-i evvel 1324/13 November 1908.

30. For an interesting iconography of female images of the nation in France, see *La France,* 1989. This guide notes, "French culture, deprived of those values which had held it together, looked for a sign sufficiently powerful to maintain itself in a secular and utopian age and found it in the image of a beloved woman, often contrasted to a darker counterpart or *femme fatale*" (p.19). In the Ottoman cartoons, the *femme fatale* role is played by the European floozy on the one hand, tempting Ottoman men, and by the Westernized Ottoman female, on the other hand, the internal threat.

31. It may also demonstrate the degree to which Ottoman cartoonists imitated tropes found in European cartoons.

32. *Musavver Papağan,* 19 Kanun-ı evvel 1324/2 January 1909. A very similar image of Türkiye, with the crescent on her head but dressed in more classical draperies, can be found in *Davul,* 13: front cover, 14 Kanun-ı sani 1324/27 January 1909. In the latter cartoon she is more sexual, the woman as beloved (her arms and neck bared) rather than as mother, but she bears the same serene, slightly smiling look.

33. *Dalkavuk,* 25:1, 21 Şubat 1324/6 March 1909. Unfortunately I could not obtain a copy of this cartoon for reproduction.

34. *Kalem,* 85:5, 22 Nisan 1326/5 May 1910.

35. Peirce, 1993:20-23, 91-112. On the old woman figure in Otto-
     man satire, see Brummett, 1997.
36. See, for example, *Kalem*, 94:3, 12 Ağustos 1326/25 August 1910;
     and 115:6, 17 Şubat 1326/2 March 1911.
37. *Kalem*, 92:10, 26 Ağustos 1326/9 September 1910.
38. *Davul*, 16:8, 11 Şubat 1324/24 February 1909.
39. Images of conspicuous consumption are most often associated
     with women. This, however, is not unique to the Ottoman
     cartoon space. British and French cartoons of the same period
     also targeted women as conspicuous consumers. Medieval Euro-
     pean sumptuary laws also ordinarily targeted the dressing of
     women.
40. Women seldom appear in institutional spaces, such as schools,
     public buildings, or parliament (except by allusion, when men
     are dressed in drag). Male figures are occasionally dressed in
     women's clothing, but not always to ridicule them. For example,
     an official could be shown in women's clothing to illustrate his
     engaging in a "woman's" task, such as sewing up the tattered
     nation. One cartoon showed role reversals, with the man mind-
     ing the baby and the woman chopping wood, although each
     retained her/his identity by retaining dress appropriate to her/his
     sex (Kalem 58:1, 8 Teşrin-i evvel, 1325/21 October 1909).
     Gender lines were also blurred in the androgynous figure of the
     old woman mascot for the gazette *Cadaloz* (1911), suggesting
     that a woman with an aggressive voice in public affairs is
     defeminized.

IN PURSUIT OF THE OTTOMAN WOMEN'S MOVEMENT

Aynur Demirdirek

Translated by Zehra F. Arat

SINCE THE LATE 1980S, we, as women involved in the new feminist movement in Turkey, pondered the conditions of womanhood and the mechanisms that sustain male dominance. We scrutinized and questioned everything that had been taught to us, including Turkish history. As a member of a feminist group, I was compelled to search for similar women's groups in Turkish history. By examining eight "women's journals" from the late Ottoman era, I wanted to meet and know women who had previously demanded their rights and struggled to establish and legitimize a new life different than what they had been experiencing in the 1890s-1910s. I tried to understand their demands and how they presented and justified them.

My research, which included translating some excerpts from various journal articles written by women, became a book, *Osmanlı Kadınlarının Hayat Hakkı Arayışının Bir Hikayesi* (A Story of Ottoman Women's Demand for the Right to Life). In this chapter, drawing on my book, in a way by summarizing it, I will present the Ottoman women's movement as it was reflected in journals oriented toward women readers. More specifically, I will highlight demands raised in various journals, the significance of the journal *Kadınlar Dünyası*, as well as an interesting but not well-known conference series, *Beyaz Konferans,* and its keynote speaker, Fatma Nesibe.

JOURNALS, THEIR PUBLISHERS, AND CONTENT

For the period prior to the establishment of the Republic, we can identify over forty publications oriented toward women. Starting in 1868 with *Muhaddarat,* the supplement of the *Terakki* newspaper, these publications include *Şükûfezar* (1886), *Aile* (1880), *Âyine* (1875), *Hanımlara Mahsus Gazete* (1895), *Demet* (1908), *Mehasin* (1908), *Kadın* (1908), *Kadınlık* (1914), *Hanımlar Âlemi* (1914), *Kadınlar Dünyası* (1913), *İnci* (1919), and *Süs* (1923). Most of these journals were owned and published by men. Some of them had male owners but were actually published by women, and a few were owned by women and had only women writers. Some of these publications, reflecting the effect of the Westernized lifestyle, focused on topics that were assumed to be of interest to women (such as child care, family and society, housework, and health) and implied that by attempting to educate women readers in these areas they pursued the goal of serving both women and society. Another group, the publications that I am concerned with, rather than enlightening women about their traditional activities, aimed at putting women's conditions and demands on the public agenda. Among these is *Kadınlar Dünyası,* which held the stated purpose of "promoting women's legal rights." This group of journals not only constitutes an important source of information about the pre-Republican women's movement but also serves as evidence of the existence of a group of Muslim women who opposed their treatment as the second sex. These journals, in which women wrote from every possible ideological perspective about the circumstances they wanted to change and the struggles they endured, include the following: *Şükûfezar* (Bloomed Garden, 1886), *Hanımlara Mahsus Gazete* (The Newspaper for Women, 1895), *Demet* (A Bunch, 1908), *Mehasin* (Virtues, 1908-1909), *Kadın* (Woman, Selanik, 1908-1909), *Kadın* (Woman, İstanbul, 1911-1912), *Kadınlar Dünyası* (Women's World, 1913-1914/1918-1921), and *Kadınlık* (Womanhood, 1914).[1]

These publications document that women had begun the struggle for their legal rights (which they would later acquire under the Republic) after the initiation of the modernization process of the empire; they show how women had struggled to be equal citizens with men, had tried to expand their social life and space, and had organized to achieve their goals. In other words, by writing articles, publishing journals, and establishing associations, Ottoman women had embraced every opportunity that had been provided in their times, although within the constraints and challenges imposed by their Muslim-Ottoman identity. Of course, women who found the opportunity to speak out, and who considered this necessary at a time when women's movements were on the rise around the world, were educated women from major cities such as İstanbul, Selanik, and İzmir. They were either graduates of the new schools for girls or were educated at home by private tutors. A careful examination of the journals also reveals that there were a few contributors from other cities such as Edirne, Konya, Manastır, and Trabzon.

Most of the journals indicate that their "pages are open to Ottoman women"; however, "Ottoman" seems to mean the member of the Muslim-Turkish community, as such usage of the term was the common practice at the time. Thus, pieces by Jewish, Armenian, or Greek women are not found in the journals. Similarly, the language of the publications addresses Muslim-Ottoman women. However, the content of the publications are not restricted to the world of Muslim-Ottoman women. News, photographs, and opinions about women from all around the world, with a special emphasis on Western women, are presented, and they seem to have served as a stepping stone for the literate Ottoman women in articulating their own demands and assessing what they could accomplish given their own circumstances.

WOMEN'S DEMANDS

The Demand for Education

The demand for education is the most frequently referred to and most clearly expressed demand. All publications include numerous articles that address the issue of education from various angles. They range from explaining the significance of women's right to education to complaining about the statesmen who originally supported women's education but later lost interest; from demanding the right to higher education to proposing curricula for schools for girls.

The significance attached to education and the prestige of being educated can be observed in the way the contributors sign their pieces. While articles and letters in earlier publications were signed "*İsmail Paşa kerimesi Leyla*" (Leyla, the daughter of İsmail *Paşa*), or "*Kemal Beyin haremi*" (The wife of Kemal *Bey*), later publications appear with signatures such as "Darülmuallimat'tan F." (F. from the Teachers Training School for Girls), or "Fatma Naima, Darülmuallimat'tan" (Fatma Naima, from the Teachers Training School for Girls). With such signatures women use education as a property that allows them to exist as individuals separate from men and able to introduce themselves without using a male kin such as a husband or a father as a source of their identity.

Most of the women in the journals argue that women, as the ones responsible for raising children, should be educated in order to enable the nation's progress and development. However, women did not demand education only in order to contribute to the society by fulfilling their "duties" as good mothers and wives; the overall content and spirit of the writings suggest other reasons as well. The women emphasize and embrace education because they also believe that only through education can they establish a presence and encounter men for equality; as educated women themselves, they instinctively know that through education women can capture the sense of self-confidence that they had been lacking.

It should be noted that at the turn of the century Ottoman women were confined to a limited domain, and they had nearly no access to opportunities and areas (such as work outside the home) that would help develop self-confidence. For some brief periods, due to the wars, some employment opportunities appeared for literate urban women. After each war, however, many women who had been working as civil servants and clerks were forced to give up their positions to the returning men.

We can argue that the demand for education in a way is also a demand to have the right to enter into the other exclusive domain, work life. A woman writer notes;

> It appears that in civilized societies first men advance in knowledge and science and women follow their path. [But m]en, as they enter this treasure house, get jealous of women who follow them and want to deny

them the gems of this treasure. When we say this has always been the case, it means how they [men] have done it. However, since *Cenab-ı Allah* [the Almighty], who is the possessor of the virtue of knowledge bestowed it to all of his subjects, male and female, [then] is it within the power of men to deny it to women?[2]

In their concrete demands for education, women want the number of schools for girls to increase and the number of publications for women to multiply; they also report various obstacles encountered by women as they attempted to "improve themselves." The journals also reveal that some women writers not only wrote extensively about education but also took action and dedicated considerable time and energy to this cause. The most important contributors in this group were Zekiye *Hanım* from the journal *Kadın* (published in Selanik), Aziz Haydar of *Kadınlar Dünyası,* and two members of the *İttihat ve Terakki Cemiyeti* (the Committee of Union and Progress), Emine Semiye and İsmet Hakkı. From the journals we learn that Aziz Haydar donated her jewelry to have a girls school open in Erenköy, İstanbul; she also founded and ran an elementary school.

The Demand for Employment

The starting point for women's demand for employment appears to be an effort to legitimize the situation of women (whose primary duties were still defined as being mothers and wives) who had to seek work outside the home because of necessity (poverty, the death of the main male provider, or having nobody to look after them). However, women also wrote that they wanted to work for the country and help its development. As in all other demands, they justified their demand for employment by emphasizing its usefulness and contribution to society. Emphasizing the social benefits of their demands as a legitimizing device or a mechanism to gain their acceptance, however, sometimes eclipsed their ability to make demands for themselves. Nevertheless, each and every time the demand for employment was raised, some other desires revealed themselves: their desire to have women's "existence" accepted, to change their status as second-class citizens, to be able to enter spaces that were closed to them, and to do work other than "women's work." The force of their desires and their enthusiasm can be observed in the following piece of news and commentary:

> Now, I am giving you the great news about another step we have taken. The Ministry of Mail and Telegraph opened for us a new area of activity by admitting a sister named Feride Yaver to the post of stamp clerk. You cannot imagine the great happiness I felt today, when I went to see Feride Yaver, as I was given the duty of congratulating her on behalf of the *Müdafaa-ı Hukûk-ı Nisvân Derneği* [Association for the Defense of Women's Rights]. . . . Yes, till now we have been oppressed, oppressed, oppressed, and the main reason of this oppression is our livelihood being provided by men. If we too were working , if we too were earning, we would not be this feeble.[3]

How women's work outside the home brings economic independence and how important this is for women are frequently discussed, especially in *Kadınlar Dünyası* and by Aziz Haydar, the author of the article quoted above.

The demand to work in some areas, such as medicine, is not based only on the desire to expand women's living space and economic independence; it is demanded to protect women and to serve women's immediate needs. For example, *Kadınlar Dünyası,* while condemning men who do not take their wives to male doctors and accusing them of being reactionary and cruel, rather than further debating male behavior, suggests that women themselves become doctors. This way, the authors argue, women would prevent their sisters' deaths.

The Subject of Marriage

Women expressed their immediate thoughts about marriage by discussing the disadvantages of arranged marriages. With the exception of a few hesitant approaches displayed in a couple of journals, almost all women who wrote on this subject opposed arranged marriages.

The kind of marriage the women desire is set forth most clearly. The desired marriage is the union of a man and a woman who choose each other as partners. Although the traditional family relations at the time would not have supported nuclear family structures, the discourse of women's articles reflects that women wanted to live in nuclear families. However, we should not see this preference for nuclear families as stemming from the exposure to various alluring images and discourses of Westernized lifestyles in cities such as İstanbul, Selanik, and İzmir. Women's writings on this subject clearly state that their insistence on independent domiciles (*mustakil hane*) stems from the discomforts of their own living arrangements (the difficulty of living with the husband's family) and their yearning for breathing space.

Two journals published in 1908, *Mehasin* and *Kadın* (Selanik), frequently addressed topics such as problems with arranged marriages, unnecessary marriage traditions, and the need for suitable matches. The writers considered increasing educational opportunities as necessary for women to catch up with men who were "ahead" and to be able to share everything with men. *Kadınlar Dünyası* further emphasized the empowerment of women within nuclear families, women's right to divorce, and the transformation of demands into legal rights. *Kadınlar Dünyası* also included articles on polygyny. However, this topic was not assigned a priority, (probably because at the time polygyny was not common and usually not well received within educated and wealthy circles in cities like İstanbul). When it was raised, women referred to polygyny as unacceptable and expressed their belief that it would disappear once women could earn their own living.

The Demand for Changing the Attire, or the Debates on *Tessettür*

The debate on *tessettür* (the concealing of women's hair, face, and body) and the demand for a change in women's "street attire" were most frequently addressed in *Kadınlar Dünyası*. In fact, the resolutions of the association that published the journal, *Müdafaa-ı Hukûk-ı Nisvân Derneği,* included working toward changing women's attire. In line with this resolution, the journal provided articles on the issue, as well as appealing photographs of fashionable outfits such as suits.

Initially, the writers of *Kadınlar Dünyası* felt the urge to consider their demands on this inciting issue from the perspective of Islam and confidently defended them as compatible with the religion. Aziz Haydar argued that women wanted to have an attire that was "religious," "moral," and "healthy," and she added that the veil and *çarşaf* met none of these criteria.[4] Moreover, the journal directed attention to the fact that women wore different costumes in different parts of Anatolia; by publishing photographs of the attires of Muslim women from different regions, under captions such as "Kisve-i Nisvân [Women's Costumes] in Anatolia" and "Kisve-i Nisvân in Kurdistan," women tried to eradicate the belief that the veil and *çarşaf* were the "correct" attire for Muslim women.

In later issues, a more secular tone gains strength in their advocacy. Women, who had been trying to advance their demands carefully by monitoring the mood of the country, presented their demand for change in attire in a nonreligious framework and justified it as "*zamanın icabatı*" (a necessity of times) and as a way for Ottoman women to take their place within the "*medeni dünya*" (civilized world). Articles reveal that *Kadınlar Dünyası*, as well as the Association of *Müdafaa-ı Hukûk-ı Nisvân*, rather than debating the philosophy of concealing, addressed the issue by emphasizing how Ottoman women's dress was perceived by outsiders, by the "*medeni dünya*," and tried to convince the public in favor of change. In fact, women's outfits, composed of the veil and *çarşaf,* had already demonstrated an evolutionary change, "along the lines of European fashion, [it evolved] first by being split into two pieces as cape and skirt, and then into the Western style suit."[5] During this process of change, the journal continued with its uncompromising position and struggle for change by printing articles, responses to criticisms, and photographs of the members of the Association of *Müdafaa-i Hukûk-ı Nisvân* in their "exemplary" outfits.

Whenever *tessettür* and other issues are debated in relation to Islam, we can notice how assessments and judgments are shaped according to men. In addition to identifying the androcentric structures and discourses within various institutions, it is important to follow how assertions and values within those systems are interpreted according to male interests. This way, women who live in different patriarchal societies with different beliefs, even if they do not question the whole system and its beliefs, still manage to see their predicament and point out similarities to each other. Of course, this does not allow women to move beyond simply demanding some rights, but it does enable them to see that social structures continue to evolve in the interest of men.

The Demand that Waits for Its Time:
The Electoral Rights

Journals show that in the early twentieth century the echoes of the women's suffrage movement in Europe reached Ottoman women. It is included in all of the journals, at least as a news item. We see women writers feel the need to address this subject for various reasons. Almost all of them follow the developments in Europe with envy, and without skipping the "for now" qualifier, they indicate that they do not demand the right to vote but will struggle for it when it is the right time. They consider it to be untimely, because they find demanding the right to vote meaningless when they are not able to leave the house to work and participate in public life as citizens. Of course, making no attempts to justify women's right to vote with any reason other than establishing equality between men and women, restrain them in their demands. Nevertheless, they note that the impact of women's awakening will be seen and that women will demand the right to vote in the near future. In fact, *Kadınlar Dünyası,* when it resumed publication in January 1921 after a brief period of discontinuity, included the right to vote and to run for office among its goals for the first time.[6]

KADINLAR DÜNYASI

Among the journals, I choose to focus on *Kadınlar Dünyası* because it was the publication of a women's organization, the Association of *Müdafaa-ı Hukûk-ı Nisvân,* that was different from other, mostly charity, organizations. Moreover, first published in 1913, *Kadınlar Dünyası* holds a unique position among the journals due to an ability to keep women's demands on the agenda, a determined and confident attitude, a platform completely formed and constituted of women, and an ability for continuously stirring debates (as done by other activities of the Association).

From its first issue in 1913 to its last in 1921, the journal was owned by Ulviyye Mevlân (Nuriye Ulviye). While the first 100 issues were dailies, later the journal became a weekly. Its publication was suspended during the First World War (1914-1918); although it reappeared in 1918, it experienced a second interruption, and then it resumed publication, but only for a brief period, in 1921.

Several women, including Ulviyye Mevlan, Aziz Haydar, Belkıs Şevket, Mükerrem Belkıs, and Nimet Cemil, wrote for *Kadınlar Dünyası*. Their articles raise some concrete demands (such as change in women's attire and women's right to higher education), report and comment on the advances that women have made (for example, Bedra Osman and her friends' employment at the telephone company, or Belkıs Şevket's ride on an airplane), and analyze and interpret the status of women. These writers express their opinions in a lively and warm environment. Even when they fall short of making demands, they repeatedly state that women are treated as second-class citizens, do not enjoy equal rights with men in marriage, and are dependent on men for their livelihood. They also point out that men hold an attitude that is restrictive and oppressive toward women, and they criticize such an attitude and the mentality behind it. Criticizing arranged marriages, they advocate marriages that would be formed by two people who meet and choose each other, marriages that would give the wife an equal say and that would have the couple live in a domicile as independent of their families. Here is an example of their assessment and its articulation:

> Let us confess, today a woman lacks the rights to live and be free. Because she can never express her ideal, will, desire and tendency to obtain and sustain it [a free life]; her life is dominated by a father, a maternal or paternal uncle, a husband or a brother who takes advantage of traditions and customs. It is impossible for her to set a goal or an ideal for herself.... In our society, a woman does not have an individual existence, she has never had [one].[7]

Kadınlar Dünyası seems to have closely followed all developments and expressed opinions and comments on them. As stated earlier, it demanded and struggled for a woman's right to higher education. In 1914, when some classes for women were initiated at Darülfünun (the university in İstanbul), the authors criticized the program for offering what they considered to be the most important course, "Hukûk-ı Nisvân" (Women's Rights), at an hour inconvenient for women. Similarly, important events elsewhere, such as the stagnation of the suffrage movement in England, were not missed, but addressed with care.

Kadınlar Dünyası was also the first journal that published photographs of Muslim women. The women who were photographed happened to be the authors of the journal and members of the Müdafaa-ı Hukûk-ı Nisvân Derneği. Through Kadınlar Dünyası, we learn that the association had some foreign membership; the journal published their articles, as well as articles about them, and some issues included supplements in French.

The contributors to Kadınlar Dünyası demonstrate mastery in polemical writing in the way they answer reactions and criticisms. As a response to various accusations about being an "imitation," instead of providing superficial defenses they calmly explain the meaning of their work both for women and society. A fine example of this attitude is seen in Nimet Cemil's article, "Yine Feminizm, Daima Feminizm!" (Feminism Again, Feminism Always!), written as a response to Yakup Kadri, a famous male novelist:

> . . . Yakup Kadri Bey takes the absence of a word that would be equivalent to feminism in our language as evidence of the absence of feminism [in our lives]. He should excuse us for rejecting this statement. Because there are some very important things that every nation has, but again many nations lack the words or even translations to name them (telegraph, automobile, ship . . .). Therefore, we feel no need for [employing] words like nisâsilik or nisâiyyun [as alternative translations]. We prefer to use the word "feminism" just like that. Let's have another foreign word in our language, what is the harm? However, it is impossible to deny the existence of feminism.

> I wish the Turkish woman had as many rights as Yakup Kadri Bey thinks and that we were in the position of working on expanding our rights; unfortunately the situation is completely different. Although, due to the feminist movement of the last five or ten years, some rights were acquired, we were not able to reach our goal. There are still some important rights to acquire. Especially in marriage, women's legal rights are far behind men's legal rights. How can a woman who does not even have the right to see and meet her prospective husband be an equal of a man who can divorce his wife any time he wants or who is

completely free to take another wife while already married to one? If you approach this issue from a woman's perspective, you can easily understand how tragic it is.[8]

A 1914 issue of *Kadınlar Dünyası* notes that *Müdafaa-ı Hukûk-ı Nisvân Derneği* receives no financial assistance from the state, unlike other associations such as *Hilâl-ı Ahmer Kadınlar Cemiyeti* or *Esirgeme Derneği*, but that it receives moral support from some prominent members of *İttihat ve Terakki Cemiyeti*: Cemal Paşa, the Minister of the Navy; Enver Paşa, the Minister of Military Affairs; Talat Bey, the Minister of Internal Affairs; and Cavit Bey, the Minster of Finance.

In sum, *Kadınlar Dünyası* served as the intellectual foundation of the *Müdafaa-ı Hukûk-ı Nisvân Derneği*, which held the goals of establishing educational institutions for women, improving the existing institutions, integrating women into work life, developing an outdoor attire that would be appropriate for the religion and would allow women to be active outside the home, abolishing all unnecessary and wrong traditions related to marriage, strengthening women's position within the family, educating mothers who would raise children following the new pedagogical guidelines, and bringing women into public life. In a dynamic and vibrant milieu, it brought together different women who tried to develop the conditions suitable for the kind of existence they desired. This is why in its pages you can see an article with a heading such as "İnsanlığın İki Kanadı, Feminizm-Sosyalizm" (Two Wings of Humanity: Feminism and Socialism),[9] or meet a woman who has a lot to say about her daily life.

THE WHITE CONFERENCE:
FATMA NESİBE *HANIM* AND P. B.

In 1911 in İstanbul, 300 women met ten times to listen to the lecturer Fatma Nesibe at the mansion of P. B., who organized the conferences. Since the entire hall was painted and decorated in white, as desired by P. B., these meetings were referred to as "the White Conference" (*Beyaz Konferans*). Although we can develop some impressions about P. B. and feel her energetic presence through her reporting of the conference in the journal *Kadın,* the only biographic information we have about her is that she was the daughter of a reformist *Paşa* or another high official.

After the establishment of the constitutional monarchy in 1908, one of the educational activities of women was organizing conferences on various topics. These conferences were generally sponsored by associations and included both male and female speakers (for example, Celal Sahir *Bey,* Süleyman Nesip, Cavit *Bey,* Halide Edib). The White Conference stands out for a number of reasons: it was not affiliated with any associations; it was continuous; and its lecturer, Fatma Nesibe, gave lectures that did not reflect the restraint demonstrated by other women who were engaged in the struggle for women's rights. While almost all conferences were published in a journal, the way the White Conference was reported was also different; while conveying Fatma Nesibe's lectures, P. B. added her feelings and her observations about the women in the conference hall.

Fatma Nesibe *Hanım,* in her detailed discussion of Stuart Mill in one of her lectures, reveals her considerable knowledge about the women's movement in the West. She comes across as an angry woman who would not hesitate to declare men as enemies. However, she also seems to be aware that change would not happen soon; in addition to indicating that she believes in patience, she notes that it is necessary to properly assess the actual conditions for action. Fatma Nesibe *Hanım* defines women as the oppressed sex and as a group whose existence should be developed for the happiness of society. This approach shapes her demands; she is one of those rare women who do not compromise in formulating policies exclusively for women. In reference to the work of some women's associations that raise funds and hold meetings for the benefit of the navy or the army, she states, "Of course, it is much more beneficial to work for our women and girls than serving navies and armies."[10]

In another lecture, Fatma Nesibe *Hanım* tells the story of Adam and Eve from a woman's point of view. Her "reinterpretations" of events and old stories from a woman's perspective show her level of consciousness about male dominance and male gaze. What Fatma Nesibe *Hanım* says in her narration of Adam and Eve and during her other lectures often resembles some approaches prevalent within today's feminist movement (such as embracing peace and compassion as feminine traits, or emphasizing women's reproductive ability). Like

Fatma Nesibe *Hanım,* many women of the era also claimed compassion, peace-seeking, intuition, and self-sacrifice as feminine traits. However, they referred to these characteristics without making any theoretical distinctions between biological femininity (sex) and womanhood as a social identity (gender). Nevertheless, their discourse implies that compassion and peace-seeking were seen as stemming from women's nature. On the other hand, some negative characteristics typically attributed to women (untrustworthiness, manipulativeness, passivity, etcetera) were treated as embedded in their social identity (womanhood), as a result of women having been stripped of their rights and freedoms, and such characteristics were expected to vanish upon women acquiring those rights. Here is a short excerpt from one of Fatma Nesibe *Hanım's* lectures:

> . . . So, what do we have? The law, tradition, pleasure, indulgence, property, power, appreciation, arbitration . . . they are all favorable to them [men]! . . .
>
> Pay attention to every corner of the world, we are at the eve of a revolution. Be assured, this revolution is not going to be bloody and savage like a men's revolution. On the contrary, it will be pleasant and relatively quiet, but definitely productive. You must believe this ladies![11]

CONCLUSION

Women's journals show that starting at the end of the nineteenth century, upper-class Ottoman women found the opportunity to articulate their demands within the context of the intellectual agenda and the changes produced by the modernization process. By the time their first journal, *Şükûfezar,* was published in 1886, there existed several secondary schools for girls with increasing numbers of students. The graduates of these schools, along with those of the Teachers Training Schools for Girls (Darülmuallimat), which had been established in 1870, established a body of readers and contributors. Male reformists, by emphasizing the significance of the "woman question" for the modernization and development of society, were generally supportive of the women's demands.[12]

Ottoman women's demands were parallel to the struggle for women's rights in the West. They followed women's movements around the world but underlined the fact that living in an Islamic society set different conditions for them. When they discussed their demands within the framework of Islam, they provided supportive examples from "*asr-ı saadet*,"[13] the "undistorted" days of Islam, but they refused to compromise.[14]

At the turn of the twentieth century, when social issues started to be addressed in a secular framework, women participated in the debates by raising secular arguments. The structure of Ottoman society and living by Islamic rules allowed women to see the hierarchal order and power relations between men and women; many women did not ignore the gender dimension and defined their problems in terms of manhood and womanhood. However, in the transition to the Republican era, the emphasis on gender was weakened, partially as a result of some positive responses to women's demands and partially due to the emphasis put on the ideal of a new united society.

Beginning to speak, write, approach issues from their life experience, and make diagnostic observations about male domination allowed women to generate a "speech" that explained their situation, first of all to themselves. In the process of writing and publishing articles by the journals' authors, as well as letters and articles sent by readers, a definition of desirable womanhood appeared: it included the right to education, the right to work outside home, the opportunity to be a good mother, and the right to make one's own decisions about her life, her education, her marriage, etcetera.

However, when we examine women's associations and the content of the journals, we do not see different feminist perceptions. From our current approach, we may be able to identify some different tendencies, but no theorized differences can be found. Differences are observed mainly in the ways the writers attempted to articulate and justify the same, shared demands: while one group stressed the "benefit to society," others, though still emphasizing "social good," reflected a rebellious tone against restrictions on women and their confinement into traditional roles. Nevertheless, those who wanted women to be good mothers and wives and those who wanted women to be able to enter nontraditional areas still agreed on the need for women's education.

Yet, it should be noted that whenever the right to work or the right to education were mentioned, there was an unspoken, a priori notion that women and men would be engaged in these activities at different sites. Nevertheless, this notion of segregation was loosened during the First World War and the War of Independence.

During the early 1990s, Turkey witnessed an increase in the number of studies based on primary sources and undertaken with the purpose of meeting and introducing the Ottoman women who had first rejected their place as the second sex, had struggled to move into areas beyond their traditional domains, and had attempted to obtain legal protection and changes in their status.[15] My own work had this purpose of "getting to know and bringing into the sun light." I would like to think that the next group of studies will be more analytical and will provide some answers to questions about when women raised their voices, when they pulled back, what their roles were in acquiring some rights, what conditions stimulated women's movements, and what heritage they left to the new Republic of Turkey that considered women's struggle for their rights as progressive, right, and beneficial.

Notes

1. With one specified exception, these journals were all published in İstanbul.
2. Fatma Aliye, 1895:2-3.
3. Aziz Haydar, 1914:4.
4. Aziz Haydar, 1913:3-4. *Çarşaf* is a large piece of cloth that wraps the body from the head down to the ankle.
5. Şeni, 1990:59.
6. Later, in 1927, *Kadınlar Birliği* (Women's Union) announced its plans for pursuing electoral rights for women.
7. "Kadın ve Hürriyet-i Şahsiyye" (Women and Personal Freedom), *Kadınlar Dünyası* 135 (March 1914/1330).
8. Nimet Cemil, 1921:2.
9. Mükerrem Belkıs states in a sentimental tone that they will make humanity gain the socialist ideals of equality and freedom along with feminism. She indicates that these two currents did not emerge as an adventurous desire but that they were developed— by women, scientists, and workers through centuries as a

response to people's needs—as a means of relief that would elevate society. Current studies on early leftist movements in the Ottoman Empire reveal that there was no comprehensive knowledge of socialism; the articulated leftist thoughts did not have much depth. Although Mükerrem Belkıs does not claim to be a spokesperson for those groups, her article reflects the traces of their writings and intellectual framework. See Mükerrem Belkıs, 1918:3-4.

10. P. B., 1912:2-7.

11. P. B., 1911:2-7.

12. As pointed out by Deniz Kandiyoti, men had their own interests; they "were seeking romantic relationships and love; desiring to have educated wives with whom they could exchange ideas and views." See Kandiyoti, 1990:346.

13. Literally meaning "the age of happiness," the term is used to refer to the early Islamic period when the Prophet ruled.

14. Some of the best examples of writings that followed this strategy include a series of articles by Gülnar Hanım entitled "İslam Kadınlarında Hürriyet" (Freedom in Women of Islam), translated from Arabic and published in Kadın (Selanik) in 1908, as well as an article by Fatma Aliye entitled "Meşahir-i Nisvân-i İslamiyeden Biri: Fatma Bint-i Abbas" (A Famous Person from Women of Islamic Community: Fatma Bint-i Abbas), published in two parts in Hanımlara Mahsus Gazete in 1895.

15. Yaraman-Başbuğu, 1992; Demirdirek, 1993; Kızıltan, 1993; Kadın Eserleri Kütüphanesi Bibliyografya Oluşturma Komisyonu, 1993; Çakır, 1994, 1991, and 1989; Işın, 1988; Z. Toprak, 1988 and 1981.

THREE

THE WOMEN OF TURKEY AS SEXUAL PERSONAE: IMAGES FROM WESTERN LITERATURE

İrvin Cemil Schick

FOR SEVERAL CENTURIES, Western attitudes toward Turkey, and toward Islam generally, have been shaped by a combination of moral outrage and irrepressible concupiscence focused on the trope of "Oriental sexuality"—a theme deploying an entire arsenal of fictional-ized devices such as the harem, the public bath, the slave market, concubines, eunuchs, polygamy, and homosexuality. From painters like Ingres, Gérome, and Lewis, to writers like Loti, Flaubert, and Burton, sexualized images of Turkish women have long been a staple of European culture.[1]

Although this fact is frequently noted by present-day critics, it is explained only too often in rather simplistic terms, primarily as a masculinist metonymic expression of the West's drive to possess the world. In fact, while it undoubtedly did serve that purpose, "Oriental sexuality" also played a much more central and polyvalent role in Western thought than is usually acknowledged. It is not that the Orient/other was as a rule feminized (although this happened often enough), but rather that gender and sexuality were deployed in various ways in colonial discourse to construct the imaginary spaces that non-Europeans occupy, thereby creating a geography of contrasts that served both Europe's self-definition and its imperial ambitions.

Places have significances transcending their physical/geographical characteristics, and these significances mediate our relations with our environment. Endowed with layers of symbolic meaning, socially constructed place is "half topology, half metaphor," writes Rob Shields, "an emotive ordering or coded geography."[2] But how do places acquire these layers of meaning? Following Foucault's use of the term "technology" to denote the discursive tools with which knowledge of social realities and institutions is constructed—for example, technologies of power, sex, and order—I describe as *technologies of place* the discursive instruments and strategies by means of which space is constituted as place, that is, by which place is socially constructed and reconstructed.[3]

In this chapter, I argue that gender and especially sexuality are fundamental (imputed) attributes of socially constructed space. Sexualized images of women *and* men were used, in Europe's discourses of the other, as key markers of place, and hence as determinants of identity and alterity. In other words, these images were among the building blocks with which a political discourse of spatiality was constructed and the world discursively territorialized. I focus on sexually explicit writings produced during the late nineteenth and early twentieth centuries in Europe and Euro-America, but staged in or otherwise related to the Middle East and more specifically Turkey. I concentrate especially on lesser-known books such as travelogues and erotic works printed "for subscribers only" and distributed "privately"; since these latter usually enjoyed relatively limited circulation, their primary significance lies not in the breadth of their influence, but rather in the fact that they present perhaps the purest, most distilled examples of the eroticization of the Orient and its inhabitants.

SPACES OF OTHERNESS

As a socially constructed, socially recognized complex of significations deriving from an individual's membership in such collectivities as class, race, gender, sexuality, generation, region, ethnicity, religion, and nation, identity plays a decisive role in human behavior: an individual acts from a particular position and in accordance with a certain worldview or set of values, interpreting data with the help of certain conceptions or mental models and reacting to them within certain parameters. But the construction of identity is inseparable from the construction of alterity—indeed, identity itself only makes sense in juxtaposition to alterity. It is discursively constructed through a process of sifting, of inclusion and exclusion, in which an "other" is dialectically endowed with properties that are disavowed by the self.

Notions of identity and alterity, of "us" and "them," are intimately related to the sense of place, that is, to the notions of "here" and "there." One's relation to place is a key element in the construction of one's identity.[4] To put it another way, an entire constellation of places, with which one engages in discursive relationships of inclusion and exclusion, attraction and repulsion, acceptance and rejection, figure prominently in the definition of self and other. The sites of discourse with the aid of which European ruling classes defined themselves included not only the domestic social topography but also foreign lands—indeed, these two were related, race and ethnicity often functioning as metonymies for class. Thus, the narratives that helped them construct their world, the "narratives of space" (*récits d'espace*), as Michel de Certeau calls them,[5] were fundamentally important to Europe's signification of itself, to its self-definition and its spatial practices.

The experiences of Europeans in foreign lands—ranging from the dilettante travelers, the writers and artists, to the occupying armies, surveyors, colonial administrators, and metropolitan officials—were therefore overdetermined by narratives of space. Indeed, not only genuine travelogues, but also tales of imaginary voyages, novels set in exotic places, and works of erotica provided Europeans with a certain unquestioned, background awareness of their global positionality—a kind of geographical *habitus*—that is key to understanding their politics of spatiality. Of course the transformation of the earth into a constellation of places did not occur in a vacuum: even seemingly innocent territorializations were intimately related to the exercise of power and must be analyzed within that context. Like eddies, the movement of power creates places of identity and alterity, both mimicking and reproducing the mechanisms of inclusion and exclusion prevalent in society. Analyzing the social construction of the outsider and the spaces to which outsiders are relegated, David Sibley has shown that marginalization "is associated not only with characterizations of the group but also with images of particular places, the landscapes of exclusion which express the marginal status of the outsider group."[6] In other words, segregation reproduces itself: spaces

of otherness become not only repositories of "others" but indeed one
of the primary indicators of alterity.

SEXUALITY AS A TECHNOLOGY OF PLACE

Often the process by which spaces of otherness are created is consciously sexualized. For example, eighteenth-century London brothels
catering to certain specialized tastes were known as *bagnios* and
serails,[7] while Gustave Flaubert wrote in 1869 of a brothel owner
known as "*La Turque*," a nickname that "added to the poetic character
of her establishment."[8]

Since to affirm that place is socially constructed implies, *inter
alia,* that it inevitably bears the imprint of society's systems of
signification, it is hardly surprising that a place is profoundly
gendered and sexualized. In the seventeenth century, Greece, and in
the nineteenth, Italy, served as symbolic sexual idylls in French and
British cultures.[9] During the eighteenth and nineteenth centuries,
such developments as the European discovery of the South Sea
Islands and the changing relations between Europe and the Middle
East (from threat to potential or actual colony) brought about a
generalization of this trope. "Thanks to the narratives of travellers,"
write Yvonne Knibiehler and Régine Goutalier, "the westerner could
. . . believe that countries overseas would offer him an abundance of
women who were compliant, loving, and completely naked." Indeed,
it was "as if the colonies were the harems of the West."[10] As travel
gained popularity, sexual exploits abroad began to make their way
into erotic works such as Riza Bey's *Darkest Orient* (1937)—which
purports to be the record of travels in Port Said, İstanbul, Ankara,
and other cities—and William Fitzpatrick's *İstanbul After Dark*
(1970), one of a long series of such "guidebooks."[11] The sexualization of geography thus came into sharper focus as libidinized spaces
of otherness acquired names; in the process, the *topoi* in which the
erotic tales were set were transformed by the tales—the erotic
reconstructs place in its own image. In Suzanne Rodin Pucci's
compelling phrase, the "mystery" of "the exotic Orient . . . is
*embodied in the representation of the harem, a realm of seemingly
radical political, and especially erotic, alterity.*"[12]

The question that remains is, "Why erotica?" Why, in other words, have recourse to sexuality for the narrative construction of spaces of otherness? Foucault writes that "sexuality is not the most intractable element in power relations, but rather one of those endowed with the greatest instrumentality: useful for the greatest number of maneuvers and capable of serving as a point of support, as a linchpin, for the most varied strategies."[13] Thus, sexuality can be a tool with which to imagine difference between "us" and "them," a litmus test for inclusion and exclusion. It is a technology of identity and alterity, and hence, a technology of place.

Sexually explicit writing lends itself particularly well to such a function. As the writer Angela Carter observes, "pornography involves an abstraction of human intercourse in which the self is reduced to its formal elements. . . . Any glimpse of a real man or a real woman is absent from these representations of the archetypal male and female."[14] In pornography, all depth and individuality are subordinated to a fundamental typology of active and passive, giving rise, in Nabokov's words, to "the copulation of clichés."[15] Given the basic essentialism in which personae distinguish themselves at best by their physical characteristics, culturally recognizable stereotypes such as the oversexed African or the lascivious harem girl were naturally quite compelling. Writers of what might be called *ethno-pornography* thus reduced all global differences to those based on sexuality, constructing sexualized spaces of otherness.

ORIENTALIST EROTICA

Since the seventeenth century, the image of the harem has, to borrow a phrase from Foucault, "not ceased to provoke a kind of generalized discursive erethism."[16] Works such as Michel Baudier's *Histoire géneralle du serrail* (1624), Ottaviano Bon's *A Description of the Grand Signor's Seraglio, or Turkish Emperours Court* (1650), and Jean-Baptiste Tavernier's *Nouvelle relation de l'intérieur du Serrail du Grand Seigneur* (1675) laid the foundation for fantastic and eroticized descriptions of imperial harems. Since their authors never personally witnessed the interior of the harem, these accounts were typically largely based on fantasy as well as a practice of mutual citation. By the eighteenth century, an array of stock motifs were available from which writers could pick and choose, and so they did, in large numbers. Indeed, the very work that provided Foucault with the metaphor to describe the modern Western obsession with talking about sex was, perhaps not coincidentally, a novella set precisely in an "Oriental" harem (more precisely, in the Congo): Denis Diderot's *Les Bijoux indiscrets* (1748), a tale based on the rather amazing premise that a magic ring caused women's "jewels" (that is, genitalia) to speak out and confess their sexual escapades.[17]

Norman Daniel has shown how the institutions of polygamy and divorce, as well as certain Islamic motifs such as Paradise, were insistently interpreted by medieval Christian polemicists as incontrovertible proof that Islam was a sensuous religion that granted its adherents boundless sexual license, that its prophet was hopelessly debauched and corrupt, and that it was therefore a false faith.[18] The accounts of Baudier, Bon, Tavernier, and many others thus merely rode the coattails of earlier anti-Islam polemics. By the eighteenth century, a synchronicity encompassing the Age of Exploration, the confinement of women, the rise of the bourgeoisie, and the decline of the moral and ideological hegemony of the church created a context wherein the sexual doings of the "other" became a topic commanding great interest.[19]

This process greatly intensified during the nineteenth century, when the sexual became "a central structuring feature of systems that relate difference to pathology."[20] In addition to better-known works by famous novelists, numerous pseudoscholarly books on sex in the Orient were published during the late nineteenth and especially the early twentieth centuries, including Bernhard Stern's *Medizin, Aberglaube und Geschlechtsleben in der Türkei* (1903), whose second volume (the one on sex, naturally!) was translated into English and "printed for subscribers" in 1934 as *The Scented Garden: Anthropology of the Sex Life in the Levant;* and Pinhas ben Nahum's *The Turkish Art of Love* (1933), which was almost entirely plagiarized from Stern's book, with the addition of a few ribald tales from a French anthology and a good deal of racist claptrap.

THE POLITICS OF TRANSLATION

Another fount of motifs was the growing pool of translations and pseudotranslations of "Oriental" works. The motif of translation was frequently used by European writers starting in the late seventeenth century, often in epistolary form, and so-called Oriental tales, like Montesquieu's celebrated *Lettres persanes* (1721), abounded. By the end of the eighteenth century it had become difficult to distinguish between genuine translations and Western imitations of Middle Eastern works. In the appendix to his translation of the *Thousand and One Nights* (1884-1886), Sir Richard Burton, who had some experience of his own in forging Eastern texts, classified the fairly large corpus of "Oriental tales" into seven groups: "satires on the Nights themselves, satires in an Oriental garb, moral tales in an Oriental garb, fantastic tales with nothing Oriental about them but the name, imitations pure and simple, imitations more or less founded on genuine Oriental sources, and genuine Oriental tales."[21]

The etymological roots of the word notwithstanding, *translation* is hardly ever mere transposition: it involves both an act of appropriation and a praxis, conscious or otherwise, whereby material is selected, paraphrased, and restated. In other words, not only must one be concerned about any new meanings with which a text may have been infused in the process of rendering it into a different language, but one must also problematize the very choice of text to be translated. An instructive case is that of Jean-Adolphe Decourdemanche, a French orientalist who published myriad books of translations from the Turkish. Generally speaking, Decourdemanche leaned toward popular works, including fables, proverbs, and the folk humor of Nasreddin Hoca. While these do contain a good deal of information relevant to the representation of women, still more interesting is Decourdemanche's translation of Enderunlu Fazıl *Bey's Zenân nâme,* published as *Le livre des femmes* (1879). Now it must be said that for all his wit and clever figures of speech, Fazıl *Bey* was by far not one of the greatest Ottoman poets; the question that perhaps first comes to mind therefore is why anyone would choose to translate his work at a time when Ottoman poetry was all but unknown to the Western reading public. Decourdemanche explains his choice first by his belief that Fazıl *Bey* was one of the rare Ottomans whose poetry is not so opaque nor his imagery so contrived as to turn a Western reader off; and second "in view of the subject it treats, which is precisely in line with the kinds of ideas—women and harems—that most excite our Western attention when there is question of the Turks. To make known the opinion of a

Turk on the women of each country seemed to us something altogether titillating."[22]

Another translation by Decourdemanche—the anonymous collection of tales entitled *Mekr-i Zenân,* published as *Les ruses des femmes*
(1896)—portrayed women as faithless, cunning, and mischievous. To
be sure, this notion is not foreign to the Muslim world, and one could
perhaps argue that in societies in which women are deprived of direct
power, the strategies to which they necessarily turn are likely to be
viewed by men (who do not lack direct power) as devious.[23] Nevertheless, the image of women as liars or tricksters was quite widespread
in the West independent of these translations of Islamic sources. Thus,
the publication of *Les ruses des femmes* amounted to little more than
"Oriental" confirmation of preexisting Western sexist stereotypes.
Another collection of tales that has been attributed to Decourdemanche, the anonymously published *La fleur lascive orientale* (1882),
also featured variations on the same theme.

By the end of the nineteenth century, translations of Eastern
erotica had become big business. Charles Carrington, a prolific
publisher of erotic works, issued *The Old Man Young Again, or Age-
Rejuvenescence in the Power of Concupiscence* (1898)—generally
(though not uncontroversially) attributed to the Ottoman scholar
Kemâl Paşa Zâde and possibly translated by him from a work by
Tīfāshī—and *The Book of Exposition* (1896), attributed to the highly
prolific Egyptian scholar Suyūtī. Along with Ernest Leroux, who
published much of Decourdemanche's work, a number of other
publishers also joined the fray. Isidore Liseux printed French translations of several "Oriental" erotic works first published in English.
Kleinbronn and Gustave Ficker initiated a series entitled "Contributions au folklore érotique: contes, chansons, usages, etc. recueillis aux
sources orales" with *Contes licencieux de Constantinople et de l'Asie
Mineure* (1906) compiled by Jean Nicolaïdes, who had already published two collections of folklore from İstanbul and Anatolia. The
newspaper and book publishers Société du Mercure de France brought
out a series of anthologies of love poetry, including *Anthologie de
l'amour turc* (1905), edited by Edmond Fazy and Abdul-Halim Memdouh.[24] Gustave Le Rouge's *Turquie: mariage, adultère, prostitution,
psychologie de l'eunuchisme. Anthologie* (1912) appeared in a series
entitled "Encyclopédie de l'amour." E. Powys Mathers's monumental

anthology *Eastern Love* (1930) was composed entirely of "Oriental" erotica translated from the French, including the *Zenân nâme*.

An intriguing case is that of *El Ktab des lois secrètes de l'amour d'après le Khôdja Omer Haleby, Abou Othman* (1893), translated (or perhaps written) by Paul de Régla (pseudonym of Paul André Desjardin). De Régla, who had several books to his credit treating the underbelly of Ottoman society, claimed in his introduction to have translated a manuscript given to him by an old scholar he had met in İstanbul, and the book became enormously popular: according to the preface to the second (cheap) edition, the first edition sold more than 21,000 copies.[25]

What is most noteworthy is not only the number of such translations, or their wide dissemination, but the precise nature of their reception in the West. Foucault has distinguished "two great procedures for producing the truth on sex," which he termed *ars erotica* and *scientia sexualis*. The former, found according to him in Southern and Eastern Asia, the Muslim world, and Ancient Rome, was "understood as a practice and accumulated as experience . . . [and] deflected back into the sexual practice itself, in order to shape it as though from within and amplify its effects"; the latter, on the other hand, only emerged in post-Enlightenment Western European society and consisted of "procedures for telling the truth of sex which are geared to a form of knowledge-power strictly opposed to the art of initiations and the masterful secret," namely "the confession."[26] Foucault's taxonomy sheds new light on the translations mentioned above, casting them as works of *ars erotica* appropriated by Westerners as raw material or "data" for their *scientia sexualis*. In other words, what had originally been written as part instructional manual, part philosophical disquisition on the art of love became "evidence" of the ways in which sexuality is actually practiced in the Orient.

Thus, for instance, tales about Arabian women engaging in sexual intercourse with bears or monkeys were viewed not as entertaining, or humorous, or allegorical, or didactic, or whatever their original audiences might have thought of them, but as true accounts of sex in the Orient. It was not hyperbole, then, for Count Gobineau, "the father of racism" as he is known, to state that "with every step one takes in Asia, one understands better that the truest, most exact, most complete book on the kingdoms of this part of the world is the

Thousand and One Nights."[27] Translations of Eastern erotica thus served a dual purpose: they provided some of the basis upon which European authors built their own erotic tales staged in the Orient; and they were a technology of place that constructed the Orient as a particular kind of location—one in which people copulate often and in ways quite shocking by European bourgeois standards.

TROPOLOGY AND VARIETY

Reading through the enormous corpus of orientalist travelogues and novels, one is struck by two qualities that are at first sight contradictory, and yet somehow seem to coexist. On the one hand, one finds a recurrence *ad nauseam* of the same motifs, anecdotes, and stereotypes, each culled from a previous work that was merely quoting yet another—a process, in other words, of reality-construction through the instrumentality of citation and repetition. On the other hand, one is confronted by a dizzying wealth of mutually contradictory assertions that, by a curious mechanism of intellectual denial, mysteriously fail to undermine the credibility of the literature as a whole: thus, for instance, "the Oriental woman" is described as both harpy and sylph—-both repulsive and alluring, crude and refined, disgustingly filthy and obsessed with bathing, unspeakably ugly and fabulously beautiful, ragged and elegant, shapeless and perfectly proportioned, clumsy as a duck and graceful as a gazelle, languorous and a beast of burden, a wily manipulator and a helpless prisoner, a scheming evil-doer and innocent as a child. Yet, in the midst of this dazzling plurality, one also regularly encounters sweeping statements like Suzanne Voilquin's 1866 claim that "one peculiarity of Arab women is the physical and moral uniformity that produces but one single type."[28] If Arab women can be all of the above and still belong to "one single type," then the functioning of Orientalism must be much more complex than some of the less sophisticated readings of Edward Said's work have implied.

The power of Orientalism (or, more generally, of alteritism) derives not from its manifest content (specific images, individual stereotypes) but rather from its epistemology: it is the very existence of difference that is operative, not particular differences.[29] Stereotypes arise to address particular circumstances, and mutually contradictory stereotypes can coexist without undermining one another's effectiveness; indeed, they reinforce each other at the very moment that they reciprocally contradict or negate one another. It is the ability to make a claim such as Voilquin's that lies at the root of the power of alteritist discourse, as well as the representational violence inherent in it. Correspondence to the "truth," or even internal consistency, are simply not germane to its functioning. The great achievement of this discourse was not the creation of a coherent tissue of representations—whether a "realistic" simulacrum of a given society, or its deliberate or unintentional "mis"representation—but rather its ability to present arbitrary and sometimes mutually contradictory statements as fact. In other words, the most fundamental product of alteritist discourse was its own credibility.

But how was it that a person could read in one place that "the Oriental woman" was revoltingly dirty, and in another that she was obsessed with her toilette, and not question the truth-value of *both* texts at once? I think the answer is that alteritist discourse was really nothing more than a collection of tropes that, while not necessarily mutually consistent, each fulfilled a certain function in the colonial project and in the process of Europe's self-definition through othering. For instance, the trope of the dirty Oriental woman was central both to the self-consciousness of the rising European bourgeoisie as clean and proper (as distinct from the filthy working classes, "the great unwashed") and to the imperial effort that justified itself in part through its claim to bring hygiene and health to the "primitive" colonies. On the other hand, the fixation of orientalist discourse upon Turkish baths served the function of portraying the Oriental woman as inordinately preoccupied with her body, hence excessively sensual and licentious, *ergo* once again unlike the hard-working, self-sacrificing, essentially asexual European bourgeoisie; moreover, such inveterate sexuality militated against the "other's" ability to self-govern, and hence argued in favor of colonization. Each product of orientalist discourse was a medley of such tropes, whose effectiveness derived from membership in a larger entity: each text benefited from the aggregate authority of alteritist discourse as a whole; and while individual works frequently took issue with one another or criticized earlier writings, the truth-value of the discourse itself and its episteme were not called into question.

This resolves the apparent contradiction between the citationary aspect of Orientalism, emphasized by Said, and the internal inconsistencies that characterize it: there were many more motifs to cite than any single work could accommodate; an individual author would pick and choose from this vast repertory—by a process that was, of course, not arbitrary but determined by the conditions under which he or she labored—and would often end up with a set of motifs that contradicted another writer's choices. This did not matter, for, as Said puts it, "every one of them kept intact the separateness of the Orient, its eccentricity."[30] In other words, every one of them was a technology of place.

ORIENTALIST TROPES
AND THE WOMEN OF TURKEY

I will use the few pages that remain to give some examples of the more salient tropes characterizing the eroticized representations of the women of Turkey in Western literature. I say "the women of Turkey" rather than "Turkish women" not only out of political correctness, but also because the women in tales about Turkish harems are seldom depicted as Turkish: they are usually either Christian (for example, Italian, French, Georgian, or Greek) or, in those rare instances when they happen to be Muslim, generally Circassian—a people obsessively depicted in orientalist writing and painting as extremely fair-skinned. Although the imperial harem certainly did contain many foreign women—some received as tribute, others captured as war booty—this was not true of the average Ottoman household. It is important to interpret this apparent inconsistency correctly: it is not that this fiction was "inaccurate" and happened to represent "the wrong women"; rather, it pointedly represented the women occupying the Turkish space *as* non-Turkish. Mary-Louise Pratt has observed that lovers in New World romances were "rarely 'pure' non-whites or 'real' slaves . . . [but] typically mulattoes or mestizos who already have European affiliations."[31] There as here, this motif no doubt served the important function of creating a fantasy of exogamy that was safe, because its women were not *really* "other."

If the woman of Turkey was seldom Turkish, she was equally seldom *a* woman. Rather than an individual, the harem woman was always portrayed as a multiplicity, a *plurality* of women. The obverse of this multiplicity was the representation of the Turkish woman as de-individualized, a nameless member of an undifferentiated mass. For example, Mario Uchard's *Mon oncle Barbassou* (1877) tells of a young Frenchman who, upon the assumed death of his uncle (a captain who had "turned Turk") inherits not only a large fortune, but also a harem. The book recounts his efforts to introduce the four "Turkish" women in his harem to French—that is, "civilized"—ways. Although he is initially unable to distinguish his "wives" from one other, as they become more Westernized he gradually comes to see them as individuals—particularly the beautiful Circassian Kondjé-Gul ("*gonce gül*" means "rosebud" in Turkish) who "de-Orientalizes" fastest thanks to her knowledge of Italian and quick mastery of French. She first becomes his favorite within the harem, then his mistress, and finally his lawfully wedded wife.

The role of education in the Westernization (and hence differentiation) of Kondjé-Gul is not incidental. In a book rather pretentiously entitled *The Real Turk* (1914), Stanwood Cobb stated that "*Ennui* is the fatal disease of the Oriental woman. She does not, as a rule, know how to read; her head is empty of ideas, and her language is vile. The talk of the harem, in which wives, servants, and little children join, is pornographic to a degree."[32] The idleness and indolence of harem women is a recurring theme in orientalist discourse, and it is closely related to the process of sexualization: as Foucault points out, "the first figure to be invested by the deployment of sexuality [in Western discourse], one of the first to be 'sexualized,' was the 'idle' woman."[33] Associated in part with the supposed "indolence" of Eastern life, and in part with the warm climate (as heat and boredom were believed to arouse sexual desire), the image of the "other" as omnisexual, prone to engage in sexual relations with anyone or anything, animate or inanimate, runs through the literature. Translations of "Oriental" works included numerous tales about bestiality,[34] that were taken as evidence of actual practices. When people or animals were not available, masturbation was of course always an option—indeed, a much favored one. In a description of the Ottoman seraglio originally written in 1608, Ottaviano Bon says of harem women that "it is not lawfull for any one to bring ought in unto them, with which they may commit the deeds of beastly, and unnaturall uncleanesse; so that if they have a will to eat, radishes, cucumbers, gourds, or such like meats; they are sent in unto them sliced, to deprive them of the means of playing the wantons."[35] This is only one of many such references, and it is noteworthy that they greatly multiplied as masturbation became a virtual fixation for the European medical establishment, resulting in an all-out "war against onanism"; in this manner, a connection was drawn between the alien and the pathological, another recurring theme in alteritist discourse.

It is interesting to note that such accounts of omnisexuality constitute the site of yet another inconsistency—or polyvalence—in orientalist discourse. The harem is often described, by present-day authors, as a monument to the male scopic desire, a phallocratic fantasy in which a multiplicity of women exist only to sexually service a unique male despot; yet, it also harbors, as Lisa Lowe has pointed out, "the possibility of an erotic universe in which there are no men, a site of social and sexual practices that are not organized around the phallus or a central male authority."[36] True, the animals in the stories of bestiality are male, and the phallic significance of cucumbers needs no elaboration; nevertheless, the woman is always firmly in control in these episodes, and it is her sexual needs and desires that take center stage. Not surprisingly, therefore, female homosexuality was also extremely central to these writings, and early travelers' accounts, such as George Sandys's *A Relation of a Journey Begun An. Dom. 1610* (1615), made sweeping claims about the prevalence of lesbianism in harems. Thus "Oriental" women were pictured as "at once passive and insatiable, oppressed and duplicitous, lascivious heterosexuals and sly homosexuals."[37] But this conflicted personality ascribed to "Oriental" women was not accidental: they were believed to engage in lesbianism not out of choice or predisposition but merely in order to satisfy their generalized lust when men happened to be absent. Flaubert epitomized this view when he wrote in 1853 that "the Oriental woman is a machine, and nothing more."[38]

Western commentators also spent a great deal of time discussing the personal grooming habits of "Oriental" women, lavishing particular attention on the application of henna to the hands and feet, and on the removal of body (particularly pubic) hair. For instance, in his *Voyage dans la haute et basse Égypte* (1798), Sonnini de Manoncourt described in painful detail how women "are unmercifully stripped of the veil of nature" since they are "anxious to preserve over their whole bodies an exact and uniform polish."[39] This point is particularly significant when one considers that eighteenth- and nineteenth-century mainstream pornography in Europe generally tended to emphasize a thick growth of pubic hair. The modes of personal hygiene and grooming practiced by or ascribed to the women of the Orient thus worked to set them apart in the Western imagination, to underscore their difference.

Billie Melman has recently pointed out two instances in which the sexuality of Turkish women was invoked as a metaphor for a woman's control over her own body, but in diametrically opposite ways. In the letters of Lady Mary Wortley Montagu and in those of Lady Elizabeth Craven, two eighteenth-century British writer-travelers, the veil, and the promiscuity they believed it enables, became a metaphor for freedom: thus, in a well-known passage, Lady Montagu wrote of Ottoman women that "'Tis very easy to see, they have in reality more liberty than we have. No woman, of what rank soever, is permitted to go into the streets without two Mu[s]lins, one that covers her face, all but her eyes; and another, that hides the whole dress of her head, and hangs half way down her back. . . . This perpetual masquerade gives them entire liberty of following their inclinations without danger of discovery."[40] While this passage is, in itself, not unlike innumerable other references to the wiles of "Oriental" women, and the impunity with which they habitually cheat on their husbands, there is an important distinction, namely the fact that both Lady Montagu and Lady Craven read sexual freedom as indicating economic independence. Thus, they used the figure of the sexually free Turkish woman to articulate a critique of their own economic precariousness and lack of liberty (both women eventually separated from their husbands and, without independent means, lived at the mercy of their good will).

A century later, interestingly enough, the trope of "Oriental sexuality" was utilized to the exact opposite effect: as Melman writes, "'Liberty' for the Augustans is licence, the liberty to indulge the natural sexual drives. To the Victorians it is freedom *from* sex, within marriage."[41] This time around, it was the motif of slippers—which, according to some travelers, would customarily be placed before the entrance to the harem in order to indicate a wife's desire for privacy—that gained center stage: to the nineteenth-century English woman, her "Oriental" counterpart seemed to have greater freedom not because she could hide behind her veil and seek sex, but because she could hide behind her slippers and avoid it. The diversity of discursive uses to which sexuality has been put is truly remarkable.

CONCLUSION

My main argument in this chapter is deceptively simple: that the function of sexuality in orientalist (or alteritist) discourse was not merely to create the image of a male/active colonizer penetrating a female/passive territory, as is often claimed, but rather to assist in the construction of Europe's spaces of otherness by establishing the alterity of the non-European. Beyond supporting the colonial project, and probably much more fundamentally, this discourse was instrumental in helping Europe signify itself, that is, define its own identity and place in the world. The sexuality of Turkish women was, in other words, a technology of place.

Notes

Author's note: The present article is based upon a forthcoming book entitled *The Erotic Margin: Sexuality and Spatiality in Alteritist Discourse*.

1. See for instance Martino, 1906:66-73, 265-272.
2. Shields, 1991:264-265.
3. Foucault, 1988:18.
4. Entrikin, 1991:1, 4; Stallybrass and White, 1986:194.
5. De Certeau, 1984:Chapter 9.
6. Sibley, 1992:107.
7. Porter, 1982:9. *Bagnio* is Italian for bath, and *serail* is French for palace; they both connote the Orient.
8. Flaubert, 1904, 2:327.
9. See for instance Douthwaite, 1992:45-46; Buzard, 1993:130-136.
10. Knibiehler and Goutalier, 1985:21, 29; translation mine.
11. I am grateful to Pelin Başcı for supplying me with a copy of this rare work.

12. Rodin Pucci, 1989:115; italics mine.
13. Foucault, 1978:103.
14. Carter, 1988:4, 6.
15. Nabokov, 1970:315.
16. Foucault, 1978:32.
17. Foucault, 1978:77, 79.
18. Daniel, 1960, Chapter 5, particularly 135-146 and 148-152.
19. Van Den Abbeele, 1992:xxiii, xxviii; Brown, 1993:3.
20. Gilman, 1985:38.
21. Burton, n.d., 10:507-513. See also Conant, 1908.
22. Fazıl-Bey, 1879:3; translation mine.
23. On harem women's intrigues as reflected in Western travel literature, see F. Davis, 1986:Chapter 10. On the theme of the trickery of women in Islamic culture, see Malti-Douglas, 1991:Chapters 2 and 3; also Aït Sabbah, 1986:70-72. On misogyny and sexuality in Islamic texts, see Boudhiba, 1975:Chapter 10.
24. I am grateful to Sara Yontan for supplying me with a copy of this rare work.
25. De Régla, 1906:1.
26. Foucault, 1978:57-58.
27. Gobineau, 1859:170; translation mine.
28. Voilquin, 1978:241; translation mine.
29. See for instance JanMohamed, 1986:78-106; Bhabha, 1994:66-84; Yeğenoğlu, 1992:45-80.
30. Said, 1979:206.
31. Pratt, 1992:100-101.
32. Cobb, 1914:68.
33. Foucault, 1978:121.
34. For an unscholarly but nevertheless useful survey of bestiality and other manifestations of sexuality in the *Thousand and One Nights*, see Dehoï, 1963.
35. Bon, 1650:59.
36. Lowe, 1991:48.
37. Douthwaite, 1992:96.
38. Letter [of 27 March 1853] to Louise Colet, in Flaubert, 1980, 1:181.
39. Sonnini [de Manoncourt], 1800:179.

40. Letter XXVI to the Lady—[Mar] (1 April 1717), in Montagu, 1763, 2:33-34.

41. Melman, 1992:88, 111.

FOUR

SHADOWS IN THE MISSIONARY GARDEN OF ROSES: WOMEN OF TURKEY IN AMERICAN MISSIONARY TEXTS

K. Pelin Başcı

A GREAT PART OF AMERICAN MISSIONARY ACTIVITY through the end of the nineteenth century was directed toward evangelizing, reconstructing, and restructuring societies in the Middle East, particularly in the Ottoman Empire. The American Board of Commissioners for Foreign Missions (ABCFM), the chief missionary organization in the United States at the time, invested more money and human power in Ottoman Turkey than in any other country.[1] Many historians aptly discuss the significance of American missionary activity in Turkey in the context of American political interests and capitalist expansionism in the Middle East.[2] There has also been controversy generated over the impact these missionaries had in constructing ethnic identity during the late Ottoman period.[3] However, recent research on the subject rarely addresses the missionary perception of women and the attempts of the missions to gain influence over gender relations in the Ottoman Empire. These attempts, nevertheless, played an important role in the way American missionaries worked, lived in, and perceived the Near East, and they need to be contextualized in the overall process of Westernization in Turkey.

At the turn of the nineteenth century a considerable amount of missionary work targeted the women in the empire and was carried out mostly by women. Both male and female missionaries wrote about their work and the people of the region, but it was often the missionary women who addressed the importance of gender roles and Ottoman women for their work. In this chapter I will trace the images of Ottoman women as depicted in the nineteenth-century literature produced by American missionary women. Looking at the intensity of the circulated imagery and its use, I intend to illustrate that "Women's Work for Women," a favorite term of the missionary texts and histories, had an ironic twist. While I wish to show that images of the native women were directly related to the increasing presence of the American women in the region at the end of the century, I do not intend to evaluate the sociological accuracy of these images. Instead, I will question the representational truth that emerged from the missionary texts and shaped the way American women related themselves to Ottoman women. Focusing on the images is likely to result in a better understanding not of Turkish women and their historical circumstances, but of the American missionary women and their cultural baggage; after all, facts are forged into images in the eyes of the beholder.

I will use the term "Ottoman women" to refer to the diverse female population of the empire—women of Turkish/ Muslim, Greek, Bulgarian, Armenian, and Jewish origins. I will focus largely on the geographical region stretching from Trace to eastern and southern Asia Minor. In the nineteenth century this area still reflected a multicultural social texture. It contained a religious, linguistic, and ethnic diversity of women, all of who were living under the rule of the *millet* system.[4] Therefore, unless specified otherwise, occasional references to "Turkish women" in the nineteenth century do not exclude Christian and Jewish subjects of the empire. On the other hand, references to American missionary women are limited largely to Protestant (Presbyterian and Congregationalist, white, middle-class) women from the nineteenth-century American Midwest and New England.

In addition to valuable secondary sources on missionary activities, my analysis is based on a reading of a limited quantity of rich first-hand missionary texts such as annual reports, journals, magazine articles, collected letters, and missionary histories. In these texts we see missionaries capitalize on the orientalist discourse that was already circulating in the Western hemisphere.[5] Research has shown that missionaries frequently exaggerated the hardships of life in the mission field in order to increase the amount of financial and spiritual support for their work at home. Nevertheless, missionary texts offer images of life in Turkey and of Turkish women that claim to have a representational value for their contemporary audience during a period when the West was attempting to understand and change the nature of the object portrayed. Moreover, it is precisely these useful distortions that this article will address.

RELIGION, CIVILIZATION, AND PROGRESS

Even though the ultimate purpose of any missionary activity was to evangelize the population, missionaries recognized that the spread of the Gospel required the establishment of "civilized Christian institutions." In the United States, many were convinced that social reform through Protestant dogma was the only way to rectify an imperfect society and its citizens.[6] Abroad, the ABCFM regarded Christian and Anglo-American goals as being inseparable and interdependent.[7] The missionary enterprise was perceived as a "universal struggle between the children of light and the children of darkness, led by an American nation in covenant with God."[8]

Although missionaries viewed religious conversion as being valuable in and of itself, they felt that its real value was in pulling Near Eastern societies out of "the dark" in order to "open their eyes and behold the universe as it is."[9] To this end, they undertook a wide range of activities, such as establishing educational institutions, congregations, hospitals, and a printing press; translating various texts; paying home visits to local people; and creating employment opportunities in industry. They believed they were contending against "certain well-known features . . . of the Oriental world which are a necessary bar to all progress," and they hoped that their activities would "eradicate" such obstacles.[10] Boarding schools and colleges for boys and girls were seen as instruments to transform minds and reconstruct the society.

The American college . . . introduces an Anglo-Saxon element into the Oriental mind and character. . . . . It is a mental transformation. . . . Every student becomes in turn a teacher. The Anglo-Saxon mind will steadily gain influence over the course of events. It will be a peaceful and civilizing influence. . . . It will . . . carry with it the blessings of a true Christian civilization. . . . [A college] . . . is also demanded for the defense of Freedom of Conscience.[11]

Missionary historian Samuel Bartlett praised the missionary schools for offering students not only a Protestant education, but an "Anglo-American mind" and "Yankee reasoning," "even in wild Kurdistan."[12] He believed that through these schools evangelical liberties and more tangible items of American influence such as clocks, chairs, tables, agricultural implements, cotton-gins, saw mills, sewing machines, and even flowers would penetrate the remote regions of Asia Minor.[13]

EDUCATION AND
"WOMEN'S WORK FOR WOMEN"

At the turn of the century, most missionaries praised "women's work for women" as one of the greatest accomplishments of the ABCFM and other Protestant organizations in the Ottoman Empire. The missionary movement as a whole represented the largest women's organization in North America and was financing two-thirds of the mission force in Asia, Africa, and the Middle East.[14] In other words, much of the American presence in the Middle East and elsewhere was perpetuated by the financial and spiritual gifts of the American women and their devotion to the Protestant church. Female teachers and missionary wives connected with the board helped bring education to urban centers and Anatolian villages where modern schooling for girls was rare or virtually nonexistent.[15] In 1909, the ABCFM employed 68 single American missionary women and 63 wives—a total of 131 women—to assist 68 ordained ministers, laymen, and male physicians (which in some cases included women) in the Ottoman Empire.[16] In 1902 the board's *annual report*, which consisted of statistical data from the mission fields in Turkey, listed a total of 8,586 female students enrolled in 366 schools. Only one of these schools was listed as a college, with a total of 156 students. Of the remaining schools, 22 (6 percent) functioned as boarding and high schools, instructing 1,705 students altogether, and an additional 343 (94 percent) were designated as common schools, with a total enrollment of 6,725.[17]

That same year, in Saimbeyli (Haçin) alone, female missionaries organized regular mid-week women's meetings, made regular home visits, instructed native women in reading the Bible, gathered some 400 women for Sunday afternoon church meetings, and brought together 150 female students for Sunday school. There were also girls' schools in four out-stations. In these areas, missionaries worked predominantly with Armenian—both Protestant and Gregorian—women. In the home schools, female missionaries even managed to collect contributions from Ottoman women for the Shao-wu mission in China.[18] In many places they established kindergartens and orphanages and worked with impaired children as well.

By 1910 there were a total of six board colleges for both boys and girls with 1,219 students, as well as 424 kindergartens and primary and secondary schools—a total of 23,474 pupils in all stations.[19] Uygur Kocabaşoğlu indicates that there were 122 Turkish, 339 Greek, and 4,385 Armenian boys and girls attending American intermediate and higher education institutions during the 1913-1914 academic year.[20] Among the schools established before World War I, there were 16 chief institutions with 4,023 students exclusively devoted to women's education. Scattered all over Anatolia, most of these schools (14) were primary and/or secondary institutions. Only two, the American Collegiate Institute for Girls in İzmir and Central Turkey College for Girls in Maraş, functioned in the capacity of colleges.[21]

Frank Stone states that in these schools, "girls were expected to exhibit proper self-control and exercise rigid economy."[22] While self-reliance was not entirely dismissed in girls' schools, unlike in boys' schools, it never quite became the focus of attention. Young men were expected to master industrial skills and crafts, whereas girls were encouraged to improve their domestic skills.[23] Every Monday was set aside as a "recreation day" in which the girls would wash, mend, iron, and scrub.[24] Industrial skills taught to girls in orphanages consisted of weaving cloth and carpets and sewing, as opposed to cabinet-making and book-binding crafts, which were restricted to the boys.[25]

Missionaries hoped to instill pride in students by offering them the benefits of a practical education in everyday life. Industrial schools furnished the students with practical and industrial skills in order to provide students with the means to sustain themselves, contribute to their congregation and schooling expenses, and in the case of banishment, survive outside their immediate native community.

Missionaries' approach to higher education in the age of science was equally pragmatic. According to Esra Danacıoğlu, American missionary schools set the standard for innovative techniques and positivist education in the Ottoman Empire during the nineteenth century.[26] Missionary religiosity was ironically led by the "gospel of science." Science was seen as a great friend of religion and incorporated into both male and female education. Frank Stone argues that the orderliness of God's universe was exhibited through the study of zoology, botany, astronomy, chemistry, and physiology.[27] Most of the women who received a college education were expected to become enlightened wives and mothers. According to Bayard Dodge, some of these students themselves became teachers or trained nurses.[28]

In creating educational programs for women in Turkey, missionaries were inspired by various women's institutions established in the United States between the early 1820s and late 1830s. Emma Hart Willard's Female Seminary in Troy, Catharine Beecher's Hartford Female Seminary in Connecticut, Zilpah Grant's Ipswich Female Seminary, and Mary Lyon's Mount Holyoke Seminary all served as models for missionaries.[29] In fact, a girls' school with the name of Lyon's Mount Holyoke was listed in the 1902-1903 annual report of the Eastern Turkey Mission.[30] Like Emma Hart Willard, who was known to be an ardent supporter of female education and women's suffrage in the United States, many of the founders and graduates of these schools also became involved in social reform movements.[31] At home, religious zeal drove their fervent determination to change the society and redirect its misguided citizens through the work of a "temperance army," "whisky war," or a "crusade" for the improvement of a God-loving Republic.[32] Abroad, as in the Ottoman Empire, women were "enlisted" in the "army" of missionaries and engaged in a "warfare" to educate and evangelize "those sad-hearted women across the seas."[33]

DAUGHTERS OF DARKNESS:
VEILED MYSTERY WOMEN

American missionaries began raising "the woman question" during the war in Greece, the first Ottoman territory to become an independent state, in 1830. Interested in the role women and family played in the birth of a nation, the board instructed one of its members, Rufus Anderson, to gather information on "the treatment of the female sex; the state of morals among women; and the desire for education of girls" in Greece.[34] The concern with "the female sex" in the Balkans, as well as in the European, central, and eastern lands of Turkey, grew steadily as the number of American women actively participating in the missionary effort increased. "The treatment of the female sex" soon became a key to understanding the social structure of Oriental cultures. Some American women, like Dorothea Day of New York, claimed that the study of the treatment, problems, and status of Middle Eastern women should be taught as a proper subject of scientific research in missionary schools. American women were asked to examine, from a respectful distance, "the things of others," the nature of the family unit, and women's place in the family and society.[35] Missionary observations published in *The Missionary Herald* and *Life and Light* emphasized the binary opposition between the light diffused by the progress of Christian civilization and the darkness of other traditions and cultures. When, in 1914, Mrs. O. E. Brown entitled her article on women in the Ottoman Empire and Islamic countries "The Shadow of Islam," she was borrowing her imagery from a rhetoric already in wide circulation among the enlightened Christian men and women of the New World.[36] In the article, she argued that the destitute women of the Near East were awaiting salvation from their Christian sisters. Brown believed that the women lingering near her door to sell her "their dainty, handmade lace" during her visit to Palestine were actually reaching out for spiritual guidance that only American women could provide.[37] She declared that there were "none more to be pitied"; due to their spiritual poverty and ignorance, they had to be entrusted to the pious work of their Christian sisters.[38] However, acknowledging the difficulty of reaching out to them, she lamented how Christian women "wished to know something of their homes and daily lives."[39]

Islamic women tended to veil not only their physical selves from outsiders, but their homes and lives as well. With the veil, Brown complained, "nothing [was] visible."[40] The true nature of things was hidden, and the scenery was obscure. She was convinced that Muslim women, covered by the veil, spoke to no one and were spoken to by no one.[41] The obstructed vision, the silence that was the veil, made the sight of Muslim women all the more desirable, and it loaded meaning into what would be an ordinary encounter with "sisters" of a contrasting world. Brown's symbolic references to the veil in her writings were typical of other missionary texts. The fact that the veil represented a closed society did not serve to dampen the missionary desire to conquer the secret behind it. Like plucking the apple from the tree of knowledge, knowing the secret behind the veil would, it was assumed, expose one to a world of sin and heighten one's obligation to reform it. It was as if the veil enveloped all the fundamental aspects of social life; it obstructed a great potential. If the obstruction could not be removed soon, it would ultimately bar all progress. Furthermore, the veil propagated a society that refused to open its doors to science, modernity, and evangelism. Therefore, the idea of "the veiled city," a romantic metaphor Albert Hubbard used on his arrival to İstanbul, was more than just a spontaneous display of emotion by a missionary on his way to Sivas.[42]

Brown, attentive to changes in fashion, closely scrutinized the various styles of veiling in her article; she noted that women who wore thick, black gauze over their faces—as opposed to a large, white, all-enveloping sheeting—embraced a relatively progressive attitude, as in the case of İstanbul women.[43] Nevertheless, the presence of the veil indicated "the lower and subordinate place held by all women in the Moslem world," where the relationship of the sexes was "the sorest spot in the lives of these little, veiled creatures."[44] It expressed a type of bondage that tied these women to one another in harem life as it enslaved them. As Nancy Cott argues, New England women were indeed familiar with a similar "bondage" of the "home sphere," which denied them political organization, public life, certain legal rights, and higher education until the 1830s.[45] On the one hand, missionary women were not as concerned that the "proper sphere" of the Middle Eastern female was designated and segregated as they were with the nature of the relationships being cultivated and nurtured within this sphere. On the other hand, the transformation of the latter depended on removing the veil from the true protagonist, "the Oriental woman."

During a meeting of the ABCFM in 1892, an African-American woman from the South was given the privilege of addressing the distinguished assembly of guests on the place of women in contemporary American society. Anna Julia Cooper began her speech—which later became the opening of her progressive narrative, *A Voice from the South*—with the following note:

> In Oriental countries woman has been uniformly devoted to a life of ignorance, infamy, and complete stagnation. . . . Mahomet did not know woman. There was no hereafter, no paradise for her. The heaven of Mussulman is peopled and made gladsome not by the departed wife, or sister, or mother, but by *houri*—a figment of Mahomet's brain, partaking of the ethereal qualities of angels, yet imbued with all the vices and inanity of Oriental women. The harem here, and—"dust to dust" hereafter, this was the hope, the inspiration of the *summum bonum* of the Eastern woman's life! With what result on the life of the nation, the "Unspeakable Turk," the "sick man" of Europe can to-day exemplify.[46]

Anna Julia Cooper's concern about the place of women in Turkish and Islamic societies stemmed from her desire to stress the achievements of American women and to glorify their status by contrasting them with women from "uncivilized" cultures. References to the impure home life of "the Turk"—a concept often discussed in female missionary texts—served to victimize Middle Eastern women and make them culpable in the perpetuation of a world based on material gains. Clearly, "the Muslim woman" was the object of man's sensual pleasures—merely a toy "with which he plays as the whim of the moment dictates."[47] The lifting of the veil would reveal the Muslim woman's "bitter anguish."[48]

The missionary rhetoric associated "the Oriental world" and "the Oriental woman" with the veil. According to Brown, when a man said, "Veil yourself; Thou art free," the woman was released into a world of self-degradation.[49] In the world outside, as in marriage, she was perceived as being a toy in the hands of other men. In fact, the author of "The Shadow of Islam" reported from her reliable sources that Ottoman women claimed to have no soul: "She obey[ed] her instincts as blindly as an animal," and was no more than a grown-up child.[50] Brown's article ends in a typically sentimental mood as she, no longer able to contain herself, dedicates a poem of her own to Ottoman women:

> Sick and weary and defiled,
> And the saviour's healing word
> They have never, never heard;
> Ever hungry and unfed,
> Left without the living bread—
> Waiting! Waiting![51]

Until the turn of the century, missionaries thought of the Muslim/Turkish woman as the epitome of all known social ills, yet endowed with influential powers in the family and the potential for social progress. A few missionaries also made comparisons between Turkish women and those from Persia, often concluding that it was "the Turkish woman" that promised a more progressive future.[52] Some also compared the "idle" Muslim/Turkish woman of the city with the economically more important yet out-of-reach peasant woman of the same background in Anatolia.[53] The peasant woman contributed to the maintenance of the household and livestock and actively participated in the agricultural production. According to the missionaries, given the *idle* seclusion and *impure* imprisonment of the former, salvation could hardly reach the urban Muslim/Turkish woman, even when delivered by a Christian woman.

Still, it was believed that education would symbolically unveil the women and awaken them from the surrounding "darkness." Unlike Muslim fundamentalism that treated unveiling of women as an act of exposing the flesh and therefore a sin, missionary women perceived unveiling as a spiritual act—revealing and freeing a woman's soul and availing it for spiritually uplifting and socially gratifying work. Therefore, for the missionaries, modernizing, educating, and unveiling women were virtually the same, and, conversely, the veil was but a symbol of their ultimate subjection to a materialistic Oriental world.

However, Turkish parents were prohibited from sending their sons and daughters to foreign schools. Before the 1908 revolution, there were three Muslim/Turkish girls who attended the American school in

Üsküdar, İstanbul: Gülistan İsmet, whose mother had been in the harem of Sultan Aziz; Halide Edib, whose father was an official in the palace of Sultan Abdul Hamid; and Nazlı Halid, whose mother was from a rich and influential family. All three had to risk the threat of persecution.[54] The missionaries, on the other hand, saw the education of Muslim/Turkish girls, as well as the school itself, as the only indication of improvement and hope in Ottoman Turkey.

Even before the First World War, there was talk about how the missionary school in Üsküdar could become an organizational base for the Muhammadan women's liberation. School teachers were familiar with and sympathetic to Muslim/Turkish women's organizations in the country. Two of these teachers, Ellen Deborah Ellis and Florence Palmer of the American College for Girls in İstanbul, acknowledged the work of Muslim women in an article entitled "The Feminist Movement in Turkey," written for the British journal *The Contemporary Review*. They referred to the awakening of the Muslim women in the Ottoman Empire as the most remarkable phenomenon for feminist movements all over the world. They also elaborated on the careers, public lives, and concerns of women in Turkey, taking most of their examples from İstanbul, and they praised the women's organization Mudafaa-i Hukuk-u Nisvan (Society for the Defense of the Rights of Women), as well as their weekly publication, *Kadınlar Dünyası* (Women's World). Having listed the demands of this women's organization—for education, active participation in social life, and opportunities for work—the article finally declared that Muslim/Turkish women urged that the veils "which hang between them and *the world* be removed."[55]

Around the turn of the century, as missionaries' work on Muslim/Turkish women intensified with the reforms of the Young Turk government, images of Turkish women in the missionary texts were inverted. Persecution was no longer a threat for the families of those who attended American colleges. Powerful members of the Union and Progress Party and the constitutional government, Enver and Cemal Paşas were supportive of the missionary interest in educating Muslim/Turkish women. There was, in fact, an increase in the attendance of these schools by Muslim girls and the new government established several scholarships for Muslim women, as in the case of the American Girls' School in Üsküdar.[56] Reports, including the one by Reverend James P. McNaughton of İzmir, indicated that Enver Paşa had recognized the work of the missionaries, had thanked them for building "the splendid system of schools," and had promised to take these schools as models for reorganizing the Ottoman education system.[57] It seemed that, after more than half a century of work, American women were finally able to capitalize on the Ottoman interest in Westernization and the demand for education of both sexes. They saw the opportunity to sweep away the European influence and leave a distinct mark of Americanism on this process. Missionary texts and teachers, connected with the ABCFM, began to emphasize the achievements of the female graduates of American schools and colleges. For example, Mary Mills Patrick, retired president of Constantinople Woman's College, stated that it was a "thrill" for the American teachers "to welcome groups of these black-robed students, eager for a life of study. Once across the threshold, the black veils disappeared, and modern seekers for knowledge came to view."[58]

Among the achievements missionaries considered to be their very own, Halide Edib—her personality and work—almost always topped the list; Mary Mills Patrick's *Under Five Sultans* opens with an unveiled picture of Halide Edib on the inside cover, and the inscription reads, "Halide Edib. Bachelor of Arts, Constantinople Woman's College, Author, Educator, Statesman."[59] The photograph is a symbolic depiction of both the work of the American women and the beginning of a new life in the modern Republic of Turkey. Mills Patrick's book continues with a positive note on the modern Turkish Republic, relates the story of life under the rule of the Sultans, tracing a period from 1871 to 1924, and closes in full circle with the founding of the Republic.

Halide Edib's own writings reflect the influence of the missionaries. Emphasizing Edib's early, universalistic interpretation of religion as a fusion of the spiritual teachings of Islam and Christianity, Duygu Köksal argues that Edib respected Christianity out of "an admiration and respect for the simplicity, tastefulness and orderliness of the missionary life" and, as such, that Edib believed Christianity could be "categorized with the Sufi tendencies in Islam."[60] There is also a striking similarity between the missionary concept of ideal womanhood and Halide Edib's vision of a woman in the service of her country. Both see women as an instrument of social transformation. Tempered by her nationalism, Edib's position reflected the conviction that improvement of women's status in society was directly related to the improvement of the nation as a whole. According to her, while striving to be an individual with access to education, public life, and social mobility, a woman's prime duty still lay at home, in the rearing of her children and the raising of a new, enlightened generation of patriots.[61] Missionary women, similarly, held the belief that a woman's role both at home and in public life revolves around her ability to influence people, to shape the character of her children for the sake of maintaining a God-loving republic.

Steps taken in the course of Westernization in Turkey were often treated in missionary texts as the evidence of missionary success. Just as Halide Edib's picture on the inside cover of Patrick's book stood for half a century of progress in the right direction, Grace T. Davis's history of the Woman's Board of Missions of the Interior illustrated the missionary women's success in the Near East with pictures of young women. The fifth chapter of Davis's *Neighbors in Christ,* entitled "Through Years of Stress in the Near East," depicted the contrast between veil and modern attire. The change in mentality and the greatness of the achievement were illustrated by two pictures: "Adana School Girls as They Used to Come," in veils and herded by men; and "Adana School Girls as They Come Today," at exactly the same spot of the school entrance but in fashionable sailor uniforms.[62]

DAUGHTERS OF SORROW:
WOMEN OF "ETHNIC RELIGIONS"

Missionary narratives often reveal missionaries' amazement at the diversity of languages, religions, and ethnicity in the Ottoman lands. In a letter to her friend "M," Henrietta Hamlin wrote;

> The streets are only narrow foot-paths, imperfectly paved with stones of every form and size; and the multitudes who throng them are from every nation under heaven, each speaking his own language, and wearing the costume of his own country. Most of them are of such wretched appearance that it gives the impression of a street full of beggars.[63]

While the missionaries were seeking to develop the means to attend to the needs of each group, their work, by their own admittance, had become intriguing. According to nineteenth-century missionary texts, the filthy and brutal lives led by women slaves was not unique to the Muslim community within the Ottoman Empire. The local Christian population was perceived as barbarous, too. "Barbarism and ethnic religions combined to degrade womanhood."[64] In Anatolia, the morals of "the subservient Greeks and Armenians" were not better in comparison to the Muslims, though they were certainly more accessible.[65] Reforming the "Oriental churches," and the "nominally" Christian people was seen as necessary not only for the salvation of the people who were observing a "corrupt" form of Christianity, but for the spread of the Gospel among the Muslims as well. Missionaries believed that the "unreformed" ceremonialism of the Oriental churches, namely Greek Orthodox, Gregorian, and Catholic, misinterpreted Christianity and impaired the spread of "true" Christianity to the Muslims.

An article by a male missionary in the annual report of ABCFM also drew attention to the Jewish residents of Anatolia: "Then there is the Jew, the ubiquitous Jew, first cousin to the Arab Moslem."[66] According to Cyrus Hamlin, founder of the Bebek Seminary (which later grew into Robert College), the Jews of the empire were ignorant, superstitious, filthy, lying, covetous, greedy, and servile.[67] The American missionaries targeting Jews found this group as difficult to reach as the Muslims, even though the original missionary goal was to influence these two religions in particular.

The self-appointed saviors of the people in the region had to work with yet another group in Anatolia, the Kurds. Missionary narratives often identified the Kurdish people with the wilderness that characterized their surroundings, but writers were unable to form any clear opinion about them. One declared that they worshiped "certain heathen forms," and therefore could not be "correctly classified as Moslem, Christian, or Jew."[68] This, of course, was an exciting observation, since real "heathens"—people not defined by standard religious categories—were the most attractive targets for ambitious missionary work. Still another female writer relayed the comment made by a young Kurdish woman speaking at a missionary conference in New York: "I am very glad," she had reportedly said in her own language, "that in such a free land, you have gone so far forward that you may worship Christ."[69] This address, along with other speeches presented by women, made such an impact on the audience of the missionary conference that one participant, General Harrison, claimed, by figure of speech, that he would be more than happy to invest a million dollars for a single female convert.

During the nineteenth century, most of the missionary work and educational activity—for both men and women—took place within the Armenian community of the empire. Despite the fact that Armenians were identified as "primitive" Christians, they were still entrusted with God's work of evangelizing the rest of the natives. In fact, it was through the recognition of the first Protestant Armenian community as a *millet* that the missionaries had secured a legitimate place for their activities in the empire. Armenians, who tended to cluster in rural areas, were seen as readily malleable, as opposed to urban Greeks, who were, according to the missionaries, more articulate and eloquent.[70] However, missionaries also worked closely with fewer wealthy urban Armenians. Henrietta Hamlin described the Armenian ladies in İstanbul as people of "courtly ease and grace of manners," but entirely uneducated.[71] Cyrus Hamlin admired the respect Armenian children displayed toward their parents and highly praised the Armenians for their interest in child-rearing; he claimed that Mr. H. Dwight's *Parents' Guide* had become one of the most popular books among the publications for Armenians distributed by the mission of western Turkey .[72]

Nevertheless, Armenians too were part of a crude and semibarbaric world. Like the rest of the vast millions of women living in "Christless lands," the women practicing "ethnic religions" in the empire were labeled as "daughters of sorrow" by the "daughters of the covenant" who pitied and wanted to save them.[73] Only through a process of modern Christian education could "sweet, ladylike girls" scatter over the Ottoman land, nurse the sick and the needy, teach the ignorant and the poor, and make their own homes centers of "silent" spiritual influence.[74] It was characteristic of the missionary work to instill a sense of superiority in the evangelized and reformed elements of society. For instance, in collecting contributions for a mission in China from female students at Saimbeyli (Haçin), the missionaries prompted one little girl in the mission's custody to say, "I am so thankful I wasn't born a girl in China."[75] The world outside the mission was much like the "dark river" that took the missionaries "back an age from the advancement of the American world" to a place of ignorance, superstition, and moral degradation.[76]

THE IMAGE MAKERS

The intensity of the negative imagery attached to Ottoman women, regardless of their social class, ethnicity, and religion, increased in the missionary sources of the mid-nineteenth century. This was in great part due to the debate that raged in the United States over women's place at home and in public life. Religious rhetoric was freely incorporated into these discussions.

A woman's sphere was "naturally" the home. However, with the onset of industrialization and the introduction of academies, seminaries, and secondary schooling for women, women's significance in household production was gradually diminishing, and new spheres in need of "proper" spiritual guidance were evolving.[77] The cult of domesticity focused on women's reproductive power and their service to the physical, spiritual, and social regeneration and well-being of a moral republic. *Home,* a world of spiritual influence as opposed to the materialistic *world* outside, was a sanctuary, a haven of good works and moral elevation.[78] The "self-contained" and "self-denying" lives and work of women—as missionary texts often described them—consisted of rearing children and influencing husbands, friends, and servants at home while remedying all of the social ills of a rapidly changing world.[79] According to Nancy Cott, the early nineteenth century witnessed the feminization of the Protestant religion.[80] For many New England women, church activity and related reform movements—from temperance and antislavery to prison and education reforms—provided the basis for social organization, gender solidarity, and self-assertion. At a time when "church-related voluntary associations commanded a much larger membership . . . than did the women's rights movement proper," it was only natural that missionary work was perceived as an area in which women could assert themselves.[81] By the 1840s many women began to argue that a "woman's blessings" could also be put to use in reforming the materialistic world outside, in teaching, nursing, and religious/missionary work. It was only logical that the same influence could be employed to fight against the "corruption" of societies abroad, and "*the* stronghold of Satan" in the Near East. In this way, American women could justify their presence in foreign lands and in the Turkish field. But in order to serve outside of their capacities as mothers or wives as prescribed by the cult of domesticity, their roles as reforming missionaries had to be submerged within the rhetoric of civilizing and evangelizing the daughters of darkness.

In America, religion could be a liberating institution; it could be used not only to glorify the role of women at home, but also to transgress the boundaries of domesticity. But abroad, in the mission field, religion turned into an instrument of manipulation and control. Women's missionary work served evangelical and American goals, as it empowered American women to regulate, control, and change the lives of others.

Women entered the Turkish field as wives and mothers, since male missionaries sent to foreign bases such as Turkey were strongly urged to bring spouses. Later, single female graduates of academies joined the missionary ranks. Women promoted the argument that only they could reach the women of Turkey. Their work could also serve as free advertisement for the ever-expanding missionary business. Mrs. Moses Smith, a Mount Holyoke graduate and the president of the Woman's Board of Missions of the Interior, declared that in the final analysis it was the mothers at home who determined the character and condition of any people.[82] Mrs. J. A. Barker, a Baptist missionary, stated boldly that "If . . . woman can be won to the truth, the viewpoint of the whole nation will be changed."[83]

By attributing great importance to all women in society, missionary women sought to enlarge their sphere of influence and hasten their entry into the public arena through the spiritual threshold of evangelism. One would expect, then, that these women would promote elevating images of women all over the world. Yet it was the missionary women themselves who demonized the women of the Near East by claiming that the latter were obstructing the way to progress and civilization by manipulating children and men with their dark influence. The application of the cult of domesticity and an unthreatening version of women's liberation in Ottoman society glorified the evangelized woman as a role model in family and public life while it denigrated all those who did not subscribe to "civilized"—that is to say, evangelical— ideals. The church, too, unfavorably compared other cultures to the American-Protestant culture, using historical references to reassure American women that they were better off due to the progress of

Christian civilization. After all, the Gospel had "civilized" society as well as men's relations with women.[84] As Barbara Welter explains, "Christianity was characterized as the liberator of women; only in Christian lands were women accorded respect and dignity."[85] In other words, just like a government, a religion should fit its people. One got what one deserved by remaining in the dark and ignoring the truth.

If Ottoman women benefited from the educational, medical, and philanthropic activities of American women, one can also argue that American women benefited from the superior position they occupied as providers of "civilized" necessities and ideas. Promoting their own self-interest and American commerce at the expense of their Ottoman "sisters" might have not been the intent of American women. In retrospect, however, this was largely the outcome of "women's work for women."

CONCLUSION

Throughout the nineteenth century, the "woman question" was merged with the "Eastern question" within the orientalist discourse. Long before the first American missionaries set foot on Ottoman soil, the European style "for dominating, restructuring, and having authority over the Orient," had been informing the educated American perception of the Near East.[86] This same discourse was also a convenient means to spread the Gospel, republican ideology, and capitalistic interests in the Middle East. Even though at times two visions—civilizing the heathens as opposed to converting them—had been in bitter conflict with each other, missionaries in practice promoted both of them throughout the nineteenth century. The premise for American missionary work was that the backwardness of the region, the darkness of its life, the despotism of its rule, the crudeness of its people, and the lack of modern facilities altogether necessitated the evangelization—and thus the "modernization"—of its people. Until 1923 American missionaries took advantage of British diplomatic and German cultural influences yet conveniently dissociated themselves from European imperial powers. Even during the Turkish War of Independence, U.S. interests in the region were not yet defined as imperialistic. Therefore, American influence, as opposed to European, generally maintained a privileged position and a safer distance from the scrutiny of the Turkish intelligentsia.

However, it was the emergence of female missionary careers, rather than a specific interest in the "woman question" by male missionaries, that brought the Ottoman women under the spotlight of missionary rhetoric in the mid-nineteenth century. American women's missionary work contributed to a discourse of paternalism, authority, and Western self-empowerment through the circulation of negative imagery.

Today, it is probably very hard, if not impossible, to assess the success of the missionary work and the amount of influence exercised by American women over their Ottoman sisters. Moreover, it has not been my purpose here to repaint the picture of Ottoman women as passive victims of a forceful transformation. Any interaction naturally involves both sides; furthermore, it would be equally misleading to talk about *the* way in which Ottoman women, as a single, unified entity, reacted to American women. Nevertheless, I would like to suggest that there is a striking similarity between the missionary perception of women in the service of a God-loving republic and the official rhetoric of the Turkish Republic, which enlists women in the crusade to modernize the country.[87] Both demand loyalty from women to their rhetoric and neither willingly acknowledges other voices and definitions of womanhood. An example of the fusion of religious, nationalistic, and republican ideas of womanhood was the work of Halide Edib, who was also embraced by the missionaries as one of their own. In *Turkey Faces West* (1930), she volunteered to play the advocate of the modern republic for the American audience.[88]

Missionaries in general, and missionary women in particular, came from a country of diversity and often talked about the creation of open minds and liberal perceptions. However, they projected a universal, unchangeable "woman nature" and promoted a uniform lot and purpose in life for Ottoman women. In a similar way, the Turkification process that started in the late Ottoman era and continued into the Republican period responded to the "woman question" as it addressed the questions of ethnicity and class—by means of melting them all in the hot tin pot of modern nationalism. Thus, women, as mothers, wives, nurses, teachers, and physical objects, rather than as individuals in their own right, have occupied a central position in the grand narratives of both religion and nationalism.

Notes

Author's note: I am indebted to Esra Danacıoğlu, who shared with me some of her research on missionary activities and increased my understanding of the topic. I would like to thank Shelly Fisher Fishkin for encouraging me to pursue this project and Irvin Schick for being supportive of this work in countless ways. I am also grateful to Stephanie Robinson, Christos Stathopoulos, and James Grehan for their invaluable suggestions.

1. *Almanac 1891,* cited by Danacıoğlu, 1987:98.
2. See Kocabaşoğlu, 1991:18.
3. For a nationalistic discussion that validates conspiratorial theories about foreign and American missionary schools in Turkey, see Sevinç, n.d.; and Clarke, 1977:421.
4. Ottoman society was politically organized on the basis of religious leadership and communities called *millet*s or nations. These communities included Muslims, Greek-Orthodox, Armenians, and Jews. For a discussion of *millet*s since the sixteenth century and their evolution in the nineteenth century, see İ. Tekeli, 1980:13-35; and Lewis, 1982.
5. Said, 1978. Describing Orientalism as a school of thought based on East/West dichotomy, Said is interested in the power-discourse relationship as it evolves in the European texts on the Orient, rather than the development of the orientalist imagery (such as corruption, sensuality, despotism, fatalism) in the United States. Nevertheless, such imagery made its way to the former British colonies in America through the European texts as early as 1776 (Başcı, 1993).
6. Crunden, 1990:91. Lyman Beecher, a distinguished Calvinist preacher, was a leader of this view. He founded the Park Street Church, which gave birth to the ABCFM in 1819. He was also the father of two remarkable women of reform. Catharine Beecher was a pioneer in women's education, and Harriet Beecher Stowe stormed the American audience with *Uncle Tom's*

Cabin during the pre–Civil War debate over slavery. For a history of the ABCFM, see Hutchison, 1987.

7. Hutchison, 1987:44-45.
8. Abzug, 1994:56.
9. Harlow, 1919:9.
10. *Statements In Regard to Colleges In Unevangelized Lands,* n.d.:1.
11. *Statements In Regard to Colleges In Unevangelized Lands,* n.d.:4-5.
12. Bartlett, 1972:26.
13. Bartlett, 1972:27.
14. L. Flemming, 1989:1-10.
15. Stone, 1984:32.
16. Riggs, 1909:179.
17. *Annual Report of the American Board of Commissioners for Foreign Missions 1902,* 1902:40-64. This excludes European Turkey Mission, which consisted of Monaster Philoppopolis, Samokov, Salonica, and the surrounding area. These figures refer to the following: (1) Western Turkey Mission, which consisted of İstanbul, İzmir, Bursa, Sivas, Kayseri, Merzifon, Trabzon; (2) Central Turkey Mission, which included Antep, Maraş, and the surrounding area of Adana-Tarsus, Saimbeyli (Haçin), and Urfa; (3) Eastern Turkey Mission, which covered the surrounding area of Bitlis, Erzurum, Elazığ (Harput), Mardin, and Van.
18. *Annual Report of the American Board of Commissioners for Foreign Missions 1902,* 1902:60-62.
19. Kocabaşoğlu, n.d., 496.
20. Kocabaşoğlu, n.d., 498.
21. Kocabaşoğlu, n.d., 498.
22. Stone, 1984:18; Stone, 1980:11.
23. Stone, 1984:18; G. Davis, 1926:58, 62.
24. Stone, 1984:18.
25. Martin, 1991:311.
26. Danacıoğlu, 1987:72.
27. Stone, 1984:19.
28. Dodge, 1992:20.
29. Stone, 1984:17-18.
30. *Annual Report of the American Board of Commissioners for Foreign Missions 1902,* 1902:67.
31. Wintle, 1923:58-59.
32. Wintle, 1923:50-56.

33. Ecumenical Missionary Conference, *Report 1900,* 1900:214-215.
34. Evarts to Anderson, ABC: 8.1, Vol. I, n. 1, cited by Phillips, 1969:142.
35. Addresses delivered before the Sixth International Convention of the Student Volunteer Movement for Foreign Missions, *Students and the Present Missionary Crisis,* 1910:403.
36. Brown, 1914:179-183.
37. Brown, 1914:179.
38. Brown, 1914:179.
39. Brown, 1914:179.
40. Brown, 1914:180.
41. Brown, 1914:180.
42. Martin, 1991:56.
43. Brown, 1914:180.
44. Brown, 1914:180.
45. Cott, 1977:1-2.
46. Cooper, 1892:9-10.
47. Brown, 1914:180.
48. Addresses delivered before the Sixth International Convention of the Student Volunteer Movement for Foreign Missions, *Students and the Present Missionary Crisis,* 1910:368.
49. Brown, 1914:180.
50. Brown, 1914:181-182.
51. Brown, 1914:183.
52. For example, see Patrick, 1929:23.
53. Martin, 1991:179. Emma Hubbard was impressed by the way peasant women worked in Anatolia. Also see Ellis and Palmer, 1914:861.
54. Patrick, 1929:164-204.
55. Ellis and Palmer, 1914:861-864.
56. Patrick, 1929:209-210.
57. Addresses delivered before the Sixth International Convention of the Student Volunteer Movement for Foreign Missions, *Students and the Present Missionary Crisis,* 1910:363.
58. Patrick, 1929:210.
59. Patrick, 1929.
60. Köksal, 1993:88.
61. *Mehasin,* [Grace] n. 6, cited by Demirdirek, 1993:40.
62. G. Davis, 1926:65.

63. Lawrence, 1853:133-134. Also see Patrick, 1929:29-30; and G. Davis, 1926:59.

64. Ecumenical Missionary Conference, *Report 1900,* 1900:219.

65. G. Davis, 1926:80.

66. Riggs, 1909:169.

67. Lawrence, 1853:195.

68. Riggs, 1909:169.

69. Ecumenical Missionary Conference, *Report 1900,* 1900:47.

70. This perception may have been due to the fact that missionaries, frequently, if not exclusively, encountered urban Greeks in centers such as İstanbul and İzmir.

71. Lawrence, 1853:134.

72. Lawrence, 1853:137.

73. *Annual Report of the American Board of Commissioners for Foreign Missions 1902,* 1902:62.

74. *Light and Life,* April 1912, cited by Stone, 1980:5.

75. G. Davis, 1926:47.

76. Lawrence, 1853:152.

77. Cott, 1977:1-10, 117.

78. Cott, 1977:64-69.

79. Cott, 1977:68-69.

80. Cott, 1977:132-153.

81. Cott, 1977:156.

82. Ecumenical Missionary Conference, *Report 1900,* 1900:219.

83. Barker, 1905:25.

84. Cott, 1977:130.

85. Welter, 1978:630.

86. Said, 1978:3.

87. Durakbaşa, this volume; Durakbaşa, 1988:167-171.

88. Adıvar, 1930:46. Throughout the book Edib plays the part of an advocate for the Turkish legacy and the modern Turkish Republic. She recreates the image of "the original Turk"—before Islam and after the empire—as an embodiment of pragmatism, mobility, and stylistic simplicity. The narrative is a defense of "the Turk" to the American audience. Edib emphasizes certain aspects of Turkish life and "identity" that might be appealing to a part of her audience. Especially interesting is her defense of "the harem" as an apartment where women rule the domestic aspects of everyday life.

PART II

THE EARLY YEARS OF THE REPUBLIC

FIVE

WOMEN AS PRESERVERS OF THE PAST: ZİYA GÖKALP AND WOMEN'S REFORM

K. E. Fleming

ZİYA GÖKALP (1876-1924), arguably the greatest intellectual figure of the earliest years of the Turkish Republic, is now celebrated mostly as a rare and curious example of the academic thinker who attempts to implement his theories in the practical domain, for Gökalp was both a brilliant scholar of sociology and an active political and social reformer.[1] Gökalp's commentators have made much of the fact that Gökalp's study of history and sociology was not a matter of mere theoretical musing, but rather was designed to provide a schematic underpinning for the formulation of a defined and specific cultural policy. Indeed, Mustafa Kemal Atatürk claimed Gökalp as his intellectual mentor and father, and Gökalp's systematic formulation of a theory of Turkish nationalism provided the starting point for Kemalist ideology.[2] Less frequently discussed, however, are the peculiar theoretical premises on which Gökalp based his program for reform.

Gökalp, like many of the political and social reformers of his day (particularly in Turkey and in Egypt), rejected European "modernity" as a model for advancement, focusing his attention instead on the ancient past—both "real" and constructed—of his own nation.[3] By situating his nation's ideal state not in an imagined future but rather in an already-lived past, Gökalp was, of course, employing a logic familiar to religious and political reform alike. Indeed, the historian Mircea Eliade has shown the notion of an Edenic "*illo tempus*" to be a near-universal feature of social ideologies of all sorts.[4] What is most interesting, however, about Gökalp's construction of the Turkish nation as based on its ancient past is the role played in this construction by women.[5] In his writings on women and reform, Gökalp provides a vivid example of the way in which reform movements perennially posit women as being central and pivotal to the enterprise of cultural and religious renewal.[6] This chapter attempts to examine some of the strategies at the heart of Gökalp's vision of the centrality of women in his broader calls for reform.

Gökalp, although now perhaps best known simply as a sociologist and educational reformer, is a conspicuous figure in the history of Turkish women's liberation movements.[7] Gökalp was a major player in the CUP period of Turkish history (Committee of Union and Progress, or İttihat ve Terakki Cemiyeti), and many of his most pioneering contributions concerned the emancipation of women. Emancipation of women, according to Gökalp, was to be total, occurring in three distinct realms: socioeconomic life, education, and legal treatment.[8] His legal and religious reforms, as well as his attitudes toward politics, language, and literature—among a host of other topics of interest— almost invariably had at their core the question of the status of women. Not only was this question of women to be a central aspect of Gökalp's utopian "New Nation," but the very idea of nationalism itself was, in many ways, predicated on the proper positioning of women in society.

Gökalp's interest in women stemmed from his broader hope for the (re)discovery of the "original" ethnic foundations of Turkish culture. This, in turn, was part of his overarching concern with the question of how Turkey was best to adopt Western civilization while synthesizing it with Islam and Turkishness, identified by Gökalp as the two great historical traditions of the Turks.[9] It is my claim that Gökalp's interest in women, then, was based on his idea that they were the repositories and guarantors of the past. It is this notion that marks Gökalp's peculiar combination and use of two themes—the centrality of women and the return to an idealized and perfect past—that are common to reform movements around the world. In granting women the role of guarantors and protectors of the past, Gökalp echoed reformist movements from India to Egypt and provides a paradigmatic case study of the centrality of women to a broad array of reformist movements.[10]

In order properly to understand the logic by which women play this role of guardians and protectors of Turkey's ancient past, it is first necessary to examine the critical distinction made in Gökalp's thought between the realms of *culture* (*hars*) and *civilization* (*medeniyet*).[11] Niyazi Berkes thus summarizes Gökalp's stance as follows: "Briefly stated, civilization refers to modes of action composed of the 'traditions' which are created by different ethnic groups and transmitted from one to another. Culture, on the other hand, is composed of the 'mores' of a particular nation and, consequently, is unique and *sui generis*."[12] Culture, wherein the unique essence of Turkishness resides, must remain intact, while civilization may change. Within this conceptual cultural framework, Gökalp directed his readers in the proper attitude Turks should have regarding the civilization of the West:

> It follows from these observations that we have to be disciples of Europe in civilization, but entirely independent of it in culture . . . we Turks can recognize the Europeans as superior in civilization. In civilization we can be their disciples and their imitators. But, beware, we should never view the culture of other nations as superior to our own! We should by no means be the disciples or imitators of other nations in matters of culture.[13]

Civilization, however, can only properly change when its new forms "penetrate into the soul of the nation and become assimilated with it."[14] If the changes of civilization truly fail to take root but rather remain superficial, the result is an imbalance between civilization and culture and a culture characterized by alien and meaningless social forms. Turkey, wrote Gökalp, provided a sad example of this imbalance: "In Turkey," he stated, "the institutions of the family as well as other institutions are now undergoing severe crises because of our failure to see these fundamental differences between the progress of civilizations and the growth of cultures."[15] Many of the forms of civilization found in Turkey, argued Gökalp, had not been properly assimilated into Turkish culture, with the result that the society was disjointed and the people lacked a sense of identity.

Complex and at times apparently inconsistent as Gökalp's detailed distinction between civilization and culture is, it is nevertheless possible to see that the two categories are roughly distinguishable along gender lines. Women, it would appear, are the proper guardians and transmitters of civilization. For example, Gökalp wrote that women were of the magical realm and men of the religious. Therefore, "[i]t was only when the importance of magic reappeared under another name [that is to say, a civilization] during the *Tanzimat* period that women began to gain higher status. Culture is a product of religion, whereas civilization is an evolution from ancient magic."[16] Women, then, are singled out as providing organization for the first and most fundamental basis for society, the family, through which woman transmits civilization and guarantees the seamless assimilation of civilization into Turkish culture:

> Society has three foundations, of which the first is the family. O Woman! It is you who organize this domain of adoration; It is you who first took in your hands the cloak of civilization. In letters of gold, your name should there be written.[17]

Crudely put, as women were increasingly marginalized by the adoption of non-Turkish social norms, an imbalance was created between their realm (civilization) and the realm of men (culture). Although the association of men and women with, respectively, culture and civilization was largely inchoate, I would argue that it nevertheless played a significant role in shaping Gökalp's program for women's emancipation. Culture (*hars*), corresponding to the male gender, represents the deepest level of a nation's identity. It is, again, *sui generis*. Civilization (*medeniyet*), on the other hand, refers to actions and traditions that, having as they do far less deep roots than the features of culture, can be passed from one ethnic, religious, or national group to another.[18] Gökalp's call for reform was based in large part on the goal of stripping away layers of "alien" civilization (as manifest, for example, in language) grafted improperly onto native culture. It is for this reason that the "true" Turkish past was seen by Gökalp to reside in the female, rather than the male, realm. This theme of women being the guardians of the past because they have possession of—and the ability to transmit—the true forms of Turkey's civilization runs throughout Gökalp's writing on women. Likewise, the distinction between *hars* and *medeniyet* influenced the entirety of Gökalp's writing on the emancipation of women.

Women, moreover, are the guarantors of the past because they are "closer" to, more "in touch with" the past than are their male contemporaries. This view of women is a natural extension of Gökalp's attitude towards the "*halk*" or "common people," in whom he believes the true source of cultural ideals resides.[19] This rosy vision of the proletariat is, of course, a familiar theme in romanticist thought (Rousseau provides but the most prominent example), but in Gökalp the specific attention to women provided a new twist.

Women, then, were closest to the most basic and ancient foundations on which modern society was to be based. Paradoxically, however, this was in part the case because of oppressive, non-Turkish practices (that is, foreign "civilization") that had denied women their proper place in society. Cloistered in the harem, denied an education, and deprived of true participation in political or economic life, women were fixed, as it were, in amber, largely unaffected by the changes in the surrounding world.

This paradox in Gökalp's work is all the more pointed in that his writing on women, based as it was on the distinction between culture and civilization, reveals an attempt to divorce Turkey from the "orientalist" imaginings of the Islamic "East" so prevalent in his day. Part and parcel, of course, of this "orientalist" fantasy were ostensibly indigenous "Muslim" or "Eastern" practices regarding women. Thus, for example, such institutions as polygamy and the seclusion of women in the harem, which through the works of European travelers and writers had become powerful symbols in the West for Islamic decadence, lack of civilization, and general "otherness," became of interest to Gökalp in his effort to identify and reclaim the "true" characteristics of the "original" Turks. Gökalp, arguing that such institutions were, in fact, intrinsic neither to Islam nor to "Turkishness," rejected much contemporary practice regarding women as being the unfortunate syncretisms of Islam and Turkey with non-Muslim, non-Turkish forms. Rather than making up part of Turkey's culture, they represented the unsuccessful adoption of the "civilization" of other nations.

In addition to further elucidating the somewhat fine distinction between culture and civilization, Gökalp's rejection of social forms viewed as alien provides a typical instance of his strategy vis-à-vis such European accusations as lack of civility or backwardness. Gökalp aimed not to demonstrate that his countrypeople were not, in fact, as "backward" as they might seem. Rather, he aimed to point out that the Turks, *as* Turks, were beyond reproach, for the very practices that Europeans might identify as distasteful were not really Turkish at all but rather were the unfortunate result of past contacts with less civilized peoples. The condemnation of the Turk was a mistaken one, more rightly directed at the Arab, the Persian, or the Byzantine:

> Women were equal to men among the ancient Turks because their religion was not an ascetic one. When the ascetic conception of the Iranian and Greek Orthodox religions penetrated through to the Muslims in the Abbasid period, ideas about the inferiority of women spread among the Muslims too.[20]

This type of logic, common to both religious and political reform movements around the world, was recruited by Gökalp in his venture to emancipate the Turkish woman. Just as many of the West's "orientalist" imaginings of the Ottoman Turk—who to the European mind was, after all, the consummate mysterious, cruel, and sensuous "Easterner"—had as their basis images of the Ottoman woman (behind the veil; locked in the harem; sharing her husband with other wives), so too did Gökalp identify woman as one of the central images in his quest for an "authentic" Turkish state. By elucidating the true nature of the Turkish heritage, Gökalp sought to prove the illegitimacy of such Western stereotypes.

Moreover, a return to the purism of ancient Turkey was fundamental to the foundation of a new Republic. Witness, for example, the logic by which Gökalp situated the question of women's status at the very heart of the nationalist enterprise:

> The ancient family and sex morality of the Turks, which had reached high standards, is completely lost today. Under the influence of the Iranian and Greek civilizations, women have become enslaved and have sunk to a low legal status. When the ideal of a national culture arose among the Turks, the revival of, and return to, these traditions were inevitable. It was for this reason that feminism in Turkey developed alongside the rise of nationalism.[21]

Since the development of national sentiment is dependent on the question of group identity, a concern that often involves a quest for origins, the Turkish endeavor had of necessity to eschew all non-Turkish elements in its midst through a systematic, historical examination of all components of latter-day Ottoman society. By identifying that which was *not* authentically Turkish, that which *was* would come into focus. In the process, claimed Gökalp, feminism would naturally develop, for the natural state of the ancient Turkish peoples was a feminist one. The proper expurgation of Arabic, Persian, Byzantine, and other foreign influences would both highlight the national character and improve the lot of women, for all things degrading to them have sprung not from Turkishness but from unfortunate foreign mutations. As Gökalp continued,

> Turkish nationalists are both popular and feminist, not only because these two principles are values in our age, but also because democracy and feminism were two bases of ancient Turkish life. Other nations, in their efforts to adapt themselves to modern civilization, have had to keep far away from their past, whereas for the Turks it is enough to turn and look at their ancient past for inspiration.[22]

The index for advancement against which modern Turkey should be measured was not Europe, but rather Turkey itself. Turkey need not be a player in the great rush to escape the past, to hurtle forward into modernity, but rather had only to look to its ancient past for guidance. The "advancing" nations who frame their notions of modernity by means of comparison with Europe had to do so because their own history is bereft of material providing guidance. The result for the women of such countries was that they gained no true advance, for in the hollow mimicry of European women they were drawing on social norms that, because they were alien to their own past, could not hope ever to take root. Gökalp was explicit in his rejection of such an approach: "Turkish womanhood certainly will better itself by benefiting from the progress of modern civilization," he asserted. "But the Turkish woman will not be a copy-cat of French or of English or of German womanhood."[23] Once again, Gökalp's argument was based both on his belief in the centrality of women's liberation to the project of reform, and on the distinction he was so eager to make between culture and civilization. Rather than merely copy the forms of European civilization, Turkish women must blend them fully with Turkish culture, thus producing a holistic and meaningful syncretism, rather than a meaningless and shallow adaptation of that which is alien.

The feminism that benefits modern Turkish womanhood, then, could be *fostered* by "the progress of modern civilization," but by no means was modern civilization its source. Rather, feminism, along with democracy, was a "basis" for Turkish life in ancient times. Democracy and feminism were not to be adopted simply because they were now all the contemporary rage in Europe, but rather because they were foundational elements to true Turkishness as discovered in the ancient past.

Thus, we see that Gökalp's brand of reform was predicated on a clever, if not wholly unique, strategy. Through constant reference to an ancient and pure Turkish past, Gökalp was able to make of the new the old, to convert the foreign into the indigenous. Concepts commonly thought to be part and parcel of modernity, such as "democracy" and "feminism"—even "nationalism"—were, through Gökalp's brand of history, found instead to have come from the most ancient of times. Similarly, the "European-ness" of such concepts was denied, as they were portrayed instead as foundational elements of a pure "Turkishness." Again, the appeal to antiquity was not a new one in the context of reform. Contemporary U.S. society is replete with examples of ideological appeals to the past; the "rediscovery" of the ancient goddess in feminist New Age circles is but one of many. What is most interesting, however, to Gökalp's formulation of this familiar dynamic was the role he granted in it to women.

I have said that Gökalp, in his identification of women as somehow being the guarantors and protectors of a pristine past, is representative of a broad array of reformist thought. One particularly clear example of this identification is found in Gökalp's views on religion. Additionally, it is in his discussion of religion that Gökalp most clearly aligned civilization with women and culture with men.

Gökalp, a secular rather than religious reformer, was not interested in reclaiming the purity of Islam, but rather of "Turkishness," of a national identity in which Islam played but one small part. The question of religion was, however, linked directly to Gökalp's discussion of women's liberation. According to Gökalp, religion was, if anything, a culprit in the demeaning of the status of women, for religion was the domain of man, not of woman:

> Among the ancient Turks, the magical system was represented by shamanism and the religious system by *töre* [pre-Islamic customary law]. As these two systems had an equal value among them there was equality between men and women . . . the more the antagonism between religion and magic deepened, the more the inequality of men and women widened.[24]

Religion, then, was the domain of man, while "magic" was that of woman. Moreover, religion was aligned with culture, and magic with civilization: "Culture is a product of religion, whereas civilization is an evolution from ancient magic."[25] Algebraically, at least, we see once again that woman was aligned with civilization and man with culture.

These two systems—religion and magic—were, according to Gökalp, happy and equal bedfellows up to the earliest years of Islamic Turkish history. Religion, however, (in this case "pure" Islam), came in contact with the "ascetic" religions of Persia and Byzantium. The asceticism of Zoroastrianism and Christianity manifested itself in a rejection of the ecstatic and sexually liberated qualities of female-governed magic. Furthermore, as the idea of asceticism is predicated on the rejection or overcoming of desire, an object *of* desire was needed. Thus the increasing negative objectification of women, which drew its breath from the asceticism of such religions. The result was the adoption within Islam of a series of social codes designed to stifle the magical libertinism of women. Hence, such practices as the sequestering of women and the wearing of the veil, although in origin alien to Islam, grew to be associated with it. Gradually, as the rift between religion and magic deepened, so too was the relative status of men and women forced further and further apart.

It should be noted, however, that Islam, along with Turkish, was seen by Gökalp to be one of Turkey's greatest cultural traditions. Islam, then, through peculiar exegetical logic, was excused from the blame to which other religions (Judaism, Zoroastrianism, Christianity) were subject. Islam, as a religious rather than a magical system, is of the male realm. In its pristine state, however, (that is, before the polluting qualities of asceticism took hold) it was balanced by female magic. It should be noted that this is directly analogous to the ancient balance, now lost, between culture and civilization. The contaminating effects of contact with other religions (that is, alien, improperly assimilated "civilization") necessitated that Islam, like Turkey itself, be purged of foreign, "ascetic" elements. As for Islamic jurists who argued for the inferiority of women, Gökalp wrote, "surely the commentators have made a mistake."[26] Correct religious practice was not to be found in following the *ulama*, but rather in the rituals of women. It was women, based as they were in magic (the ancient manifestation of civilization) who had in their ritual activity most closely preserved the forms of the ancient civilization; in short, who now played the role once played by ancient magical systems. Asceticism, then, was the *ur* source of the disparity between the status of the sexes. The "magical," "spontaneous" dimension of woman had to be restored and the ascetic dimensions of Islam purged to bring the two into alignment.

The imbalance between men and women would be rectified through attention to the ancient forms as manifested in the current-day practices of women. Just as women's rituals provided the template for proper religious practice, so too did their behavior provide guidance in other realms as well. Gökalp's interest in language reform, for instance, had as one of its bases the notion that women provided a crucial key to the past. Gökalp's infatuation with the *halk* was part and parcel of his great hope to break down the barrier dividing Turkey's intellectual elite and the masses. This barrier, he felt, was based largely on the peculiarities of the formal Ottoman language, which was inaccessible to all but the most educated. The Ottoman tongue's recondite grammatical forms and vast—and largely foreign—vocabulary required years of formal education to master. Gökalp advocated that a new, common "language of the nation" should be substituted in its stead. While not so radical a purist as Fuat Raif and the *İkdam* newspaper circle, Gökalp nevertheless stood out as a language reformer.[27] And, as with his views on religion, central to Gökalp's approach to the reform of language was his view that women provided the most accurate model of the past. The new national language was to be based on the vernacular of the masses of Istanbul, especially, he wrote, as spoken by the city's women. For it was women, he argued, who had most effectively preserved the language's native "spontaneity" and "harmony."[28] Conversely, it was men, particularly men of the religious establishment, who had weighed language down with Arabicisms and Persian borrowings.

The return to the forms of the past would not merely give women parity with men, but would moreover be based on the model of women. That is to say, women's culture and behaviors were to point the way to that past, to embody it. Just as woman's religious rituals and speech represented a preserving of ancient language and religion, so too did her role within the family provide a model on which to base the modern Turkish home. Gökalp thus urged a transition from the large, extended, patriarchal family living in a *konak* to a small, nuclear, monogamic family living in a *yuva* (literally, a nest)—a nice image drawn, not coincidentally, from the realm of nature rather than that of culture.[29] Only in the context of the small, nuclear family—thought by Gökalp to represent the original form of the Turkish family unit— would women finally be able to reestablish a balance of power.

Again and again in Gökalp's arguments—on language reform, religion, and family structure, to survey but a few—we see his distinctive methodology at work. By hinging the entirety of his reforms on an appeal to the past of his own nation, he was able to subvert the symbolic power of Western concepts and ideals. By claiming that Turkey held within its own history all of the materials necessary for the structuring of a "modern" state, he converted the external into the internal, the future into the past. And time and again we see that his ubiquitous interest in women was part and parcel of his method. By viewing women as the guardians of the past, he granted them a position vital to the enterprise of reform and provided a vivid demonstration of the gender themes common to reform movements.

Notes

1. Berkes, 1964.
2. Devereux, 1968:ix-xi.
3. Lewis, 1968:351. The literary expression of this "Turkist trend" was the review *Genç Kalemler* (Young Pens), to which Gökalp was a regular contributor. In Egypt, this rejection of the notion of European "modernity" and supremacy is presently seen in such reformist thinkers as Mustafa Kamil and Sa`d Zaghlul.

4. Eliade, 1954.

5. Mardin, 1969. For more on this question of a return to a pristine past in the context of Turkish reform movements, see Mardin, 1960.

6. For an excellent discussion of this, see, for example, Baykan, 1994.

7. Ziyaeddin Fahri gives a compelling argument for the absolute centrality of Gökalp's views on women to the entirety of his thought (Fahri, 1935).

8. Cited in Y. Arat, 1989:27, n. 30.

9. Berkes, 1959:7.

10. Baykan, 1994:101ff.

11. As Heyd points out, the term *hars* "was formed by Gökalp from an Arabic root as an exact equivalent of the French *culture*. Before Gökalp defined culture as the totality of national values he used the word *irfan,* or '*medeniyet*'" (Heyd, 1950:63, n. 3). From 1918 on, Gökalp made a clear distinction between the three terms.

12. Berkes, 1959:23.

13. Berkes, 1959:251.

14. Berkes, 1959:250.

15. Berkes, 1959:250-251.

16. Berkes, 1959:254.

17. Fındıkoğlu, 1936:Appendix I; translation mine.

18. See, for more on this, Berkes, 1959:23ff.

19. See, for example, the poem "Hakkın muradı halktan fırladı" in Gökalp, 1914-1915:80.

20. Berkes, 1959:254.

21. Berkes, 1959:303.

22. Berkes, 1959:303.

23. Berkes, 1959:254.

24. Berkes, 1959:254.

25. Berkes, 1959:254.

26. Heyd, 1950:95.

27. Heyd, 1950:116.

28. Gökalp, 1923:11, 29, 97-98; Gökalp, 1918:31, 47-48; Gökalp, 1941:15.

29. Gökalp, 1941:17ff; Gökalp, 1922-1923:21; Gökalp, 1923:162.

KEMALISM AS IDENTITY POLITICS IN TURKEY

Ayşe Durakbaşa

THE SO-CALLED MIDDLE EASTERN SOCIETIES OF TODAY have undergone the impact of Westernization for more than a century, and this is, in fact, the major characteristic of their social histories now. Hence the social history of those societies for the last century is the story of their encounter with the West. In most of the societies with a majority Muslim population, Islam functioned as the only ideological source for the definition of authenticity and authentic national identity. Women's emancipation was considered an integral part of the nationalist resistance movements against colonialism and the economic and cultural hegemony of the West. It was formulated as central to the nationalist ideologies that fostered a new national and cultural identity for which the image of the "new woman" was a marker not only of cultural authenticity but also of being "civilized" as a nation.[1]

However, within the framework of Turkish nationalism, the cultural reference for authentic national identity shifted from Islamic culture to the original culture of the Turks before they accepted Islam. Kemal Atatürk and the other leaders of the Turkish nationalist struggle and the Turkish Republic made a radical break with Islamic law and tradition that had a direct impact on the area of legislation related to women's position in society. Hence the efforts for reform in women's status culminated in the "state feminism"[2] of the new Turkish Republic, which provided all Turkish women with some equal rights in the area of law, education, and political life. Kemalist elites realized the project of modernization to its full extent, which up to the present day has proved to be the major source of "Kemalist pride."[3]

In this chapter I will try to mark some of the particularities of Turkish nationalism and feminism, mainly as reflected in the official ideology of the Republic—namely Kemalism—and explore the impact of the related reforms in the making of modern femininities and masculinities in Turkey. I will argue that Kemalism, although a progressive ideology that fostered women's participation in education and the professions, did not alter the patriarchal norms of morality and in fact maintained the basic cultural conservatism about male/female relations, despite its radicalism in opening a space for women in the public domain.

TURKISH FEMINISM
AND TURKISH NATIONALISM

Ziya Gökalp, in his book *The Principles of Turkism,* wrote a section on "Turkish Feminism" in which he maintained that in Shamanism, the religion of the ancient Turks, women were attributed certain powers, and in the nomadic Turkish tribes women held positions equal to men.[4] In the same canon with Ziya Gökalp, Halide Edib, a pioneering Turkish feminist, characterized Turkish feminism as different from Western feminism. In one of her lectures at the Jamia Millia (Muslim) Institution in India in 1935, she identified "the most salient features" of Turkish feminism as seeking "the gradual emancipation of Turkish women and their evolution as useful and beneficial social units," and then she highlighted the differences:

> . . . features in which it differs from Western feminism are, first, that it was not the revolt of one sex against the other's domination. It was a part and an integral part of Turkish reform and accepted as such by all progressive parties in Turkey.
>
> Second, as against other reforms, the conflict of East and West has in this one played only a minor part. It was considered a natural revival of the best both in Islam and in the racial culture and tradition of the Turks. This, I believe, gave it its greatest force.[5]

Halide Edib and Ziya Gökalp emphasized the idea that "feminism," that is, equality between the sexes, was endemic to the Turkish national character and characterized the social life of pre-Islamic and early Islamic Turkish societies. The same view was repeated in speeches and books by the Kemalists, and Turkish feminism was defined within this framework.[6] Gender equality was presented as a part of national identity; in fact, the equality of the sexes in the original nomadic culture of the Turks was the basic theme in the writings of the first generation of Kemalist women.[7]

Kemalist Republican ideology incorporated in its modernist reforms a project of "degendering" and "regendering." New forms of masculinity and femininity were brought about by the Kemalists, who condemned some of the traditional gender notions as backward and praised some in a new context. Most significantly, "new women" became the symbols of the new Turkey as a civilized nation. In some ways Republican ideology of "sexual egalitarianism" echoed French thinkers of the Enlightenment, yet these egalitarian and liberal ideas were basically formulated in a corporatist-nationalist framework. Within the Kemalist-nationalist framework, the equality of men and women was put forward as the equality of the male and female members of the new-born Turkish nation, who shared the same ideals and responsibilities in the nation-building process. In this process, alongside the legal reforms, a new institutional make-up for a desegregated society was also brought forth. New conceptions of the relationship between the state and the individual were introduced. Members of Turkish society were no longer thought of as "subjects" but as "citizens"; that is, members of a political community with legally delimited rights and duties. The ideas of citizenship were closely linked with the making of a national culture and history.

In an effort to create a citizenry with a distinct national identity, a new theory about the origins of Turks was presented. The "Turkish history thesis" argued that Turks had contributed to civilization long before they had been part of the Islamic world and the Ottoman Empire, and that they had maintained their cultural identity, which originated in Central Asia, even though they were a minority in a multinational empire.[8] A pioneer of this theory, Afet İnan, an adopted daughter of Atatürk, was assigned the mission of writing the national history by Atatürk.[9] Atatürk was also directly involved in the formulation of the thesis; his house at Çankaya was turned into a workshop for discussions on which Afet İnan took notes. In fact, as a result of her regular attendance at these intellectual meetings, Afet İnan became a student of national history and later was chosen to head the Committee for the Investigation of Turkish History by the General Assembly of the Turkish Hearth organizations.[10] Hence in the 1930s, recording of history, especially by this group of nationalist historians, took on a special character of fabrication due to the official ideology in which history was conceived to be the prime mover for "national consciousness" and citizenship. Afet İnan, in due course, wrote *Vatandaş İçin Medeni Bilgiler* (Civil Instructions for the Citizen, 1931), a book about the new concepts of citizenship and the new institutions of the Republic, which was not only supervised by Atatürk but later was recommended by him to become part of the secondary school curriculum of the Republic.[11]

The champions of Turkish nationalism were after an ideal of a society built equally by Turkish men and women who were all sturdy, hardworking, and austere. Young Turkish men and women were visualized as the guardians of the reforms, progress, modernization, and enlightenment. The statues and monuments, installed in main city squares during the Republican period, displayed images of *"femme forte"* side by side with strongly built young men, both carrying torchlights.[12] A prominent professor of pedagogy and a nationalist intellectual, İsmail Hakkı Baltacıoğlu, wrote about how equality between the sexes was understood within the Kemalist framework in his 1934 article, published in the intellectual periodical *Yeni Adam* (The New Man):

> . . . There is no difference between men and women in the Turkish land anymore. Sexual difference is not a difference that the nation should regard or deal with. These are the possessions of a single man (person), why should we bother . . . What we need are men or women, people who have adopted the national values, national techniques, that's all! . . . [13]

THE NEW WOMAN AS AN
AGENT FOR SOCIAL FEMINISM

In the modernist views of the late Ottoman period, the image of the "new woman" was basically defined as the "social woman"; that is, the contribution of women to the community and to society in general was stressed. This emphasis was a characteristic that early feminism in Turkey shared with philanthropic feminism or social feminism in Western societies of the nineteenth century. Kemalists also defended the idea that women should participate in social life and take on social responsibilities and roles as professional women alongside their traditional sex roles of mother and wife. The image of the "new woman" was quite important for the cadres of the new Republic who wanted to acquire a "civilized" outlook and present the image of a modern state to the Western world.

The most outstanding challenge that Kemalists brought to women's sex status was women's participation in the public domain as professionals. Later, most of these professional, elite women, in their memoirs, emphasized their professional identity as the basic area of definition for themselves, while their domestic identity and domestic relations such as marriage and motherhood were de-emphasized.

Süreyya Ağaoğlu, a pioneer female lawyer, is a good example of a woman who actively worked in organizations, both professional and political, in the Kemalist period. She displayed the organizational skills and professionalism required to allow her to work and share power with her male colleagues. Similar Kemalist women of the period were expected to have "masculine" character traits, unlike the Ottoman ladies who regulated and organized the activities in the private domain among women. In the Kemalist period, the private domain continued to be considered a woman's area, but women entered the public domain, and at the same time their control over domestic affairs declined as men became more influential in the education and socialization of children.[14] We can also argue that women's role in the regulation of social relations became less significant as the family transformed into more of a conjugal unit and women were isolated from their kinswomen.

MAKING OF MODERN FEMININITY IN TURKEY

The cultural model that the Kemalists advocated was different from the earlier approaches in that women's public and social responsibilities were evaluated as superior to their traditional roles and domestic responsibilities. An educated professional woman was highly regarded in comparison to a traditional housewife and attributed a higher status. Although women's social recognition in the public domain did not challenge the direct male/female relations in the private domain[15] and even narrowed their power there, women's domestic duties took on a new character with the "rationalization" of housework and the advent of the science of home-economics. Information about hygiene, scientific upbringing of children, housework technology, and homemaking were instructed through the family and women's magazines and courses taught at schools, and adult education programs offered courses on those subjects.[16] A Kemalist woman, above all, had to be a modern woman:

> Modern woman . . . means social woman in the first place. She is the woman of a vigorous society. These vigorous institutions are science and industry. Modern woman is a woman who is cultivated in science and industrial culture. Motherhood is a woman's duty; she has always done it, she must do it just the same. However, bearing children is not a profession, it is one of the physical needs and duties, just like a man's need and requirement to impregnate. . . .[17]

As reflected in the above quotation, motherhood was still stressed as a woman's traditional role, along with her new role as a professional woman. However, motherhood was perceived within a new framework, as merely a "biological function," and in a sense its traditional cultural value was de-emphasized. This image of a "biological woman" could perhaps be considered as the guarantee of the womanliness of the Kemalist woman.

A new understanding of female beauty as linked with health was an underlined theme, especially for the upbringing of the new generations. Young women and young men dressed in sportswear participated in parades organized for the celebration of the national holidays and displayed the robustness of the nation. The following quotation from an editorial indicates how important sports was in marking the new national identity, as well as in assigning the identities of the "new men" and "new women."

> Today's regime requires healthy and active, agile bodies. . . . This generation who have been able to overthrow the black veil from their

faces and the *çarşaf* from their backs should also be careful about the beauty of their bodies. For the mothers who are going to bring up the healthy generations of tomorrow, sports is as important as for men. . . . In the national holidays for the youth, we witnessed our young girls with dismay, who did not exercise their bodies except for one class hour of physical education per week: Our young girls usually displayed a fat and clumsy body with big breasts and fleshy legs. Those young girls who have the greatest beauty of the Turkish race by birth. . . . Today's regime requires a healthy and agile body, not a sloppy, clumsy one. The Republican regime that requires a healthy and sturdy generation reformed the physical education and sports classes within the school curriculum while the law of physical education was being prepared. Since there is no inequality in law between men and women, we impatiently look forward to the new attempts that the Ministry of Education will put into application.[18]

Another indication of the new femininity in the 1930s was that Turkey participated in international beauty competitions for the first time. Keriman Halis was chosen Turkey's first beauty queen and honored by the last name "Ece" (which means "Queen" in "authentic/ pure" Turkish) by Atatürk. The newspaper that sponsored the beauty competition issued article after article to convince the public that it was not a disgraceful event:

We thought that the revolutionary Turkey should not stay behind the other countries in which beauty competitions have become popularized just like other activities that have globally come about. What is lacking in Turkey? Why should it not adapt to this new current of the world? On the contrary, new Turkey had to get involved in this movement with zeal and enthusiasm and more than any other country; because it announced and realized the emancipation of Turkish women who had been helpless victims under captivity for centuries. Finally, we needed to show to the world with actual deeds that the ideas and beliefs, shared by the world for centuries, about Turkish women, are merely myths that are out of place at present. Turkish women have been exalted to the status of equality with their sisters in the liberated countries of the whole world. Being beautiful is not disgraceful; beauty is something that all the world bends before with respect and admiration. . . . In the civilized world, we know that great attempts are being made to shape the bodies of children, especially girls, according to certain physical diets. Gradually beauty is becoming twins with health.[19]

As a result of these changes in attitudes and prescribed roles, some women among the first generation of the Kemalist Republic enjoyed various opportunities and privileges. They were mostly related to bureaucrats or military officers, or themselves were professionals engaged in teaching, medicine, or law. They were active in the philanthropic organizations of the day such as *Yardımsevenler Derneği* (Association for Volunteers for Helping the Poor), *Hilâl-i Ahmer Cemiyeti* (The Red Crescent Society), or *Halkevleri* (People's Houses), the cultural clubs of the Republican People's Party. However, independent women's organizations were discouraged by the closing down of *Kadınlar Birliği* (The League of Women) in 1935; the members of this association were encouraged to take on philanthropic work in the women's auxiliary of the Republican People's Party.[20]

Women were also active in the campaigns for the development of a national economy. Members of *Milli İktisat ve Tasarruf Cemiyeti* (Association for National Economy and Thrift) regarded themselves as soldiers in the struggle to build a national economy; they promoted domestic goods and campaigned for "buying and using Turkish brands," rather than imported goods. Nakiye *Hanım,* a leading teacher and a leading figure in the association, invoked this as a nationalist duty at a meeting:

> Turkish women who could die for their country, could they not learn how to accord with principles of thrift for a while? National economy does not require that we do not dress up, but it does not want to let money go to imports for the goods that we possess in our country. Women will be in the front lines in this struggle for national economy and thrift like they have been so far in all other struggles.[21]

The image of the "modern woman" was reinforced by the femininity that Kemalist women exhibited in ballrooms when they attended "modern" "Republican balls" and parties (held by various associations and clubs of the regime, especially the People's Houses) dressed in "modern gowns" and holding the arm of their cavalier. A newspaper reporting on a "Ball in İzmir" in 1930 notes that women exhibited night-dresses made of Turkish fabric:

> The annual ball of the Red Crescent Society took place yesterday in the reserved halls of government offices. All the notables of our city and some foreigners attended the ball. The ball started with the national anthem at 20:30.
>
> ... Almost all the ladies who attended the party wore dresses made of "national fabric," and in that way contributed to the national mobilization of resources.[22]

KEMALIST FEMALE IDENTITY

The Kemalist female image reflected the pragmatism of the Kemalist ideology and was basically a combination of conflicting images: "an educated-professional woman" at work; "a socially active organizing woman" as a member of social clubs, associations, etcetera; "a biologically functioning woman" in the family fulfilling reproductive responsibilities as a mother and wife; "a feminine woman" entertaining men at the balls and parties. While the first three images had been circulating in previous eras, the last was new and attempted to establish a Western style of gender relationship in Turkey. It signified the regime's desire to Westernize, that is to imitate the West and its civilization. If the first two images implied a change in women's place in society, the last two asserted a boundary that assured that the new roles would not alter a woman's subordinate position as a "female" in the male-female relationship.

Among the generations of modernist elites in Turkey, the Kemalists were certainly the most eager for women to take part in public life, although the leaders and administrators of "new Turkey" remained predominantly male. Thus, the Kemalist women who became active in the public domain, which typically meant to work within a predominantly male bureaucratic structure, had to present a "suitable" body image, a new femininity that was somehow connected to the image of a *male* body. This meant transgression and transcendence of traditional feminine roles in certain instances and subjection to the almost "formal" control of their bodies by men in other instances. The uniform-like suits that Kemalist women, especially teachers, wore were a pictorial representation of this fact. Kemal Atatürk himself undertook the mission of encouraging women's emancipation from traditional bondages and promoted the new woman of national ideals and morality by touring the country with his wife, who wore a "modernized" headscarf and an almost military uniform.

While a segregated Muslim society underwent secularization and desegregation with a series of institutional reforms, Kemalist women emphasized their professional identities rather than their individuality and sexuality and viewed themselves as prestigious representatives of the government. Their ideological and institutional affiliations with the new Republic helped them to present a sexually modest and respectable picture that would not threaten the patriarchal morality. Thus, however modernist an ideology it was, Kemalism could not alter the traditional norms of morality that guaranteed a biologically defined and socially constraining femininity for women. The notion of female modesty—that is, the traditional values of virginity before marriage, fidelity of the wife, and a particular public comportment and dress—was carried over with an even heavier emotional load to the new generations of Kemalist women and became the basic theme of the "new morality" for the Kemalist elite.

Most of the speeches made by Atatürk about women were related to the issue of change in women's style of dress and "veiling"; more substantive issues were introduced in connection with this emotional and easily politicized issue. Atatürk, as a pragmatic leader, reinterpreted a religious obligation (to veil) from a functional perspective, emphasizing the need to adapt to the necessities of modern life. He cautiously added, however, that modesty was essential to the morality of the community; that is, if the purpose of "veiling" was to preserve virtue, this purpose would be cautiously acknowledged in reforms that applied to clothing. In his speeches, Atatürk tried to persuade the people that his reforms were not against true Islam or the true spirit of the Turkish nation. He tried to legitimize his reforms by referring to the new thesis of Turkish history; what he was doing was not in fact alien but indigenous, a revival of the ancient culture of the nation. In a speech made to the people of Kastamonu in 1926, Atatürk revisted the issue:

The *concealing* that our religion requires is applicable to both life and moral prudence. If our women did *conceal* according to the prescriptions of Sharia and religion, they will neither cover up that much nor undress. *Concealing* according to Sharia is simple in form that would not cause a difficulty for women and would not inhibit women's participation in activities in areas of social life, economic life, scientific life . . . with men. This simple form [of dress] does not contradict with the morality and codes of decent behavior of our social community.

If our women present themselves with a proper dress, prescribed by Sharia and religion and a comportment required by moral prudence and participate in scientific and artistic activities of the nation like this, I assure you that even the most conservative member of our nation will hardly keep himself from appreciating this situation.[23]

TRADITIONAL SEXUAL
MORALITY UNQUESTIONED

The "woman question" was dealt with within an eclectic formula of a modernizing ideology combined with an extremely conservative, puritan sexual morality. In the midst of changing gender relations in the public domain, Kemalist women adopted a new form of "femininity" and acquired the skills to "veil" their sexuality in their relationships in the male world of public affairs. The so-called modern woman carefully checked her behavior toward men and was cautious not to debase the traditional female objective identity and norms of femaleness; at the same time, probably thanks to the skills honed in a sexually segregated cultural order, she could detach herself from her sexual identity and challenge the traditional mode of "femininity," though only by being assertive and professionally ambitious in her occupational life.

In the same era, the "masculinity" that progressive men adopted was best exemplified by Atatürk, who appeared as the "emancipator" of Turkish women.[24] Progressive men showed "tolerance" and offered paternal protection to the new women and established a supposedly egalitarian professional environment. However, the main normative categories of traditional patriarchy such as *şeref* (family reputation) and *namus* (honor)[25] were preserved without much individual reformulation of morality for these men, while women were required to internalize strict self-discipline and adaptive strategies to cope with modernity and tradition at the same time. Therefore, the other face of the constitution of "Kemalist female identity" is probably the Kemalist male psyche, with its perfectionism in bringing up exemplary "daughters of the new Republic," its obsession with male honor and family reputation, and its careful attention to notions about social esteem based on conduct of the womenfolk of the family (measured both in terms of appropriate sexual behavior and in terms of achievements in accord with modernity).

However, we can argue that, however unintentionally, Kemalist socialization cultivated in women the first germs of individuation, because individual women were forced to define an ethic for themselves as they pushed forward to open up space in the public domain and challenge their gender-status. What tensions between modernity and tradition did these women live through? And how was their social conduct checked by their male relatives, male comrades, and the community in general?

A history of Turkish modernization is yet to be written from the point of view of the women who lived through the conflicts, the tensions, and pangs of modernization. Women fiction writers in Turkey took on this task more than the historians. One well-known novelist, Adalet Ağaoğlu, moved beyond fiction in her "eulogy" essay about Mevhibe İnönü, the wife of İsmet İnönü (a leading commander in the nationalist struggle who became the second president of the Turkish Republic after Atatürk's death).

> . . . Why have those women been the ones whose inner worlds have been the least of interest? Why haven't they been written about with a deep interest of seeing and knowing? When they were written about, they were written merely from the angle that showed their social missions. The wife of a statesman, head of an association, volunteer nurse, corporal, teacher, the first lawyer, loyal wife, perfect mother. . .
>
> "Those women" were women who could overcome all those "ill eyes" over them, without losing their balance. They were the ones who had to read in Latin alphabet the next day, although they were writing in Arabic script the day before; they were the ones who had to regulate the degree of intimacy with great caution and meticulous attention as

they danced with men who were total strangers to them; those who looked properly dressed although they gave up the *yaşmak* and *çarşaf*. ... Even if the Great Principles of the Republican Revolution, and the leaders of those principles were backing you, still these were not deeds easy to accomplish. .... Now, it seems easy to tell.[26]

Namus (honor) had been a subject with a special emotional load and tension; now, for women, it also acquired an aspect of "individual morality," as different from "patriarchal morality." Semiha Berksoy's memoirs reflect how *namus* acquired a revised content and became an individualized character trait for her as she lived through the tension of becoming a professional singer and preserving her virtue at the same time. Semiha Berksoy's exchange of letters with her father[27] is full of emotion in every line as both of them question and try to reinforce the "shared values" of "family status" and "woman's dignity" at the same time. The father wants assurances that his daughter is still in accordance with the basic social values and that she will lead a "legitimate" life, while the daughter tries to convey her desire (to develop her creative-artistic potential) to her father within a "legitimate formula." Age-old social norms and patriarchal codes are being encountered and pushed by a woman gifted with a beautiful voice who wants to have her own way. This can be a legitimate life, as she is backed up by the new Republican ideology that gives credit to and guarantees high status for gifted women. Hence, she tries to assure her father on the basis of the institutional support she gets from the State Conservatoire and the Theater School of the Municipality of İstanbul.

While sexuality is central to the meanings and values related to gender roles and relations, the traditional sexual morality was not ever radically questioned within the Kemalist ethic. Since the notion of "sexual virtue," defined in terms of virginity of women before marriage, was preserved, the social conduct of women with men was controlled and female sexuality was repressed without much direct intervention. This old morality was preserved by Kemalist reformers, the "emancipators" of Turkish women, because they felt that they might lose control of their women if the women discovered their own potential of emancipation. This threat was much more viable than what the men of traditional patriarchal families had felt. It seems that there was a tacit agreement between fathers and

daughters: the daughters were granted the opportunities of education, career, and certain liberties in participating in social activities;
in return, fathers expected their daughters to be extremely careful
in their interactions with men and to strictly repress their sexuality
until acceptable husbands were found for them. Women raised with
this ethic were enthusiastically involved in the "mission" ascribed
to them and fit into the ideal image of women of the reformist
ideology. Fathers and Atatürk—the symbolic father of the entire
nation, especially of Turkish women—would back up the "daughters"[28] and present them to the public under their patronage.
Kemalist women felt themselves important and privileged. They felt
they were not simply women but individuals with important social
functions, and this impression was reinforced by everybody around
them—the families, their schools, and the state.

CONCLUSION

Kemalism is not an individualist ideology; it was formulated basically
as a corporatist state ideology. Most of the observers of women's
history in Turkey today agree that the single party regime after the
Republic did not leave much room for women to voice their own
demands as the state granted women some civil and political rights
and created opportunities through reforms in education, dress codes,
and family civil laws. "Kemalism" served as "feminism" for a new
generation of elite women who could enjoy the advantages and
privileges of the new status the Republic had given them. There
developed a special relationship between women and the state, and
like any other social group, women relied on the protectionism and
paternalism of the state. However, the state-oriented nature of Kemalist feminism in Turkey has been critically evaluated by new groups of
feminists and feminist researchers since the early 1980s.[29]

In order to appreciate the distinction of the Kemalist Revolution
and its impact on the identities of today's Turkish men and women, we
must rethink the history of modernization in Turkey. Even though the
Republic does not have a long history, the socio-cultural change in the
area of secularization can now be called a tradition, a cultural heritage
that became inscribed in individual identities of the Republican

generations. The Kemalist Revolution has made a sharp break with Islam and wiped out the influence of religion in the civil institutions of the Republic. Kemalist feminism follows from the recognition that Islam and feminism are incompatible and is based on a conception of Islam as one "religious belief" among others, the choice of which pertains only to the individual. Kemalist reforms in due course have limited the scope of Islam from the realm of institutions to the realm of personal conscience and consequently emancipated women from the repressive norms of Islamic institutions and Islamic law. Because Turkish nationalism is based on a "cultural nationalism" defined in terms of national origins and citizenship rather than an "authentic Muslim identity," as has been the case in many Middle Eastern nationalisms, Turkish women have been able to evade the repressive norms of Islam in the area of gender relations and in the search for multiple cultural references for their self-perceptions and identities.

The consequences of Kemalism are meaningful for feminist discussions in Turkey today. Although most of its shortcomings in the questioning of sex roles and sexist standards of morality have been scrutinized within contemporary feminist circles in the last ten years,[30] it is a main ingredient, a catalyst for the formation of new feminist identities. As properly stated by Yeşim Arat, contemporary feminism in Turkey is a radical extension of the Kemalist legacy, and it questions the limitations of Kemalism for a feminist understanding of women's position.[31] During the last decade, it has become a more significant identity standpoint for a segment of Turkish women who see the growing radicalization of Islam as a threat to the equal rights of women that were acquired within a secular legal framework—an increasingly challenging threat that presents a rival ideological framework and the definition of a new identity, the "modern Islamist woman."[32]

Notes

1. Jayawardena, 1989:8.
2. The term first used by Şirin Tekeli (1986a), now commonly used by feminist researchers in reference to the Kemalist approach to women.

3. Göle (1991:78) uses the term "Kemalist pride" in the depiction of Kemalist women's stand against the *tesettür*, the recent practice of veiling by radical Muslim women.
4. Gökalp, 1976.
5. Adıvar, 1935:197.
6. See İnan, 1968; Taşkıran, 1973.
7. Özbay, 1986.
8. Mardin, 1981:211.
9. Ersanlı, 1987:81-104.
10. Turkish Hearth Organizations later turned into the People's Houses, an organ directly linked to the Republican People's Party.
11. İnan, 1969 (first published as a textbook in 1931).
12. An interesting painting by Zeki Faik İzer, dated 1933, is a copy of Delacroix's famous painting (1830) and portrays the French Revolution with a Turkish setting of the Kemalist Revolution, from a Kemalist viewpoint.
13. *Yeni Adam* 51 (1934):5; translation mine.
14. See Durakbaşa, 1987:124-133; also Behar and Duben, 1991:232-237.
15. Behar and Duben rightly comment, "The Republican Civil Code of 1926, a revolutionary document from an Islamic point of view, gives the legal sanction of the modernists to the traditional gender division of labour" (1991:222-223). The Code assigns the headship and the provision of family income to the husband and the following role to the wife: "The wife . . . is the assistant and advisor of the husband. She is responsible for the housework." See Velidedeoğlu, 1970:81.
16. Navaro, 1991.
17. *Yeni Adam* 96 (1935):5; translation mine.
18. "Kadınlarımız ve Spor" (Our Women and Sports) *Akşam Spor* 20 (April 1938):9; translation mine.
19. "Güzellik Ayıp Birşey Değildir" (Beauty Is Not a Disgraceful Thing), *Cumhuriyet,* 13 Kanun-ı sani, 1930.
20. Z. Toprak, 1986.
21. *Cumhuriyet,* 11 Kanun-ı sani, 1930; translation mine.
22. "İzmir'de Balo" (Ball in İzmir), *Cumhuriyet,* Kanun-ı sani, 1930; translation mine.
23. Karal, 1956:53; translation and emphasis mine.

24. Atatürk acted like a giving father in his relations with his wife Latife *Hanım,* his adoptive daughters—one of whom, Afet İnan, was his secretary—and toward women of Turkey in general.

25. For a review of the anthropological studies on the ideology of honor in Mediterranean societies and cultures, see Forouz Jowkar, 1988:45-65.

26. Ağaoğlu, 1993:148; translation mine.

27. Özbilgen, 1985:21-25.

28. It is significant that Atatürk adopted daughters, not sons, who were brought up as exemplary Republican women, were well trained in their careers, and were devoted to the Kemalist ideals as well as to Atatürk himself.

29. Ş. Tekeli, 1986a, 1986b, and 1990b; Sirman, 1989.

30. See Kandiyoti, 1987:317-339; Ş. Tekeli, 1990a; also the special issue of *Toplum ve Bilim* 53 (Spring 1991).

31. See Y. Arat, 1992:75-95.

32. For a group portrait of professional, Islamist women who can be counted as the members of a counter-elite in opposition to the Kemalist elite, see İlyasoğlu, 1994. Also see İlyasoğlu in this volume.

SEVEN

EDUCATING THE DAUGHTERS OF THE REPUBLIC

Zehra F. Arat

EDUCATION WAS A PRIORITY for the founders of the Republic of Turkey. Mustafa Kemal was addressing the issue as early as 1919 in Sivas, where the independence movement was launched.[1] The Grand National Assembly, about ten days after its own creation, founded the Ministry of Education on May 2, 1920, which presented its education program to the assembly the following week. In 1921 the Ministry organized a *Maarif Kongresi* (Public Instruction Congress) in which Mustafa Kemal emphasized the need for the formation of a *national* educational system.[2] The link between economy and education was emphasized at the Economic Congress, convened in İzmir in 1923. Also in the same year, a month-long education convention, the First Convention of Education (*Birinci Heyet-i İlmiye*), was held. Implemented in 1924, the decisions of the First Convention of Education included setting primary education at five years, which was to be followed by three years of middle school and three years of high school education.[3] "Education of all" had been already set as a goal, and elementary education had been made mandatory and free for both sexes in 1923. In 1924, this principle was incorporated into the first constitution of the Republic, as Article 80: "Under the supervision of the State all types of education are free. Primary education is mandatory and free in public schools." Thus, a serious campaign for education, both for children and adults, was initiated, and the numbers of both schools and enrollments showed a steady increase during the first ten years of the Republic, with the "most significant progress" noted in "girls' enrollments."[4]

This chapter examines the education policies of the Republic of Turkey in its formative years, mainly in the 1920s and 1930s, and the experience of the women who went through the educational system during that period. Based on both secondary data and in-depth interviews with thirty women (conducted during the summer of 1993), my purpose is to identify the underlying goals of women's education and how they were experienced by its recipients.[5]

The lag between the time events were experienced and the time they were narrated might have caused some distortions, and the accounts of participants may not be the "actual" representation of events. Thus, with no pretense of "fully grasping" the past consciousness and reconstructing it, I will treat the information revealed during the interviews as the "perception" of the generation in question and juxtapose them with *my* reading of secondary data. As Elspeth Probyn puts it, "we may live within patriarchy but at different levels, and in different ways the struggle to rearticulate the locale continues."[6] This chapter is a part of that struggle, even though the articulation of the earlier generation will be inevitably presented through my lenses.

PRINCIPLES OF THE REPUBLICAN EDUCATION POLICIES AND REFORMS

In addition to its significance for economic development, education was stressed by the Republican leaders because it was seen as the most effective way of transforming the Ottoman subjects into "nationalist" citizens with modern and secular minds. A government document summarized the objective of the educational system to raise "Republican, nationalist, populist, secularist, statist, reformist citizens," and defined "The Republican Public Instruction" as an "apparatus that operates to raise nationalist citizens."[7] The Law of Unification of Instruction, enacted in 1924 (no. 430), sought secularization, centralization, and standardization of the curricula for the schools that provided the same level of education and issued the same type of diplomas and established the state's control over all schools.

Nationalism was incorporated into the curricula at all levels. The objectives of Turkish classes in middle schools included "inflicting students with noble ideals, and national, patriotic and heroic sensibilities" as a part of the "national, social and moral goals."[8] Civic classes focused on "explanation of the principles such as nation, state, democracy, republic, independence, and equality; subjects of elections, taxing, and military; and the essentials that would serve to the understanding of the current regime."[9] At teachers training schools, an ethics course,"Morals and Knowledge on Civilization and Law," was replaced with "Knowledge of the Motherland," a course "designed to inflict the merits of the Republican regime."[10]

Among the tacit but still underlying principles of the educational reforms can be listed universal access, improved quality, and Westernization. Western education experts were invited to offer proposals for the new system,[11] and students were sent to Europe to be trained as teachers.[12] The curricula for literature classes were revised; the share of Ottoman literature was reduced to increase the exposure to contemporary Turkish literature and Western classics.[13] Following the foreign expert Dr. Kuhne's recommendation, the Latin alphabet was adopted in 1928. A year later, Arabic and Persian were removed from the high school curricula, and a second European language requirement was added.

As an extension of the principles of Westernization and secularization, coeducation was also advocated. In 1923, the minister of education stated the government view as follows:

> The Ministry of Education does not and will not think of separate treatment for girls and boys either in educational instruction or as youths. Our young girls and boys will be trained within the same system, and they will follow the same path.[14]

However, not supported by the assembly, this idea cost the minister of education his cabinet post. Consequently, desegregation of schools was pursued as an incremental policy. It was first established only at the primary and university levels in 1924. Middle schools were not integrated until the 1927-28 academic year, and it took nearly another decade, until the 1934-35 academic year, for high schools to start becoming coeducational. Even then, coeducation was pursued only in those cities that had only one high school.[15]

WOMEN'S EDUCATION

The leaders of the Republic frequently criticized the Ottoman regime for neglecting women's education. A government document accused the Ottoman Ministry of Education for ignoring the "cultivation of women" and doing "very little for girls' schools." The biased approach of the old regime was attributed to the fear of "religious fanaticism," following "the convictions of those who had been hostile to women's education and girls' literacy," and to the mentality that perceived women "only as love mates."[16]

The Republican government, on the other hand, as reflected in Mustafa Kemal Atatürk's speeches, emphasized women's education and invoked a discourse of modernization to justify it:

> If it is found to be sufficient to have only one of the two sexes that compose a society equipped with the contemporary needs, more than half of that society would remain weak. . . . Therefore, if knowledge and technology are necessary for our society, both our men and women have to acquire them equally. . . .
>
> . . . Circumstances today require the advancement of our women in all respects. Therefore, our women, too, will be enlightened and learned, and like all men, will go through all educational stages. Then, women and men, walking side by side, will be each other's help and support in social life.[17]

The new regime manifested its commitment to girls' education by opening new secondary schools. Despite the emphasis put on girls' education, however, the number of schools for them remained at a fraction of the number of boys' schools.[18] Moreover, the state failed to enforce the "mandatory primary education" rule, especially for girls. Some school administrators did not take girls' education seriously. For example, a report on the village institutes in the 1940s noted that since the laundry was done by female students, they tended to "miss their classes and lag behind."[19] The goals of primary school education included "*taking measures according to the characteristics of each sex,* and turning them into citizens who can continue to work together, starting at school."[20] Fortunately, in practice, with the exception of village schools—for which "training village girls to acquire the knowledge and habits that would make the family life more hygienic, better and happier" was the goal[21]—the education of boys and girls at primary schools was uniform and coeducational in the real sense of the term. However, some gendered curricula were followed in secondary schools.

In middle and high schools, physical education and military instruction were first introduced to boys only. Girls were taught sewing, embroidery, home economics, and child care instead. Later on, physical education and military instruction were added to the curricula for girls, but classes were segregated even at otherwise coeducational schools. Moreover, the nature of the instructions and activities were different—for example, the military instruction for boys was allotted twice as much time and focused on military training rather than civil defense. In some academic years, boys in middle schools were assigned extra time for science laboratories or field trips that would complement their history and geography classes, while girls were instructed in modern techniques of housekeeping.[22] Other studio classes (sometimes listed as "lab" classes) also trained students differently; while boys were instructed in several crafts such as bookbinding, woodworking, and paper marbling, girls were trained in cooking, pickling, baking, sewing, and child care.

Increasing women's participation in the teaching profession was also an important objective, and policy was set to assure the presence of at least one woman teacher at those primary schools with substantial female enrollments.[23] However, applied courses at the teachers training schools for elementary school education were also gendered: agriculture was offered only at schools for males, and they spent twice as much time on creative subjects such as painting, hand crafts, and calligraphy; female students were offered courses on sewing, home economics (laundry, ironing, and cleaning), embroidery, and child care instead.[24] Similar gender-specific curricula were developed for village teachers training schools; while boys were trained in farming and other vocations considered as essential to rural life (such as construction, blacksmithy, and running cooperatives), the minister of education stated that the village girls and women at these schools, "like their male counterparts," would go through "a rational training" for works that would be of "concern to villages and house wives," which included activities such as "sewing, child care and nursing, and agricultural crafts."[25]

The government also established separate vocational schools for males and females. Their segregated nature was not only acknowledged but justified: "Naturally, certain schools of vocational training which demand only one or the other of the two sexes form an exception to this general rule [of coeducation]."[26] When the industrial schools of the empire were reorganized by the Republic, the vocational schools for boys continued to offer specializations in blacksmithy, leveling, lathe operation, casting, carpentry, electrical and other installations, and tailoring.[27] Girls' schools of arts and crafts, which had originally focused on textiles and tailoring, were already losing their *vocational* emphasis and becoming "finishing schools" under Ottoman rule.[28] That transformation was completed by the Republic when they were renamed as girls' institutes in 1927-1928 and restructured to offer courses mainly in home economics, cooking, sewing, and fashion. A brand-new and exemplary girls' institute was founded in Ankara, in 1928, and named after İsmet İnönü—a war hero and the prime minister at the time. A government promotion book, circulated among foreign dignitaries, expressed the pride in the "well-equipped workshops for sewing, cutting, embroidery, hat designing and making, flower making, drawing, home economics, etc." of the İsmet *Paşa* Girls' Institute and explained its mission:

> The aim of the Institute is twofold; firstly, to provide future housewives with all the modern knowledge and technique of house-keeping, and secondly, to give young women a professional education that will enable them to earn their living. This Institute regularly follows the latest fashions in women's dresses, hats, etc.[29]

To train teachers for the institutes and for home economics classes at middle schools, the Technical Teachers Training School for Girls was opened in Ankara in 1934.[30] Evening counterparts of girls' institutes were also initiated, in 1927-1928, for women and older girls.[31] Like the institutes, other vocational schools for girls also specialized in activities that corresponded to traditional female roles (that is, health care schools that were specialized in nursing, child care, and midwifery), but girls' institutes multiplied rapidly over the years and held the lion's share of female secondary school enrollments.[32]

In Ottoman times, vocational schools mainly accommodated the poor, and some even specifically required the applicants to "have no father or mother and no assets."[33] Although this tradition continued for boys' schools during the Republican era, girls' institutes tended to attract students from the upper socio-economic strata. The education offered at these schools failed to offer employment opportunities and seemed "somewhat of a luxury" to low-income families.[34]

WOMEN'S EXPERIENCE AND VIEWS

The Profile

The age of the 30 women who were interviewed in 1993 ranged from 62 to 90, and the average age was 73.2. They were born in different parts of Turkey, but mostly to urban families. Even those who were born in villages or small towns eventually moved to major cities where they attended secondary schools. Most attended public schools, and a few switched between public and private schools. Most of the participants started and completed their education during the 1920s and 1930s, but some began their education under Ottoman rule, and a few were still in school in the early 1940s. The education level of the participants can be broken down as follows:

some middle school	2
middle school graduate	1
some high school	2
high school (or equivalent) graduate	16
academic (3); business (2); teachers training (5);	
conservatory (1); girls' institute (4); nursing (1)	
some college	1
college graduate	6
post graduate (Ph.D.)	2

Figure 7.1. A *Yurt. Yurts,* like vocational schools, held exhibitions at the end of each academic year and displayed the best examples of the students' work. Two students in front of their work at a *yurt* in Malatya, c. 1938 (courtesy of Mrs. L. K.).

Six of the women also attended private programs that were called *yurts.* These programs mainly focused on training young women in sewing, embroidery, etcetera. They were founded by graduates of girls' institutes, with the permission of the Ministry of Education, which would issue a certificate. Classes for such programs were typically held at the house of the teacher-director and thus enrolled only a small number of students. The programs were set for two to three years, although depending on their abilities, pupils could be accelerated and allowed to finish in one year. (See figure 7.1.)

While the primary schools that were attended by the participants were typically day schools and coeducational, out of thirty-three middle schools attended, only nine were integrated, and the rest were girls' schools. Like primary schools, the middle schools that the women attended were mainly in cities, and most of them followed academic programs—only seven of them were vocational schools (mostly girls' institutes). While only seven women attended boarding middle schools, half of the women who attended high schools went to boarding schools. Twenty-four women attended twenty-eight different high schools or the equivalent, and they were mostly schools for girls; only five were coeducational. Slightly more than half of the high school or equivalent attendance was at academic schools, and regardless of their focus and types, all high schools attended were located in major cities.[35]

The fathers of the participants were usually men with a high standing in the community and considerable education. More than half of the fathers were high-school (9) or college (8) graduates. Only one father had no schooling, but he was literate. Mothers, on the other hand, were less educated; only two had secondary educations, and ten of them were illiterate. Practically all mothers were homemakers. Most fathers were merchants or businessmen (10), and the others were civil servants (8), officers (5), teachers (2), self-employed professionals (2), and farmers (2).

When participants were asked about their families' financial comfort during their childhood and school years, eight referred to the conditions as "poor or tight," thirteen as "comfortable," four as "wealthy," and five as "changed from wealthy or comfortable to tight." Three of the thirty participants were only children, and others were mostly from small families.

Except two, all the women in the study had married, and two of them had married twice. The age at first marriage was rather higher than average for their generation; for the study group, the average age at first marriage was twenty-six, and the median age was twenty-five. Most of the women had already finished with their schooling before they had gotten married, and only two of them left school to get married.

Most of the women worked until they reached retirement age or later. Nine worked as teachers, five as civil servants, four as professionals (two college professors, one judge/attorney, and one nurse), and four held various jobs in the private and public sectors. Eight of them were homemakers and never worked outside the home, although some of them contributed to the family budget by producing things at home.

Who Went to School and Why?

A relationship between fathers' and daughters' education levels is observed only at the upper ends, that is, all daughters who attended or completed college had fathers who were high-school or college graduates, and similarly, college graduate fathers encouraged their daughters to attend at least high school. Moreover, the more educated the father, the more likely it was for the daughter to attend an academic high school. The father's occupation seems to have affected the daughter's education; the daughters of civil servants, merchants/businessmen, and teachers were better educated than the daughters of men with other occupations. Similarly, the children of civil servants and merchants/businessmen were more likely to be sent to academic high schools.

Although some families with tight budgets were able to support their daughters through secondary or higher education, daughters from better-off families on the whole experienced more schooling. Moreover, supporting the earlier observations about the "finishing school" character of girls' institutes, none of the poor women in the study group were ever enrolled in girls' institutes.

A woman's education level seems to have held no relation to her work experience; some high-school and college graduates became homemakers, while some less-educated women worked. The *type* of education, however, corresponded to the future occupation, especially for the graduates of two types of schools: all teachers' school graduates became teachers and worked as teachers until they reached retirement, while all institute graduates became homemakers.

When asked to identify their main reason for going to school, twelve women indicated that they had never thought about a reason: "It was expected," or "It was the thing to do." Others gave as their reasons the desire to be cultured and educated (7), to earn money and make a living (5), to have a profession (3), and to help others and the country (3).

The participants typically identified their fathers as the primary person who had supported their education. Ten women indicated that their fathers took the initiative, encouraged, and supported their education, sometimes despite some resistance from their mothers. Seven stated that they had been encouraged by both parents. Some of them also emphasized the support from their siblings and other relatives.

Despite the initial support of their fathers, however, most of the women in the study could not continue with their schooling after a certain point due to the withdrawal of that support. Some women's desires to be a teacher or to pursue higher education were rejected by fathers who did not want to send "a girl far away to a boarding school," especially if they did not have relatives who lived close enough to the school to "keep an eye on her." Others were barred from occupational training or higher education due to a concern over what would happen afterward: "If you are appointed to a village or a remote town, who will accompany you?" they were asked. Nevertheless, many of those who attended high schools or teachers training schools as boarding students were able to travel between their towns and the city where the school was located without any problems. Moreover, the few who had had to go to remote villages or towns to work described the local people as "extremely accommodating," "willing to accept their city ways" (such as not using a head scarf), "tolerant," "understanding," and "friendly and helpful."

The only woman in the sample who had attended a village school stated that she had been the only girl at the school for the first three years and managed to attend thanks to her father's "progressive attitude." In her own words,

> When I was harassed by some women on the way to school—they would make embarrassing statements such as "Look at her. Her breasts are about to burst out of her chest, and she still goes to school"—I would come home and cry. But, my father would tell me to pay no attention to those ignorant women. He would say they were cruel because they envied me.

The same father, however, failed to provide support for her secondary education. There was no secondary school in the village. Nevertheless, her two brothers, one ten years older and one two years younger, were sent to middle and high schools in the city—less than 10 kilometers away—on horseback, but she was not. A few years later she was allowed to attend a *yurt* in the city, because she could stay with relatives. Only after her older brother completed his college and Master's degrees and settled in Ankara was she able to join him and attend İsmet *Paşa* Girls' Institute "with girls who were much younger."

Another women who finished high school in Adana wanted to study at the art academy in İstanbul. Her father, who had been nothing but encouraging up to that point, asked her if she would not be embarrassed to paint or draw nude models while standing next to male students. Since she could not dissent, she could not continue with her education.

Similar obstacles were pointed out or set up when women wanted to seek employment or earn money. Another progressive father, who was willing to send his daughter to İsmet *Paşa* Girls' Institute in Ankara as a boarding student, withdrew his support when she wanted to continue with her education at the Technical Teachers Training School. Later, still desiring to be a teacher, she applied to the Ministry of Education and was granted the permission to start a *yurt* at her family's house in Sarıkamış. When informed of this, the father called the whole thing off, on the grounds that in a small town, with several girls entering and leaving their house, people would gossip. "I will pay you the money that you would have earned," he proposed.

When asked if the education of sons and daughters received different levels of parental support, most participants gave a negative response. Nevertheless, the differences in the education levels of siblings and the fact that several sons were sent away to boarding schools while daughters were not indicate that sex discrimination was present in many families. Boys, in half of the twenty households that had both male and female children, were better educated than girls. Only four families had both sons and daughters educated at comparable levels. Education of children in the other six families corresponded to either family finances (that is, older children were better educated, if the family later experienced economic hardship) or the availability of educational facilities (that is, the younger ones could attend recently opened schools). All women who had a high-school education or above (including teachers' training schools, but not institutes) were only children or had only female siblings. This finding implies that parents preferred to educate their sons and tended to support their daughters' academic or professional education only if they did not have any sons.

The Experience and its Assessment

The women in the study described school uniforms and other dress codes in secondary schools as "tight and rigid." Their hair had to be either short or pulled back in braids or ponytails. Short hair was preferred because it fit well into the officially promoted hygienic image of the "modern woman." The anecdotes told by a retired teacher

Figure 7.2. Students with Hats. When school uniforms included hats that resembled those of military officers, most students derided wearing them. However, some students wore them with pride, even when they were not required to do so, probably to signify their privileged *mektepli* (attending a school) status (c. 1940, courtesy of Mrs. L. K.).

included the scare she had had at the principal's office at the Çamlıca Teachers Training School in İstanbul: the principal had made her admission to the school contingent upon cutting her braided hair.

Make-up and any headwear or accessories, except for bobby-pins and plain straps used to secure the hair, were forbidden. Similarly, the uniforms were plain with long hemlines and included stockings that had to be thick and of a dark color such as black or brown. For some years, uniforms included hats that resembled those of military officers, and were required to be worn by students when not in the classroom (see figure 7.2.) Any reflection of femininity was scrutinized and often resulted in a scolding or an insult, if not punishment. At least five women remembered an incident when either herself or a friend who happened to have "colorful cheeks" was accused by a teacher or the principal of wearing make-up and asked to wipe her face. This humiliating experience seems to have ended usually with the humiliation of the teacher, who would be proven wrong. "The teacher did not believe me when I said I had no make-up," one woman said. "She asked a friend to bring some cotton balls and, then, ordered me to clean my face. 'Wipe it out! So, we can see what you have' said she. What could I have? Only dust and dirt appeared on the cotton."

In coeducational secondary schools male and female students were seated separately in classes, girls clustering at one side of the classroom or in the front seats. Similarly, to the extent it was allowed by the architectural design of the school, boys and girls were directed to use different doors to enter or exit buildings. A high school principal in İstanbul personally supervised the students at dismissal to insure that the handful of girls left the classrooms and the building before their male friends.

School teachers' and administrators' control over the students' outfits and behavior extended beyond the school. One of the participants had been summoned to the principal's office to "identify the man" who had accompanied her and her widowed mother soon after she had attended a New Year's ball with her mother and maternal uncle. The same principal had been known to have spies among the students and had dismissed one of the students in her senior year upon the discovery that her mother worked as a prostitute.

Women in the study generally defined their relationships with teachers and administrators as pleasant, and some "loved" their teachers. Nevertheless, they mostly referred to them as "distant"; "even when we were friendly, there was respect," they noted. Some described their feelings in the presence of teachers as "intimidated," or even "fearful." Participants agreed that the sex of the teacher had not been a significant factor in determining the relationship. They had not necessarily felt any closer to a teacher "just because she was a woman," or received more support and encouragement from women. Ironically, the regulation of dress codes and appearances and the sanctioning of impropriety had been carried out exclusively by women teachers and principals, probably because scrutinizing a female student's hemline or face had been deemed improper for a male teacher. Moreover, such tasks fall into the "traditionally" female responsibilities of "social reproduction." Women who had been subject to such controls, however, seemed to have assimilated well and perpetuated the norms themselves. Several women in the study referred to them with approval. "I adored my literature teacher and wanted to be a teacher like her," one women stated before she continued with an anecdote:

> One of the girls had her hair curled, and it looked kind of fancy. The teacher called her to the blackboard for an oral exam. She failed to answer the question. Then the teacher said something I still remember today: "Instead of embellishing the exterior of your heads, embellish the inside." Isn't it a wonderful comment?

Mostly, those who had been the direct target of humiliation were outraged. However, several women claimed that such restrictions had not affected them because the same had been expected at home, and as "properly raised daughters" or "family girls" they had never suffered an embarrassing situation or faced reprimands at school.

The interview process revealed that the students had also inspected their teachers' outfits and taken their teachers as role models in configuring their own appearances, as well as intellectual aspirations. Even though they were not asked about it, the first few interviewees volunteered information about female teachers' chic outfits, fashionable hats, and overall "modern" appearance. Subsequently, during the later interviews, the participants were prompted to describe the way teachers had dressed. Although occasionally the adjective "modest" replaced "chic," "modern women" in suits who "did not wear scarfs" was the typical description. A sense of approval and pride was evident on their faces and in their voices when they talked about these "modern and educated women," and many women felt compelled to add how "progressive" that era had been compared to the 1990s, when more and more women in *tesettür* (new veiling) were appearing on the streets.[36]

In an effort to see how they perceived the gendered curricula and tight controls over expressions of "femininity," participants were asked if they had ever sensed that they, as girls or young women, had been expected to behave and act in a certain way. Most of the participants stated that they had not been reminded of their sex in any way at school. A few noted that they had not needed to be reminded because they had already been aware and behaved accordingly, and four argued that they had always been explicitly or implicitly warned about proper female behaviors and roles. Two characterized the suggestions they had been given as extensive warnings about boys and men (that they should be kept at a distance and not trusted) that had made them "fearful of and cold toward men."

The governments and school administrators seem to have been cautious, if not confused, about bringing down the barriers between sexes and ending the sex-segregated society. On the one hand, the principle of coeducation was advocated and pursued as a policy. Even when schools were segregated, students were brought together to participate in official ceremonies and sports spectacles on national holidays. At coeducational high schools in which female enrollments were low, there seems to have been an effort to distribute girls among classes in order to guarantee at least one female student in each section. However, an evident need to regulate behavior and to limit the interactions between sexes in those shared spaces led to restrictions on the relatively free time that they could have spent together. Thus, the entering/exiting of schools and the seats in classrooms were separated by sex.

Keeping curious boys away from school premises and gates was a task assigned to the janitors at girls' schools, if the principal was not a man. At some schools the windows facing the street were painted, at some others balconies or hills that had a view of the street were forbidden to the girls. One of the women in the study group remembered a movie theater school trip from her days at the Kızıltoprak Middle School for Girls in İstanbul:

> One day the principal took us to a theater to see the movie "The Last Days of Pompeii." Soon after we took our seats at the theater, boys from a nearby school walked in with their principal. Ours got furious. He ordered us to get up and leave immediately and made us open our hands at the door (just like beggars) to get our money back. Then he took us to another theater, and ironically, had to let us enjoy a love story. We could not have been happier.

When asked about discrimination by teachers, all of the participants rejected the notion that there had been any discrimination because of sex. Only a few indicated that there might have been some favoritism toward the children of the wealthy, better-educated families, or local notables. The favorite students, they all agreed, were the ones who were bright, industrious, and successful at school.

The participants were also asked if schools instructed them about a sense of duty toward their country and nation. Seventeen of the thirty women stated that there were no overt impositions. However, five noted that such suggestions were always present but that they were not overt because their generation had shared such a sense of national unity and duty. While nine of them were ambivalent about such indoctrinations, four argued that these suggestions regarding loving and serving the country had been overwhelming, even reaching the level of "brain washing."

Interestingly, older women who attended secondary schools during Ottoman times also reported extensive class discussions about patriotic duties.[37] The war and the European invasion seem to have fed the nationalistic fervor. Women referred to their Turkish literature classes and instructors as the ones that had been most explicit in bringing up the country's problems as well as the responsibilities of the new generations in solving them. A former teacher read from her old notebook: "Lamartine argues that what brings a country into being is the ashes of the dead; we want esteemed women's ashes on our land." It was the punchline of her essay for a literature class at the teachers training school that she had attended during the War of Independence; her teacher's comment praised and encouraged her both for her writing and for her nationalist sentiments.

The graduates of teachers training schools were almost unanimous in reciting the famous phrase by Atatürk, "Teachers, the new generation will be your masterpiece." Several others made statements such as "we grew up in the days of national struggle" to underline their "natural" sense of duty. The younger ones noted that they were "the children of Atatürk" and "brought up with a genuine love for him." Their generation's "special relation to Atatürk," the savior who fought for the land with courage and vision, was the source of inspiration and the reason for their dedication to the country.

The participants were asked to comment about the quality of education that they had received and to assess its usefulness. An overwhelming majority of them referred to their education as "exceptionally good"—a sentiment unanimously shared for high-school education and its equivalent. In addition to pointing to the teachers, who were portrayed as "strong," "well known in their fields," "demanding," and "modern and progressive," the high quality of education was attributed to the "outstanding facilities," such as fully equipped science laboratories, music rooms, etcetera. Referring to the educated in their generation, many said "we were lucky" and criticized the schools in the 1980s and 1990s for being ill-equipped and holding poor educational standards, and the whole system for being less serious and lacking in discipline.

The positive feeling toward their education was evident also when they discussed the usefulness of their education (even though the articulation of this usefulness proved difficult). Despite a few criticisms (such as too much memorization, inadequate opportunities to identify aptitudes, no guidance for career options), what they had learned at school was considered useful, and the whole "school experience" was appreciated. Schools were perceived as places of dynamism and change and valued as a source of animation. "Of course, the school was a great opportunity," an institute graduate responded. "What would have become of me, if I did not go to school? I would have been making house visits with my mother in Sarıkamış. Instead, I went to Ankara and made friends with girls from all around the country."

Most women in the study described themselves as "one who loved to read, learn, and study." Even those who had not cared much for schoolwork had loved their school and school experience. Some of those who had been boarding students in high school had stayed at school for some vacations, not out of necessity but because they had enjoyed the company of fellow students.

DISCUSSION

It was astonishing to me to hear quite a few participants deny that there had been any suggestions at school about loving and serving the country, while the curricula, their official descriptions and justifications, and the content of poems read and plays performed at schools indicate the opposite. But it was more amazing to discover that *all* of the women completely dismissed the gendered aspects of the curricula and that a few even claimed they had been taught in a gender-neutral system.

In my earlier assessments of the era, I argued that the Republican leadership offered Turkish women a system of paradoxes. While women's participation in both economic and social life was considered to be essential for the development and transformation of the country, all the obstacles in their way were not removed. Women's primary contribution continued to be seen as being in the domestic sphere, and as reflected in Atatürk's words, motherhood was emphasized as the most important function of women:

> The most important duty of woman is motherhood. The importance of this duty is better understood if one considers that the earliest education takes place on one's mother's lap. Our nation has decided to be a strong nation. . . . Therefore, our women, too, will be enlightened and learned and, like men, will go through all educational stages.[38]

With their primary function still mothering, "learned women" were expected to put their knowledge into practice first at home. Since it was believed that "it is the woman who gives a man the earliest words of advice and education, and who exercises on him the initial influence of motherhood,"[39] women, too, had to be educated. Recognizing the need to adapt to the changing circumstances, Atatürk argued,

> Today's mothers have to attain several high qualities in order to bring up children with the necessary qualities and develop them into active members for life today. Therefore, our women are obliged to be more enlightened, more prosperous, and more knowledgeable than our men. If they really want to be the *mothers of this nation*, this is the way.[40]

Since women's education was promoted not as a right—an end in itself—or as a means of liberating women, but as a device to improve the quality of maternal care, following a "feminized" curriculum became a rational strategy to raise competent mothers and "modern house-wives."

However, almost none of the women in the study made a connection between their education and being a good mother or wife. Only one, a graduate of the Girls' Institute in Adana, attributed her housekeeping and child care skills and her "tasteful ways of doing things" to her education. The "problems of women," however, were raised by some women as a general concern. "Unfortunately, the reforms by the Republic have not been consolidated, and the equality between women and men hasn't been achieved," commented one. Other women's remarks also reflected that they had no illusions about the progress of Turkish women, but they also treated what they had achieved as "real" and significant. In other words, the *gender divided* (masculine/feminine) character of the educational system and other reforms were discarded, while the *gender dominated* character of the present society was acknowledged. A deep commitment to secularism (treating religion as a private affair) and to women's political rights was also evident in their wording. Comparing the past with the present was tempting to the women in the study, and since the interviews took place soon after Tansu Çiller became the prime minister, and at a time when Islamist groups were becoming more visible, their comments on the present situation included these developments.

The revival of Islamist groups was watched with discontent, if not horror, by most. They saw them as intolerant and reactionary. Criticizing her own Islamist son, one woman emphasized, "I *am* a Muslim, I observe my religion. I wouldn't miss a day without fasting during the month of Ramadan. But I'd like to be able to enjoy my beer, too." Many others were upset about the new Islamist attire. To them, *tesettür,* followed especially by educated young women, was a sign of the erosion of the progress made over the years. During the interviews, they highlighted the tolerance of people in the past: how they had traveled to remote villages and rural towns in short-sleeve dresses and without feeling the need to cover their hair; how their teachers (and for some, their mothers) or the wives of civil servants had been allowed to maintain their urban and modern attire; how loose and relaxed they had worn their scarfs, if they had at all; when in school, how they had worn shorts for gym classes and, on national holidays, how they marched to and performed at stadiums or town squares in shorts. All of these examples would be concluded with the same lamenting remark: "It was not like today."

A few who brought up Tansu Çiller's political rise during the conversation did so with affection. They trusted her but were concerned that "all those men" around her would "cause problems" or "shadow her successes." "I always remember her in my prayers," an older women commented, "I hope God helps her."

Except one participant who has been a well-known "Kemalist feminist," none of the participants identified herself as a "feminist" (and no such direct question was asked). Nevertheless, the Kemalist woman image—"modern/Westernized," educated, secular, and devoted to the country—was embraced as their identification and the ideal by many.

The discrepancies and differences between the education of the two sexes that is obvious to me today did not exist for the women who had been students then. They believed that they had received a "first class" education and had not been subject to discrimination. Despite our different views, however, I do see their assessment not as impressionist but as emanating from some principles followed in government policies.

Although it appears that men's education had primacy and somewhat gendered curricula were followed, the Turkish Republican regime did not subscribe to any biological theories such as those developed and used to justify the inferior female education in Europe.[41] The deliberations on educational policies by the Republican leadership include no reference to an inherent intellectual weakness of the female or to any detrimental impacts vigorous curricula might have on girls' reproductive cycles and capabilities. On the contrary, the underlying belief seems to have been that of an equality in intellectual ability. At academic schools, equally vigorous programs were followed for both sexes. The "separate but equal" principle seems to have been followed, at least formally, and the quality of instruction was likely to be the same, since teachers for many academic subjects had to be shared by girls' and boys' schools. Girls were also encouraged to believe that they could study everything and pursue any career. Atatürk himself adopted several girls and encouraged them to study and participate in activities such as aviation that had not been previously open to women.

Deniz Kandiyoti used the phrase "emancipated but not liberated" in reference to generations of Turkish women who had been the beneficiaries of the Kemalist reforms of the Republic.[42] The women included in this study not only fit the description but also reflect this depiction in their own statements. They are proud of being a part of "the progress," but they are also aware that the progress was limited and they are afraid of reversals. What seems to distinguish them from some younger women and new groups of feminists is their unreserved vindication of reforms, not seeing the pervasiveness of gender problems in any way stemming from or related to the limitations of the reforms themselves.

Notes

Author's note: This is the third of a series of articles on gender policies of the first governments of the Republic of Turkey (see Z. Arat, 1994a, reprinted as Z. Arat, 1994b; also see Z. Arat, 1994c). For this paper, first I am grateful to the women who spent several hours to share their school memories and views with me. Second, my gratitude is extended to the directors and staff of two retirement homes in İstanbul: Atiye Yıldırım and Taner Artan of Bakırköy Huzur Evi; and Enis *Bey,* Mustafa Irgat, and Nermin and Çiğdem *Hanıms* at Emekli Sandığı, Etiler Huzur Evi. I am also indebted to Professor Nermin Abadan-Unat, who supported the project by arranging interviews with her friends, and to Professor Deborah Amory, whose invaluable comments improved my analysis and presentation significantly.

1. See his interview with the American journalist E. Brown, quoted in Başgöz and Wilson, 1968:200.
2. See Z. Arat 1994c:84 for Atatürk's address to the Grand National Assembly on March 1, 1922.
3. Hesapcıoğlu, 1984.
4. Female enrollments increased both in secondary schools (*Maarif Sergisi Rehberi,* 1933:29-30) and in higher education institutions (Abadan-Unat, 1991:184). For secondary school enrollment data, see Table 1 in Z. Arat, 1994c.
5. Due to the small size and scattered nature of the theoretical population (women who spent some years in secondary school during the 1920s and 1930s), a non-probability sampling procedure was employed. In addition to referrals by friends and relatives in Turkey, the residents of two different retirement

homes in İstanbul were contacted, and a conversational style was employed during the interviews. Although answers to some specific questions were sought, they were not presented in a uniform order or format, and the participants were encouraged to volunteer information. Consequently, the interview times varied, ranging from one to three hours.

6. Probyn, 1990:182.
7. *Maarif Sergisi Rehberi,* 1933:iv.
8. Yücel, 1938:196.
9. Yücel, 1938:198.
10. Yücel, 1938:220.
11. Teams headed by John Dewey (USA), Dr. Kuhne (Germany), Omar Buyse (Belgium), and Walter Kemmerrer (USA) issued reports in 1924, 1926, 1927, and 1933, respectively (Başgöz and Wilson, 1968:63-75).
12. *Maarif Sergisi Rehberi,* 1933:56.
13. Yücel, 1938:196.
14. Başgöz and Wilson, 1968:108.
15. *Cumhuriyetin 50.Yılında Milli Eğitimimiz,* 1973:143; Tan, 1981:19.
16. *Maarif Sergisi Rehberi,* 1933:7.
17. His address to the citizens of İzmir, on January 31, 1923. See Atatürk, 1989, Vol.2:89-90; translation mine.
18. Z. Arat, 1994c:89-91.
19. Sakaoğlu, 1992:99.
20. *Maarif Sergisi Rehberi,* 1933:14; emphasis added.
21. *Maarif Sergisi Rehberi,* 1933:13.
22. See tables of curricula in Yücel, 1938:145-236, 177-180.
23. *Maarif Sergisi Rehberi,* 1933:13.
24. Yücel, 1938:229-230.
25. Yücel, 1938:234. Village teachers training schools were first established for boys in 1927 as a response to the shortage of elementary school teachers; their female counterparts were introduced a decade later in 1938.
26. *Public Instruction in the Republic of Turkey,* 1936:19. Business schools (Ticaret Okulu) and the conservatory were exceptions as vocational schools; they were coeducational and followed relatively gender neutral curricula.
27. *Maarif Sergisi Rehberi,* 1933:66-79.

28. *Maarif Sergisi Rehberi,* 1933:69-71.

29. *Public Instruction,* 1936:45.

30. *Cumhuriyetin 50.Yılında,* 1973:150; Z. Arat, 1994c.

31. *Cumhuriyetin 50.Yılında,* 1973:155.

32. Başgöz and Wilson, 1968:176; Z. Arat, 1994c; Tan, 1979.

33. Başgöz and Wilson, 1968:180.

34. Başgöz and Wilson 1968:181-182. Some data from the 1960s indicate that only 24 percent of the institute graduates continued in higher education, while 30 percent were employed in an area that had little or nothing to do with the subject studied at school, and 41 percent stayed at home (Tan, 1979:211).

35. They were located in nine different cities: İstanbul (10), İzmir (6), Adana (4), Ankara (3), Bursa (2), Konya (2), Edirne (1), Trabzon (1), and Tokat (1). For the trend of increase in high schools, see Z. Arat 1994c: 90.

36. See İlyasoğlu in this volume.

37. The age distribution indicates that twenty-three of the women were truly "children of the Republic"—they were born after or just before the establishment of the Republic in 1923 and obtained their education within the Republican system.

38. From the 1923 İzmir speech. Atatürk, 1989, Vol.2:89-90; translation mine.

39. From Atatürk's handwritten manuscripts of 1930, published by Afet İnan and quoted in Doğramacı, 1989:164; translation mine.

40. His address to the women of Konya on March 21, 1923. See Atatürk, 1989, Vol.2:156; translation and emphasis mine.

41. See Dyhouse, 1981. A similar approach was also followed in many colonies. See Masemann, 1974.

42. Kandiyoti, 1981.

PART III

THE ERA OF POLITICAL MOBILIZATION AND DIVERSITY

CONSTRUCTED IMAGES AS EMPLOYMENT RESTRICTIONS: DETERMINANTS OF FEMALE LABOR IN TURKEY

Işık Urla Zeytinoğlu

IT IS PRETTY MUCH ESTABLISHED that investments in female human capital will not only improve women's conditions but will also stimulate the economic development of a country. In the 1920s Turkish governments started to pursue policies to enhance the participation of women in the economic development process. The earlier efforts toward transforming the Turkish economy from a primarily agricultural to an industrialized one, however, resulted in the decline of women's participation in the labor force. Since the early 1990s, the focus has been on raising women's skills and increasing their representation in the labor force.

Owing to the early Republican reforms of 1920s and 1930s, a small segment of Turkish women have been able to obtain university educations and women are represented in many professions. However, a substantial number of Turkish women remain unemployed, underemployed, or employed as unpaid farm laborers. The rapid progress of the university-educated women gave the impression that there was no need to address women's issues independent of the general development process. The resurgence of Islam as a political movement in the 1980s and its emphasis on women's roles primarily as wives and mothers, however, have increased, among women in

TABLE 8.1.

LABOR FORCE PARTICIPATION RATES BY SEX

Year	Men[*]	Women[*]	% of women in the labor force
1970	9,306	5,813	38
1975	11,180	6,204	36
1980	12,284	6,928	36
1985	13,933	7,647	35
1990 Oct.	14,418	6,728	32
1995 Oct.	15,944	6,956	31

[*]Numbers in thousands.
Source: International Labour Organisation (ILO), *Yearbook of Labour Statistics (1970-1985)*, Geneva, ILO, annual; State Institute of Statistics (SIS), *Statistical Yearbook of Turkey, 1996*, Ankara, February 1997:258.

urban centers, the awareness and sensitivity to the protection of their own standing. In this chapter I examine the employment of Turkish women in light of these developments and argue that lack of investment in education and training of women, as well as sexist norms that prevail in the culture and that are institutionalized by law, hold women back, perpetuating their status as second-class citizens in paid employment.

EMPLOYMENT OF WOMEN IN TURKEY

Women in Turkey primarily work as laborers on family-owned farms and as homemakers (housewives) in their homes. Since homemaking is not (yet) valued in monetary terms, women's work as homemakers is not included in national accounts and in the labor force statistics. Using official statistics, I am limiting the analysis in this chapter to data included in the official employment statistics.

TABLE 8.2.

DISTRIBUTION OF WOMEN
IN THE LABOR FORCE BY SECTOR, 1995

Sector	Total	Women[*]	Men[*]	Women (% of female labor force)	Men (% of male labor force)	Women (% of total labor force)
TOTAL	21,377	6,486	14,891	100	100	30
AGR	10,226	4,852	5,374	75	36	47
MANUF	2,947	538	2,409	8	16	18
OSERV	2,780	638	2,142	10	14	23
TRADE	2,162	255	2,357	4	16	12
FINAN	487	144	343	2	2	30
TRANS	855	32	823	**	6	4
MINING	131	0	131	**	1	**
UTIL	112	7	105	**	1	6
CONS	1,227	20	1,207	**	8	2

[*]Numbers in thousands. ** Less than one percent.
AGR=agriculture; MANUF=manufacturing; OSERV= community, social, & personal services; TRADE=wholesale/retail trade; FINAN= finance, insurance, & related; TRANS= transportation & communications; UTIL=utilities; CONS=construction.
Source: State Institute of Statistics (SIS), *Statistical Yearbook of Turkey, 1996*, Ankara, February 1997:265.

Sectoral Distribution of Female Labor

As presented in Table 8.1, in 1995 women's labor force participation rate[1] in Turkey was 31 percent. The table shows that participation rates for women declined from 1970 to 1995. Data on the distribution of women as a percentage of total labor force, as presented in Table 8.2, show that agriculture is the only sector in which the representation of women (47 percent) approximates that of men (53 percent). The proportion of women in other sectors, however, is very low. Within the female labor force, 75 percent of women are employed in agriculture,

TABLE 8.3.

LABOR FORCE DISTRIBUTION
BY OCCUPATION AND SEX, 1995

Occupation	Male[*]	Female[*]	% Female
Farmer	4,754	4,773	48
Clerical/Secr.	630	288	31
Professional	668	270	29
Other	107	24	18
Service	1,381	193	12
Prod.& Rel.	4,103	474	10
Sales	1,429	125	8
Managerial	360	22	6

[*]Numbers in thousands.
Source: State Institute of Statistics (SIS), *Statistical Yearbook of Turkey, 1996*. Ankara, February 1997:265-267.

with the rest constituting 10 percent or less of the labor force in each of the other sectors.

Occupational Distribution of Female Labor[2]

As presented in Table 8.3, following agricultural occupations, clerical/secretarial occupations are the second largest "feminized" occupational group. However, in comparison to the general trend in developed countries, the number of women in clerical/secretarial occupations in Turkey is small. Similarly, women's employment in sales and service related occupations is also small. Women represent 29 percent of professionals. The relatively larger share of female employment in professional occupations in Turkey is a common phenomenon in many developing countries. Distribution of women within professional occupations, however, is not even, and women professionals tend to concentrate in certain areas such as teaching, engineering, and health care.[3] As Table 8.3 shows, only 6 percent of managers are women. Production and related occupations in construction, mining, and utilities jobs reflect a similarly low female participation rate. Furthermore, female workers in these areas are employed in light manufacturing such as the textile, food processing, and tobacco industries.

DETERMINANTS OF SECTORAL AND OCCUPATIONAL DISTRIBUTION

As the above figures show, sectors and occupations in Turkey are segregated by sex. There are a few factors contributing to the occupational segregation of women and men. These can be grouped as: investments in human capital; socio-cultural factors such as norms, values, attitudes, and religious beliefs; and laws that are an extension of cultural norms.

Investments in Human Capital

The human capital model assumes that individuals will be employed according to their investment in education and training. Those who have the education and training can find jobs regardless of their sex.[4] From the human capital point of view, as presented in Table 8.4, many women and men in Turkey would have difficulty in finding jobs since they lack the basic requirement for most jobs—literacy,[5] despite the fact that elementary school education has been mandatory since 1923. Moreover, even many of those who are literate and hold a diploma fail to find meaningful employment because the training at elementary and secondary schools does not provide marketable skills.[6] Table 8.4 shows that women are far less educated than men, but that the labor force participation rates of women increase with their level of education. Investment in human capital seems to pay off especially for university-educated women.

Statistics on women's educational levels and labor activity reflect considerable differences between urban and rural areas. Most of the educated women live in urban areas;[7] newly created and better-paying jobs are also located in urban areas. For those women in the urban labor force, the literacy rate is 89 percent, close to men's 96 percent literacy rate.[8]

TABLE 8.4.

LABOR FORCE STATUS OF FEMALES AND MALES BY EDUCATION LEVEL, 1993

Education Level (Graduates)	Population 12 + Age[*]	Labor Force[*]	LFPR %
Total Labor Female Male	20,470 20,442	6,262 14,555	31 71
University Female Male	364 859	266 740	73 86
Senior High Sch. Female Male	1,135 1,688	422 1,271	37 75
Vocational SHS Female Male	247 496	111 400	45 81
Junior High Sch. Female Male	1,351 2,465	168 1,291	13 52
Vocational JHS Female Male	78 142	11 67	14 47
Elementary Sch. Female Male	13,223 13,536	3,931 10,012	30 74
Illiterate Female Male	4,072 1,255	1,354 774	33 62

[*]Numbers in thousands.
LFPR= Labor Force Participation Rate; SHS= Senior High School; JHS= Junior High School; Elementary Sch.= includes elementary school graduates and literate but without a diploma.

Source: State Institute of Statistics (SIS), *Household Labor Force Survey Results, April 1993*, Ankara, 1994:16.

The uneven distribution of public schools between urban and rural areas, the better-equipped secondary and high schools in urban areas, and the concentration of universities in major cities make education more accessible to urban women.[9] In rural areas the situation is different. Although elementary school education is mandatory, the law is not enforced, and parents prefer children help on the family farm rather than attend school.[10] Seeing no financial value in schooling, parents are not tempted to invest in education, especially for their daughters, who will be married away.[11]

Socio-cultural Factors

The subservient position of Turkish women in the labor market is determined not only by the inferiority of their educational skills but also by cultural factors—men's prejudices toward women and reluctance to give up their power over women.[12] The belief that men are more valuable is so influential that many women do not even consider themselves equal to men, nor do they demand equal educational or employment opportunities,[13] for "motherhood" is primary in importance. Only a small group of women, mostly from upper and middle-upper income groups, can overcome these barriers.[14]

Once they are employed, however, women encounter similar barriers and discrimination in the workplace.[15] There is blatant sex discrimination, particularly for those few women who would like to break into male-dominated occupations.[16] As there is extreme social tolerance for sex discrimination in employment, women are often channeled into positions that are an extension of their domestic tasks of care-giving, and they are not recruited to decision-making positions or technical jobs, even if they are as well educated and experienced as their male counterparts.[17]

The high rate of urbanization does not seem to improve women's employment opportunities. When families move from rural to urban areas, it is often women who experience difficulties in finding gainful employment.[18] Most employers and managers are men, and they have negative attitudes toward women and prefer to hire men.[19] Women are hired for jobs that do not attract men,[20] or for jobs in which employers believe women will be more obedient employees than men, willing to work in poor conditions,[21] and less likely to unionize or strike.[22]

Especially for positions that require close contact with male clientele, as in some sales, service, manufacturing, and transportation occupations, employers generally prefer men—more commonly in the conservative sections of cities and towns.[23] As an extension of centuries-old socialization, women also believe that men should be the breadwinners in the family.[24] Thus, we may say that these women voluntarily refrain from seeking employment, stay at home as homemakers, and consider themselves as "not working."

Legislation

Women's labor is addressed by Turkish law at two different levels. First, the Constitution (law no. 2709, dated 1982) which states the basic principles, and second, the three employment laws: the Civil Servants Law (law no. 657, dated 1965), the State-Owned Enterprises Employment Law (no. 3771, 1992) and the Labor Law (no. 1475, 1971). These laws regulate three main categories of employment: civil servants, contractual personnel, and workers. The wording of laws and policies is, in general, gender neutral, but this proves not to be sufficient to ensure equality in employment for women.

The Constitution. The 1982 constitution reiterates equality under law established by earlier constitutions. According to article 10, all individuals are equal before the law irrespective of language, race, color, sex, political opinion, belief, religion and sect, or any such consideration. No privilege shall be granted to any individual, family, group, or class. State organs and administrative authorities shall act in compliance with the principle of equality before the law in all their proceedings.

Despite the equality principles of the constitution, the article on the protection of the family implicitly designates Turkish women as a vulnerable group that needs to be protected. Article 41 specifies the state's responsibility for protection of the family, especially the protection of the mother and children, and for family planning education.

Under the constitution, everyone has the right and duty to work (art. 49). No one shall be required to perform work unsuitable for her/his age, sex, or capacity. Minors, women and persons with disabilities shall enjoy special protection with regard to working conditions (art. 50). Every citizen has the right to enter public service. No criteria other than merit shall be taken into consideration for recruitment into public service (art. 70). Despite such provisions, there are established administrative practices that work to the contrary. For example, until the early 1990s women were not appointed as governors and deputy governors, and there were attempts to limit the candidacy of female judges. In recent years, these practices started to change as a result of women's groups' actions and the increasing political-social consciousness of many women.[25] The influence of international organizations, particularly the European Community's insistence that Turkey improve its human rights record, has also spilled over to other aspects of life, influencing the government to initiate changes, albeit mostly cosmetic, to eliminate discrimination against women in the workplace.

Employment Laws. The three employment laws are gender-neutral in their wording in most articles but contain some sections that are discriminatory or patronizing. Their discriminatory impact is most evident for women in professional positions in both the public and private sectors.[26]

Civil Servants Law. The law regulates qualifications of civil servants and other public officials, procedures governing their appointments, duties and powers, rights and responsibilities, salaries, and other matters related to their occupation. Under this law women have been treated fairly in most aspects. In public service organizations women have been accepted into entry-level professional or managerial positions and many have reached middle-level management positions. However, the posts of governor in the provinces and deputy governors in towns were denied to women until 1991, when the first female governor was appointed. Although the legislation does not specifically discriminate against women, lack of antidiscriminatory clauses allows administrators to exclude women from the post-bachelor training programs required for appointment to these posts.[27]

The provisions of the law that are gender-specific are the ones on pregnancy and maternity leave. Women are entitled to a total paid leave of nine weeks (three weeks before and six weeks after birth) (art. 104/A). Nursing breaks, up to one-and-a-half hours a day, are provided for six months following the birth. If requested, unpaid leave for up to twelve months may be granted (art. 108). Upon request, the father is given three days off with pay after birth (art. 104/B).

State-owned Enterprises Employment Law. Starting in 1984, the State-owned Enterprises were given the legal right to employ contractual personnel.[28] These laws include no female-specific provisions. Since these laws are relatively recent, their impact on female employment has not been established.

Labor Law. This law defines a worker as "an individual employed under a labor contract and earning a wage" (art. 1). The law applies to both private and public sector workers and covers both manual and non-manual labor. Agricultural workers (as paid laborers) are outside the scope of the Labor Law.[29] The female-specific provisions of the Labor Law are as follows.

- Pregnancy/maternity provisions: The Labor Law as well as the Regulation on Conditions of Work for Pregnant or Nursing Women, Nursing Rooms and Day Nurseries, enacted in 1987, provide certain protections for female workers. They are entitled to a paid leave of absence from work for medical check-ups during the first three months of pregnancy and once a month thereafter (Regulation, art. 4). They are entitled to paid leave of six weeks before and after giving birth. If the worker does not return to her job within the six-week period following the maternity leave, her employer has the right to dismiss her without waiting for the notice period (Labor Law, art. 17/1b).

  Depending on the number of female workers, the Labor Law requires nursing rooms and day-care centers to be established or supported by employers. These places should be close to the premises. Workplaces may share the day-care and nursery facilities (Regulation, art. 7). The fact that nurseries and day-care centers have to be established in accordance with the number of female workers reveals that child-rearing is presumed to be solely women's responsibility. Some employers in the private sector manage to avoid providing such facilities by keeping the number of women employees slightly below the specified numbers.

- Prohibitions or restrictions on the employment of women in specific types of work under the Labor Law: The low participation rate of women in the manufacturing, mining, utilities, and construction sectors is also closely related to the legislative restrictions on the employment of women in underground and underwater work, night work, and in dangerous or heavy work (art. 68). Women are also prohibited from night work in industry, with some exceptions as stated in the Regulation (art. 69). Although originally intended to protect women and prevent child labor, these laws effectively exclude women from jobs that tend to pay higher wages.[30] Moreover, these provisions of the law create the image that women are the "weaker sex" and need protection. To protect them, the law restricts or prohibits women's employment in certain types of jobs rather than attempting to improve safety conditions for all workers regardless of their sex.

- Wage and severance pay: Although there has been no legislation to establish the principle of "equal wage for work of equal value," or comparable worth, the principle of equal pay for equal work has been a statutory provision in Turkey since the 1950s (law no. 5518).[31] However, it has not been applied in practice. Female workers have been paid less than their male counterparts on the basis of presumed differences in tasks, seniority, merit, or skills. With the onus of proof of discriminatory pay on women, and with the societal acceptance of the belief that women should be paid less than men,[32] there has not been many challenges to the practice. In fact, female workers have been ghettoized in a few female-dominated job classes that are generally known to be lower-paying jobs.[33]

The entitlement to severance pay upon termination of a labor contract includes a female-specific provision: if the female worker decides to leave her employment within one year following marriage, she is entitled to severance pay (art. 14 as amended in 1983). Even though this provision gives the impression that the legislation favors women, it perpetuates women's secondary role in the paid workforce and the society. Granting severance pay upon marriage encourages married women to leave paid employment to become unpaid "homemakers" and "caretakers" for their families. The tacit goal seems to be to maintain women as homemakers who will provide support and comfort to working males, and to manipulate the workforce to favor men. Thus, the overall impact of the provision has been the perpetuation of the gender-based division of labor.

Women in Professional Occupations

The relatively high representation of women in professional occupations and their uneven distribution within professions beg for some explanation. First, in most of these occupations, such as teaching, the old masculine image has been lost.[34] In addition, occupations such as medicine or law are considered appropriate for women because they are perceived as an extension of women's role of caring for the sick, deprived, and needy.

Second, certain occupations are believed to capture "presumably" inherent characteristics that women have—precision, manual dexterity, and concentration. An architect, a chemical engineer, a surgeon, or a computer programmer are perceived to require such characteristics and therefore are considered appropriate occupations for women.

Third, families counsel their daughters to enter certain fields because they presume that the work environments in most professional occupations provide physical protection and cleanliness.[35] For example, the common perception is that laboratories in which chemists or chemical engineers are employed constitute a clean, non–physically demanding environment. The same belief applies for the medical, pharmaceutical, and dental professions. Similarly, the office environment is presumed to be a clean, pleasant environment, and therefore a preferred workplace for daughters.

Fourth, the socioeconomic level of women also makes a difference in their success in professional occupations. Most women in professional occupations are from families with a higher socioeconomic status than those of men with the same occupation and educational level.[36] Because families and friends of these women are already in power, they are more easily accepted into these professions.[37] They also find jobs easily through their family contacts.

Fifth, in Turkey, in contrast to industrialized countries of Europe and North America, these professions have never had associations that controlled the entrance to the profession.[38] For example, in North America, associations of medical doctors and lawyers have been able to control the number and characteristics of students who applied to law schools or medical colleges/schools. Until recently, these associations excluded women and minorities from joining their ranks by requiring the universities to use restrictive admission criteria, eliminating the representatives of nondesirable groups in the interview process, or denying them internship or articling positions that are required prior to practicing the profession. In Turkey, on the other hand, the professions of law, medicine, engineering, or university teaching were never considered as reserved for a select few men. In the 1920s during the formative years of the Turkish Republic, the country needed professionals in large numbers.[39] To increase their number in a short time, universities accepted high-school graduates regardless of their sex or income level. Later, when the increase in the number of universities lagged behind the population, a national university entrance examination was instituted to select qualified students and place them into schools according to their performance. Thus, there have been no special educational requirements (as there are in the United States and Canada for law and medicine), other than a high-school diploma and a national university entrance exam score. Professional associations were established by law that also required the university graduates to become a member of the association in order to be able to practice the profession. The associations' task has been to ensure that members work ethically and according to the accepted standards and norms of their profession. They never adopted policies that would result in discrimination against women. On the contrary, they have been forerunners in promoting human rights, equality, and justice.

CONCLUSIONS

This paper examined employment of women in Turkey and its sectoral and occupational determinants. As the data show, most women in

Turkey are either homemakers or work in the agricultural sector. The few women who are in paid employment live mostly in urban areas. The lack of investment in women's education and training, as well as cultural prejudices and sex discrimination against women and a lack of legal protection against discrimination, all contribute to Turkish women's inferior position in paid employment and at home. Moreover, the gender-neutral laws and female-specific provisions that would help women enter the job market, such as establishing day-care centers, have not been fully enforced.

The recent international interest on investment in women, perceived as a necessary condition for a country to prosper, will improve the lot of some women in Turkish society. However, the political trend in the 1990s has been in favor of religious fundamentalists and pro-Western conservatives. Despite their differences, both of these groups hold a traditional view of women and attempt to preserve male dominance. Moreover, the gap between highly educated, upper-class urban women and uneducated, lower-class, mostly rural women is likely to grow. For the first group, even though finding employment and professional success may still be relatively easy, breaking the "glass ceiling" and moving into positions of power and decision-making will be slow.

Notes

1. The labor force participation rate refers to the percentage of persons eligible for the labor force who are actually in it. This includes employed persons as well as those seeking employment. The State Institute of Statistics data cover any person twelve years or older who is not institutionalized. Schooling is required until children are twelve years of age.
2. All occupations are coded according to the International Standard Classification of Occupations (ISCO, 1968) by the State Institute of Statistics (hereafter, SIS).
3. Zeytinoğlu, 1994.
4. Becker, 1971.
5. Kazgan, 1981.
6. Ecevit, 1992.
7. Taş, et al., 1994.

8. SIS, 1994:16.
9. Berik, 1989.
10. Kazgan, 1981.
11. Yörükoğlu, 1992; Kazgan, 1981.
12. Kabasakal, 1991a; Yörükoğlu, 1992.
13. N. Arat, 1986.
14. Zeytinoğlu, 1994; N. Arat, 1986.
15. Ecevit, 1992; Katrinli and Özmen 1991; Arbak, et al., in press.
16. Zeytinoğlu, 1994; Ecevit, 1992; Katrinli and Özmen, 1992 and 1991; Yörükoğlu, 1992.
17. Yörükoğlu, 1992.
18. SIS, 1994.
19. Katrinli and Özmen, 1992; Kabasakal, 1991b; Özbay, 1981.
20. N. Arat, 1986; Altındal, 1991.
21. Zeytinoğlu, 1994.
22. Ecevit, 1991.
23. Abadan-Unat, 1981.
24. Özbay, 1981; Altındal, 1991; Abadan-Unat, 1981.
25. Zeytinoğlu, 1994.
26. Arbak, et al., in press.
27. Z. Arat, 1994a.
28. Statutory decree no. 233, later replaced by statutory decree no. 399 and law no. 3771, dated 1992.
29. These workers, however, are covered by the collective labor legislation, which will not be discussed here as it does not have female-specific provisions.
30. Z. Arat, 1994a.
31. Ekonomi, n.d.
32. Zeytinoğlu, 1994.
33. Zeytinoğlu, 1994.
34. Acar, 1994.
35. Özbay, 1981.
36. Arbak, et al., in press.
37. Acar, 1994.
38. Zeytinoğlu, 1994.
39. Acar, 1991 and 1994; Zeytinoğlu, 1994.

NINE

IMAGES OF VILLAGE WOMEN IN TURKEY: MODELS AND ANOMALIES

Emine Onaran İncirlioğlu

And the women,
our women
with their awesome, sacred hands,
        pointed little chins, and big eyes,
           our mothers, lovers, wives,
who die without ever having lived,
who get fed at our tables
        after the oxen,
who we abduct and carry off to the hills
        and go to prison for,
who harvest grain, cut tobacco, chop wood, and barter in
    the markets,
who we harness to our plows,
and who with their bells and undulant heavy hips
surrender to us in sheepfolds
in the gleam of knives stuck in the ground—
              the women, our women
                —Nazım Hikmet[1]

"THE VILLAGE WOMAN"
IN TURKEY: CONTRADICTORY IMAGES

"THE VILLAGE WOMAN" in Turkey has an ambiguous image. On the one hand she is strong, wise, powerful, and confident; on the other, she is backbreakingly overworked, undervalued, ignorant, submissive—simply downtrodden. Interestingly enough, the same themes are used in building both images, albeit with different implications and consequences: gendered division of labor, illiteracy, separation of public-private domains, and Islam.

Kemalism has portrayed a "powerful" image: although Turkish village women were somewhat influenced by Islam, they still carried the pre-Islamic spirit of "authentic Turkic" culture. While upper-class Ottoman women were secluded after the fifteenth century and confined to the "private domain," peasant women, who worked in the fields with the men and who were never tightly veiled, continued to be a part of the "public."[2] Kemalist authors have highlighted the public participation of village women, not only in economic activities "shoulder to shoulder" with their men, but also in the political arena. Satı Kadın (Satı Çırpan) set a popular example. She was an independence war heroine; in 1930 she was elected *muhtar* (village head official) in an Ankara village, and in 1935 she was elected to the Grand National Assembly following her nomination by Atatürk.[3]

What has been later highlighted in the national and international media, however, is the "toilworn peasant woman" image, and the gap between the "sophisticated" city woman and the "backward" village woman. A *New York Times* article in early 1994, for example, reported the recent "revolutionary" changes in Turkey—"a woman as prime minister," and the "glossy" Turkish *Cosmopolitan* that sells 35,000 issues a month and publishes articles with headlines such as "I slept with a gay" and "Frigidity"—and contrasted them to "the countryside [, which] remains socially and sexually conservative." A number of successful, professional Turkish women from Ankara and İstanbul were quoted saying: "Turkish women in the large cities are as sophisticated as any in Europe"; "the new elite [is] tiny compared with the many Turkish women still held in thrall by rural and conservative

Islamic values, even some of those who migrate to the big cities"; "we represent one in 100,000 Turkish women. . . . Seventy years is not enough for a real revolution"; "The main problem in Turkey is the gap between the cities and the rural areas. . . . The women in the villages, when they are not educated, when they are under the pressure of men and Islam—they are not part of society."[4]

Not limited to journalism, the same image is produced and reproduced also in social science literature: "village women's" work in the fields is classified in the national statistics as "unpaid family labor," and the products of her labor belong to the male head of the household, be it her father, brother, husband, or son. "The village woman" carries the enormous burden of preparing dung for fuel, fetching water and wood from long distances, and processing food. Her work as unpaid family laborer is one of the justifications for the husband's family to pay a "bride price" to the wife's family. She is viewed as nothing more than a commodity (labor) to be purchased or sold, both at home and on the farm.[5] Strict division of labor by gender and women's disproportionately heavy workload go hand-in-hand with their low status. Village women's status depends on their participation in the labor force, which in turn depends on the size of landholdings, degree of mechanization in agriculture, labor-intensity requirements of crops produced, and the availability of nonagricultural income sources for men and women.[6]

Illiteracy, which is used synonymously with "ignorance" and is accompanied by subordination, is another common feature of some social scientists' image of "the village woman."[7] Where women are the least educated, their participation in the economy is the highest and their status is the lowest; they are seen as property and beaten frequently by their husbands.[8] Those Turkish women who were convinced that "their battles were won" after universal suffrage had been granted in 1934, viewed education as a means of spreading Kemalist reforms and raising awareness.[9]

The "backward," "primitive," "traditional" image of village women in Turkey usually includes a reference to Islam—implicitly or explicitly. Underdevelopment in Muslim societies, women's subordinate position, their "covering" and confinement to the "private domain" are portrayed as functions of Islam. Although women's subordination by the institutionalization of veiling can be traced to ancient Mesopotamian societies, long before the emergence of Islam (indeed, before the emergence of Semitic monotheism),[10] there is still an overwhelming ahistorical tendency to regard Islam, as an independent variable, as responsible for women's low status.[11] Ironically, Islam is used to portray both powerful *and* powerless images of village women: while early Republican images of powerful village women were linked with *isolation* from Islamic influence, almost all recent images of "subordinate village women" are associated with the *persistence* of Islamic influence in villages.[12]

The ambiguity of the image of "the village woman" is furthered by numerous ethnographic accounts that discuss village women's relative power in relation to the gendered division of labor and spatial segregation—interdependence of men and women implies a complementarity in which women's work is valued, and "independent social networks" imply women's autonomy. In addition to their informal power in the "domestic" sphere, these studies show that village women in different regions of Turkey have access to significant power resources as a result of their extensive and intensive agricultural work. Senior women do exercise control over the household income, especially money earned by female household members. In times of crisis, women work out their own coping strategies to obtain financial security and independence. And the women-centered and men-centered networks, which have existed simultaneously and autonomously in many regions, counter the image of powerless village women.[13]

One serious, probably unavoidable, problem in representing ethnographic reality is the selective use of ethnographic evidence.[14] Writing ethnography is imposing some kind of order on a complex and diverse reality by presenting "patterns," parsimonious models, and images that aim to be consistent with each other. Creating models (through both abstraction and construction) and images, however, is creating at the same time anomalies, in so far as each general statement is likely to exclude some "exceptional" cases. What we call "anomalies" are those behaviors or attitudes that are either statistically infrequent in a given society or that disturb our neat models and representations even though they may be quite frequent. Those cases, however, are not "anomalous" until and unless we portray a model that defines the "normal." Such cases may be statistically less frequent in any context, but they *are* possibilities that can and do survive in that social context. Some may disappear, some may gain wide recognition and act as "seeds" of change, some may continue to exist as exceptional cases, but if we exclude them from our models, those models will *not* represent a reality that is *able to accommodate* the so-called anomalies.

I would also argue that, by excluding "anomalies" in favor of "patterns" and neat models, we are acting *irresponsibly* as social scientists, since our representations have at least potential political consequences. I am not saying that the outcome of ethnographies should be motivated and fabricated by political ideologies, or that they should be suppressed on the grounds that they may damage a social or political movement (although it may be necessary to do so in some particular situations, for ethical and safety reasons). What I am suggesting, rather, is that it is our responsibility to point out the incongruities and "exceptional cases" because what we *omit* from our general statements about, say, village women in Turkey, may carry some different policy implications, for example, in the identification and implementation of development projects.

FIELDWORK IN TWO CENTRAL ANATOLIAN VILLAGES: SAKALTUTAN AND ELBAŞI

The women I will introduce here are from two villages, Sakaltutan and Elbaşı, both in the Kayseri province of central Anatolia.[15] They were either born in one of those two villages or moved there as brides. Some still live there, some have migrated to various towns with their families. I have been in contact with these villages since my initial collaboration with the British anthropologist Paul Stirling in 1986 in a broader research project. For eight months in 1986 Stirling and I did fieldwork in Sakaltutan and Elbaşı and in some towns where migrant households from these villages were settled. Later, in the summer of 1989, we went back to Turkey for a brief study. Almost every summer since 1989, I have visited both villages. I stay in my village friends' houses as a guest and correspond with some of them during the year. Hence, my descriptions and analyses here are based on my personal observations since 1986, as well as some earlier data provided by Stirling.[16]

Sakaltutan is a medium-size village with a population that was less than 1,000 people living in 153 households in 1 986. Elbaşı is a larger village, designated as a district (*bucak*) in the administrative structure, and had a population of roughly 2,200 people belonging to over 300 households in 1986; it became a municipality in 1992. Both are "ordinary" Sunnite-Muslim Turkish villages; they do not have any particular ethnic identities such as "Avşar," "Türkmen," or "Çerkes." In 1986, the average education level in Elbaşı was slightly higher than in Sakaltutan. In Sakaltutan most children received only a five-year primary school education, if not less, while many Elbaşı children, mostly boys, were sent to secondary school in the village. Adult literacy among women in 1986 was about 55 percent in Sakaltutan and 64 percent in Elbaşı , a remarkable increase since 1949, when virtually all women were nonliterate.[17]

Gendered Division of Labor and Status: "Toilworn Peasant Women"

Most households in Sakaltutan and Elbaşı rely on agriculture, carpet-weaving, construction work, and remittances from abroad. The significance, distribution, and combination of these income sources vary from one household to another, depending on the season, household land, and the age/sex composition of the household. Male out-migration in Sakaltutan and carpet- weaving in Elbaşı have been the most significant income sources. Nevertheless, Elbaşı has a longer history of both carpet-weaving and male out-migrations.[18] The major crops in both villages are grains (predominantly wheat), as well as onions, potatoes, garlic, squash, garbanzo beans, lentils, and beans. Most households also have a small vegetable garden for household consumption. In Sakaltutan, most girls and some women weave carpets in winter, while most young men work as pendular migrants in towns. Carpet-weaving in most households stops in summer; agricultural work takes up most of the time for both men and women. In Elbaşı, however, women spend less time and energy in farm work; in many households a few girls or women weave throughout the year. If men are in the village, they clear away the snow on the roads and the roofs; if there are no men in the household women do whatever is necessary. In addition to farm work and carpeting, in both villages women do "domestic work" and mind the household animals.

Village women's long working days and heavy workloads conform to the "toilworn peasant woman" model, while most women who migrate to towns enjoy a relative freedom from hard work. This, indeed, is why many village girls want to marry out to a town.[19] Meanwhile, several Elbaşı daughters who have been trained as teachers and nurses do work outside the village, wherever they are appointed.

Stirling's account of 1949-1952 depicted women as year-round hard workers, while the men, for about four months in winter, "have no work to do"; therefore "part of the bride price must . . . represent a good recompense for work done in the past by the women of the household." Yet this labor participation did not give women high status or decision-making power: "men decide all matters concerning the farming routine, all major sales and purchases, the marriage of children, visits to the doctor, in fact, everything of importance."[20] Women's farm work has continued to be significant in the 1980s and 1990s, though more in Sakaltutan than in Elbaşı. Villagers agree that the changes that took place in the villages since 1950, especially the mechanization of agriculture, helped reduce both men's and women's agricultural labor. Nevertheless, most labor-intensive tasks that are not mechanized, such as hoeing, weeding, harvesting the legumes, and picking vegetables, remain "women's work."

Carpet-weaving is women's most significant nonagricultural income-generating activity. A full-time weaver's day usually begins at six o'clock in the morning. Normally, a weaver takes three one-hour breaks throughout the day, for breakfast, lunch, and tea, and weaves for a total of nine to eleven hours until eight o'clock in the evening. In winter, some continue weaving after supper. Although women find weaving demanding and tiresome (as one simply put it, "*usandım*" [I'm fed up]), many still prefer weaving to housework, which includes a host of daily activities, provided that there is another woman in the household to undertake those activities. Some women weave on a part-time basis in either small teams or individually, as they find time in their routine schedule. While many women with children find it burdensome, weaving for most girls is not only an important source of self-identity and pride, but also an opportunity to socialize.

Housework is the most inclusive category. It involves food preparation, cooking, baking bread, washing the dishes, sweeping the floor
a few times a day, making beds at night and folding and stacking them
in the morning, picking up and tidying the *divan* covers continually,
doing the laundry daily on the *sallık* (porch) or right outside the
house, and mending clothes—sometimes using one of the few sewing
machines in the village, but usually by hand. Housework, however, is
not restricted to the house, and sometimes it is an outdoor communal
activity. In Elbaşı, fetching water from either the public fountain or the
household pump also is a part of housework. Washing wool, rugs,
mattresses, and pillows, done at least once a year, is a "communal"
activity that is performed by the pond or the fountain in Sakaltutan,
and in *pınarbaşı* (the spring) in Elbaşı. The laundry also becomes a
social activity when several neighbors come together to do it outdoors.
Gathering in front of their houses early in the morning everyday to sell
their daily milk to the collector also provides them with the opportunity to talk to each other and exchange news.

Men are busy, too. Some herd their own sheep, collect milk to
be sold in the province center, and repair tools or furniture when the
need arises. In a few households that have started small-scale
production and marketing of fruits such as peaches and strawber-
ries, men build fruit cases out of wood or fix old boxes used in
transportation. If a trip to town is required to purchase a household
need, to go to the bank to receive the remittances sent by their sons
working abroad, or to carry out business in a public office, men take
the early morning bus to Kayseri and come back in the evening. The
ones who remain in Sakaltutan are usually older men, who sit in
their houses most of the time, keeping an eye on the children and
talking with their neighbors who stop by. They go to the bus stop
and talk to people who come off the bus, they visit their friends, and
they go to the village mosque for prayers. Men who are away from
the village most of the year are treated like guests when they come
back home, unless it is harvest time, when they also work. In winter,
they spend most of the time "socializing"; the young ones "hang
out" with other men. In Elbaşı they spend time in one of the coffee
or tea houses. Two attempts to run a coffeehouse in Sakaltutan did
not work. However, a small room behind one of the village grocers
serves as a meeting place for some teenage boys.

It is misleading to talk about a gender division of labor without specifying the different situations and contexts within which tasks are undertaken. Since researchers are always "guests," it is difficult to observe the "routine" division of labor in daily lives. For example, because of spatio-sexual segregation, men, not women, serve male guests. Thus, "food serving" is a genderless construction; it is not categorically associated with women but is contextual. Moreover, although men actually do certain tasks that may be "normally" considered women's work in the privacy of their houses, they avoid doing such things when there are outsiders present. In an unannounced visit to Bike's house, my good friend and informant in the village, I found her busy preparing couscous on the *divan,* her seventeen-year-old daughter feeding the stove, and her husband, Bayram, sweeping the floor. As I walked in, Bayram immediately disappeared with the broom and came back after a while and greeted me as if he had just seen me. Women, too, undertake unconventional tasks, and try to be secretive and "invisible" when they do so. For example, a few women drive tractors in the farms or at the outskirts of the village, but not within, or they wear a hat and dress like a man when they drive between villages.

Why Do Men and Women Do What They Do?

Two interrelated questions that have been frequently addressed in feminist literature are "Why is women's work devalued?" and "Is biology destiny?" In the two villages I studied, I have no clear evidence to conclude that women's work is devalued. On the contrary, many men and women explicitly said that women's tasks are more important, more difficult, and indispensable—they are never looked down on as insignificant. Other ethnographies elsewhere in Turkey also suggest that women's work is not seen as "doable by anyone."[21]

One general explanation for women's "confinement" to the private sphere and their "universal subordination" is their role in biological reproduction and their socially (for some, "logically") extended duty in child-rearing. In Sakaltutan and Elbaşı, it is predominantly mothers who spend time with and look after children during infancy, until they are weaned. However, child-rearing is not restricted

to mothers or women. When mothers work in the house, infants stay
with them. Women carry their infants, and even toddlers, on their
back when they walk out in the village, everywhere except to the
fields. During the weeding season, women leave their small children at
home with their elder siblings, or alone after they go to sleep. As one
young woman casually said, "*zaten herkes dölünün saatini bilir a!*" (At
any rate, everyone knows the [sleeping/waking] hours of their children!). After weaning, however, and especially after children start
walking and talking, mothers' immediate supervisory responsibilities
decrease. Children start spending time alone, with other adults, or
with other children, usually outdoors. Fathers or male relatives look
after children only if there are no women around or if they feel like
playing. When asked about men's contribution to child-rearing,
"*bakan bakar*" (those who look after, look after) was a very common
answer. Nevertheless, it is common to see elder brothers as well as
sisters in the narrow village streets, holding a younger sibling in their
arms. And it is common for men—a father, a grandfather, or any
"uncle"—to teach, to play with, or to feed children. Men's contribution
to child-rearing is neither a new phenomenon nor limited to these
villages.[22] In single-family households in which fathers are pendular
migrants, working outside the village, child-rearing becomes the
mother's job. Nevertheless, inter-household support in child care is
quite common among neighbors, and many children spend most of
their time with both paternal and maternal grandparents.

The dichotomization of "production" and "reproduction" (or
"paid market production" and "unpaid domestic work") that is
associated with men's and women's work, respectively, does not apply
to Sakaltutan and Elbaşı. Both men and women take part in both
productive and reproductive tasks and are involved in both unpaid and
paid work. In fact, in our 1986 Elbaşı sample, more women generated
income through carpet-weaving than men did through various nonagricultural activities.

So why do village men and women do what they do? The most
common response was simply, "*işte, öyle!*" (because it is so!); the
division of labor is not questioned. One may think it is not questioned
because it is considered "natural" or "God's order." However, the
indigenous model of household and gender division of labor is more
complex. Let me address this complexity under three headings: the

complementarity and hierarchy of the gendered tasks; the "biology versus culture" debate; and the issue of "anomalies" and changes.

Complementarity and Hierarchy of Gendered Tasks. The different tasks village women and men do can be evaluated as both complementary *and* hierarchical. When comparing gendered tasks, both men and women indicated that they saw their respective jobs as complementary, equally important, necessary, and valuable—*not* in a hierarchy. Men's and women's tasks are separate, they require different skills and knowledge, but they are equally valuable. Women know how to bake, cook, and mind the animals, and men do not. To purchase a cow from another village, usually a woman accompanies the men of the household; she is the *expert.* It is women who select the seed to be planted. Concerning women's tasks, women usually write off men by saying *"Erkek ne anlar?"* or *"Erkek ne bilecekmiş?"* (What would a man know?) A fifty-eight- year-old, senior woman in a large, multifamily household, responded to my question *"Evde kimin lafı geçiyor?"* (Whose word holds in the house?) with "mine," without hesitation. *"Erkekten ne . . . olacak? Ev durumuna avradın lafı geçer!"* (What can you expect of men? Women's word holds for household affairs). Then she added, "men's word holds among men, women's word holds among women."

The notion of *ayıp* (shame) is embedded in the evaluation of men doing women's and women doing men's tasks. This "shame" goes partly to the person who is involved in an inappropriate task, and partly to others who are expected to do that task. If men have to do weeding in their fields, the villagers immediately comment on it: *"Ayıp değil mi? Utanmıyor musun?"* (Isn't it a shame? Aren't you ashamed of yourself?) Or, when a man fails to take the ill in the family to the hospital, it is *ayıp* for him.

We can also argue that men's avoidance of women's tasks is a demonstration of gender hierarchy, of the power relations between them. It can be said that it is *ayıp* for men to be involved in women's tasks because men should be able to delegate that work to women and not do it themselves. When we take into consideration that women's tasks are far more labor-intensive than men's, the gender division of labor may demonstrate a gender hierarchy in which men control women's labor. Here we can include men's control and claim over their children's labor, too. In fact, men often claim that they perform a certain task, using the first person *singular*, when it is actually undertaken by others in their house or kin group. For example, Rıdvan would say that *he* did vegetable trade ("*sebzecilik yapıyorum*"), even though he was not doing any such work at all: his younger brother would buy vegetables from Kayseri markets and carry them to Sakaltutan on the bus; his wife would open the boxes and store them in the household *kerer* (cave); his son would peddle them in the village. Meanwhile, many women used the first person *plural*, even for tasks that they performed single-handedly. Although such cases can be used to demonstrate men's control over other household members' labor (and I admit, this would provide a very "neat model"), they should not be used to portray an image of "the village woman in Turkey" for three reasons. First, I have not particularly focused on sociolinguistic problems in my research, and I do not wish to make generalizations based on limited impressions. Second, I observed on many occasions that women, in their turn, had the right to demand household labor. They would tell their husbands and children what to do and what not to do. Thus, although the use of language may not be symmetrical, language *alone* should not be taken as an indicator of domination/subordination. Finally, I made similar observations not only in Turkish cities, but also in non-Turkish households in the United States and England. In other words, as widely documented in the area of gender and language, Turkish village men are not unique in representing themselves as in charge of household property and labor. There is nothing "Turkish" or "village-like" about it.

Biology or Culture? Why do men and women do what they do? In the villages, responses have social but *not* biological references. In other words, the indigenous model does not assume essentialist reasons behind the separation of tasks; tasks are gendered because of differences in knowledge, as well as social controls and sanctions against "deviations" from the norms. I have never heard anyone in the village saying men or women, as a category, could not do a certain task because they were not biologically suited. But I have heard many people bringing up the notion of *ayıp* as a social sanction. And I have heard many villagers *marking* sex, very explicitly, in their reasoning.

The most striking example is Bike's explanation for "why girls and women do not drive tractors": she said bluntly, "because they will say, 'look, she's driving a tractor with her vagina!'" (*Amıyla traktör sürüyor derler!*). Mind you, the biological reference is not the reason here; it is not that women cannot drive a tractor *because* they have vaginas (they do indeed drive tractors), rather, what "they will say" prevents them from *being seen* when they drive tractors. And numerous other women in both villages said in response to the same question, "*ayıpsarlar*" ("they" will find it shameful).

Similarly, physical strength is seen as a personal attribute and is not associated with men categorically. Those men and women who are capable carry heavy loads, and those who lack the strength do not. Women do not step back when physical strength and heavy work are required.

Anomalies and Changes. Although there are some fairly strict norms about what men and women should do, there are also a number of "anomalous" cases. The only area in which men and women seem to stick to their spheres in the division of labor with no exceptions is nonagricultural wage labor. It is unthinkable for a man to weave carpets or for a woman to work in constructions outside the village as a pendular migrant. Otherwise, partly depending on the demographic and economic circumstances of the households, and partly as a result of personality differences, all norms could be broken.[23] For example, taking care of animals, which appears to be exclusively a woman's task, is also done by men, especially in winter. In fact, according to Stirling, the winter job of watering and feeding animals was not a gendered task in the 1950s.

In my observations, villagers did not regard the exceptions and anomalies as indicators of a change in the gender division of labor; nor did they treat them as "role models." Men and women did undertake the "other's" tasks if the situation called for it, yet the responsibility remained temporary and exceptional. A synchronic research period is, of course, too short a time to make conclusions on some possible trends. It is possible to argue that there is actually some trend toward an androgynous division of labor that the villagers do not perceive. Nevertheless, the very fact that they recognize and verbalize contingencies makes change possible in any direction.

These contingencies can lead us to draw different explanatory models, linking for example "economic development" and gender relations. Technological changes that took place since the 1950s had some impact on women's work, gender relations, and women's image. Both villages gained access to electricity, and cooking pits (tandır) were replaced with bottled gas cooking stoves. In the 1950s, in both Elbaşı and Sakaltutan women fetched potable water from the village wells and fountains. By 1986, all houses in Sakaltutan had running water either in the kitchens or the stables or both. Women used fountain and well water only for their large-scale laundry and seasonal cleaning, which are undertaken as "communal" activities. All the women in Sakaltutan who had experienced the old days, cooking with tandır and fetching water from the public fountains, told me that their lives were now far better. In Elbaşı, where fetching water remains "women's work," we may choose to highlight either the women's burden of walking to the fountain and back with heavy loads, or their advantage in gathering and manipulating news and information.

The increase in small, nuclear-family households can also be linked to changes in the division of labor. This change in household structure has at least two, and somewhat contradictory, consequences. The first is a "practical" change: early fissions intensify husband-wife relationships and make possible some shifts in roles. Especially in smaller households, men undertake some tasks that are expected of other women in larger households. On the other hand, the change from multifamily to single family households means a change from complex and multiple divisions of labor, which recognize seniority and kinship roles as well as gender, to a simple and categorical *gender* division of labor. This may create a powerful ideology in which "women's work" is not only categorical, but intrinsically unimportant simply because it is "female." In her analysis of "institutionalized gender hierarchy" in class and state societies, Gailey points out the problem: "people's functions in the division of labor come to be discernable with reference to categories of gender, age and skill, *abstracted from their particular kinship connections and meanings*," and "where people become identified independently of kinship—for instance, as constituents of a class—biological differences or functions (as defined in the culture), rather than social identities, become increasingly important."[24]

Different Worlds:
"Women in the Private, Men in the Public"

The gendered division of labor in the villages does not necessarily lead to a simple public-private dichotomization; nor to women's ignorance of the "public sphere." In 1986, one elder Sakaltutan woman identified men's and women's responsibilities as *dışarı işleri* (external affairs) and *evin işleri* (household affairs), respectively. In "external affairs," she included bringing in money, purchasing the necessities in town, and linking the household members with public institutions when the need arises, such as taking them to hospitals and registering their births and deaths. However, because "household affairs" are very "liberally" defined—including income and expense management (*gelir-gider*), deciding about profit and loss (*kar, zarar*), and thinking of the household necessities (*evin eksiği gediği*)—it does not make much theoretical sense to equate household affairs with private affairs. One of my Sakaltutan friends refused to give pocket money (*sigara parası*) to her husband because she needed the money for household necessities. Probably most women did not hold "the purse strings," but I know of a few who did.[25]

"Knowledge" of "public matters," including extra-domestic economy and politics, is not restricted to men. Many women were not only well-informed about their husbands' income, but they were also able to carry a discussion about increasing inflation, rents in cities, cost of gold in the market, or interest rates. Here some anecdotal stories regarding three village women will be illustrative. Elif, Gönül, and Güler are "typical" village women in the sense that, as members of their respective communities, they do what they are expected to do, and are by no means considered to be "deviant."

Elif. Born in a village close by Sakaltutan, Elif was fifty-two years old in 1986. She had married three times and had a total of eleven children. When I went to visit her for the first time, I found an oldish man sleeping under his rugged coat at one corner of the built-in divan. Soon I learned that he had come to collect the money Elif's husband Salih owed him, and that he was determined to wait until Salih came home. The moment Elif entered the scene and started talking, it was clear that she would control the content and the direction of the conversation. She was not very talkative, but witty, sarcastic, and somewhat ruthless in her biting remarks. Elif did not look any different in her appearance from other village women of her age, and like most of them, she was nonliterate. Yet she had something to say about everything that was going on in the household and in the village economy. She carried a huge bunch of banknotes in her bosom; she knew how much money Salih made, how much he owed, and to whom; she knew with whom he did business. She seemed to be the one who told Salih what to do in crises. She was visibly angry when she talked about Salih's "irresponsible" sons from a previous marriage because she had no control over their contributions to the household budget. When the man who was sleeping woke up to complain about Salih postponing paying his debt, Elif shut him up with a lecture. I wrote that day in my field notes,

> Salih has been in Adana for a month, waiting to get his money in return for a herd of sheep he had sold for 7.5 million Turkish Liras. Elif says there are nine men altogether waiting at this man's door, to get a total of 80 million Turkish Liras. The man, or the company in Adana, resells the herds to Saudi Arabia. I asked why the nine men, including Salih, were not paid in time. Elif's answer was sharp: "Do you know how much interest that 80 million brings in a month?" "So," I asked, "is the man holding on to the money to make profit out of it?" "Of course!" Elif said, certain of herself. Salih owes half a million to a man from Kayseri [the man in the room]; 120,000 Turkish Liras to Sefa Vacit of Mengicek; and less than a hundred thousand to another man. "That's all," Elif asserted, "but he is owed much more. He has lost two million liras just last year in Saudi Arabia." Last year he sent his sister's son . . . to Saudi Arabia to sell a herd of sheep. The Arabs did not pay him. There were also individuals from various villages who did not pay for the animals they had already received, showing various excuses. "Salih gives . . . vouchers when he owes money, but he does not ask for documentation for his credits," Elif said.

Gönül. I met Gönül in 1986 as an "informant" in Elbaşı, when she was in her early forties and pregnant with her seventh child. She has never had any formal education; however, she learned how to read and write all by herself and has been following national and international news on television on a daily basis. During the election campaign in 1992, when the Minister of Internal Affairs, İsmet Sezgin, came to the village, she confronted him in public. In the presence of 2,000 people, she told him what kinds of education and health services the village needed. In the summer of 1993, when I visited Gönül, she told me the story of this public encounter, which was later confirmed by others:

> I complained—those appointed to the village were not always doing their jobs. "I welcome you, my Minister of Interior," I said, "in the name of the people of Elbaşı. I have some complaints to you." "Tell me," he said. "First, we want education and health from you; first of all education, and second health. All these women who are looking at you right now, lack education," I said. "They cannot understand even the news on the television because of a lack of education," I said. "And concerning our complaints about health: the state built a health center here, we are thankful for that. However, the doctor comes, stays for a week, and leaves—never around, and the state knows nothing about this," I said. "And we find the midwife and the nurse in their houses doing housework," I said. "We get sick in the middle of the night, we cannot find transportation. Aren't we the citizens of the Turkish Republic? We go to the doctor, the doctor examines us on top of our dresses without much attention; and we buy the medicine, at the cost of gold, which causes an opposite reaction, so we don't take it but save it in some corner. How does your conscience take all this? We want a doctor who stays in the village all the time, and a midwife and nurse who work in the health center until their work day is over. We want a health center with medicine, with ultrasound, with an ambulance . . . For the last forty years I have been putting my stamp on your white horse;[26] but if these demands of ours are not satisfied, I'll drive nails under the feet of your horse." He said, "All right. Now I'll present all you've said to the people," and went up on the podium. "Everything this elderly sister said is absolutely right; I accept everything she said," he said. He thought I was an old woman. Well, it's all right. "At first your education," he said, "and following that, your health." He promised that he would carry out these [tasks], and that he would talk about me and be willing to receive me all the time; then he left.

Gönül also reported the developments in Elbaşı:

> On 11 June 1992 the village became a municipality; and things became even better. Our mayor . . . is from the Social Democrat Party and he is working with success. He brought municipal bus service, had a bread bakery built, brought one of those bulldozers to clean the mud, a tractor for the municipality, and a truck that we are using for the village. An ambulance is on its way, today or tomorrow it will arrive; it will be kept at the health center [sağlık ocağı]. İller Bankası, is apparently the bank for municipalities; money comes from there.

She predicted that villagers would not be moving to the city anymore. Then she started to discuss wheat production in Turkey, giving actual figures, including Turkey's rank in world food production. I could not assess if her statistics were "accurate," but Gönül was so completely in control of the discussion and so convincing that it did not even occur to me that she might be wrong. Then she volunteered her opinions on "Islamic fundamentalists":

> Erbakan's followers and Humeyni's followers wear black veils [kara peçe]. We don't have them here, but there are many in Kayseri. They wear the veil all the way that even their fingernails don't show. I say that they are worse than the PKK[27] for the future of Turkey. What is the human being underneath that veil? It can carry anything. Is it carrying a gun? Is it carrying money? Is it robbing a bank? Is it a man or a woman? Its sex is not apparent. And on top of that, they are establishing schools and claim that they are teaching the Qur'an. It is not apparent what they teach. We don't know what they have been doing. Most people cannot be aware of it, but they are brainwashing these children. In the future, if Turkey cannot find their head and eradicate them, they are more dangerous than the PKK. Turkey can hang out with the West but cannot hang out with them.

Gönül did not think attempts for such an "Islamic" education would succeed in the village, especially among women. A new cooperative official had come to Elbaşı from Sivas, and his wife, a follower of the Islamist movement, had been trying to organize village women since 1989. "Every now and then she gathers them together at the village mosque, talks to them, but in two hours, women completely forget about all she says; then she gathers them again," reported Gönül. She explained why this woman could not convince village women to follow an "Islamic way": "We milk cows, there is farm work, the dung to collect, the bread to bake, and carpets. . . . There is a lot of work in the village; no one has time to follow her. The same thing has been going on for five years now." Gönül added, tongue-in-cheek, "so, she could not gather anyone under her protection."

Güler. Unlike Elif and Gönül, Güler is a very quiet young woman. She is nonliterate, does not volunteer her opinions, and does not have an extraordinary charisma. When I first met her in Sakaltutan in 1986, she was in her early twenties, a junior bride in a large household. By 1989 the whole household had migrated to Antalya. At first they all shared a two-story *gecekondu* (squatter housing) building, but by the summer of 1993 Güler and her husband had separated from the "extended family" and moved with their two young children to their own *gecekondu* in a different Antalya neighborhood, where Paul Stirling and I visited them. In her own house now, Güler was not a junior bride but was as quiet and hard-working as ever. Her elder son had started to go to school the previous year, and she was trying to learn to read and write with him. By coincidence, the day before we visited them Tansu Çiller had been elected the leader of the Motherland Party, which would make her the first woman prime minister of Turkey. Stirling was interested in the villagers' views on this "extraordinary" event. As usual, Güler did not volunteer her ideas, waiting until she was asked; but when she was asked, she articulated both the issues and her opinions in a concise and eloquent way. Her first point was that having a woman prime minister did not necessarily mean improvement in women's conditions. "One may think that a woman prime minister will benefit all women," she said, "but that's not at all certain" (*o hiç belli olmaz*). Then, she accepted Çiller's authority. "Obviously she has confidence in herself and she knows what she is doing that she has stepped forward," she said, "not everyone can." When I paraphrased Paul's questions "Can a woman be a prime minister? Would the nation follow a woman?," Güler simply replied, "why not?" looking at me in disbelief that we were asking such bizarre questions. "*Kadının nesi eksik?*" (What does the woman lack?). I did not respond but smiled as she continued saying, "*kafası varsa yapar*" (if she's got the brains, she can do it). We read in the newspaper polls the following day that about 70 percent of the respondents considered the prime minister's gender as irrelevant. Stirling was surprised.

Elif, Gönül, and Güler, as introduced in these anecdotes, may be considered "anomalous" cases, since they hardly fit the images of village women in Turkey as depicted by social scientists and journalists, or as perceived by city people in Turkey. Their knowledge of the supposedly "men's world," self-confidence in participation in the so-called public sphere, and analytic skills in evaluating national events may seem to be "statistically insignificant." Yet, while neither of these three women are considered "extraordinary" in their villages, we need to understand that they are unique persons, not just "village women."

CONCLUSION:
REALITIES, MODELS, ANOMALIES

Turkish intellectuals have treated the issue of "women" as a central problem in social change since the *Tanzimat* period;[28] and a polarization emerged along Western/modern and Muslim/traditional lines. It is very clear to me that this polarization has been extended to the "rural versus urban" dichotomization. Thus appear two distinct images: the underdeveloped, uneducated, religious, "traditional," village woman—oppressed and repressed at different levels—and the Westernized, educated, secular, "modern," city woman, whose situation is categorically different.

"To be able to say 'I' and express themselves is a very difficult thing for women," writes Berktay, because "the dominant culture recognizes little right for the woman to be an active and autonomous subject." She continues, "in this [any patriarchal] culture, it is difficult for the woman to be the symbolizer, the representer, because she herself is the symbol. The power to symbolize, to name and to define is traditionally in the hands of the man; and he transforms the woman into a symbolized object."[29] Nazım Hikmet's "The Story of Our Women," cited in the beginning of this chapter, is a perfect example of "the toilworn village woman" who is an object both defined *and owned* by men.

What stands out in the images of "villager" and "woman" is their subordinate positions. Is it a coincidence, for example, that both images include "irrationality"? The structural similarity between the images, representations, of women and of villagers may not be so surprising once we recognize the power relations between the subjects who record these images with authority on the one hand, and the objects of these images that are recorded on the other. After all, neither women nor peasants wrote about themselves using their own theories. Thus, "the village woman" is objectified twice—once by men and again by the "urban elite," both men and women.

Clear-cut models, whether they portray powerless, helpless, sub-ordinate images of women (whether with a "male bias" or a "feminist" critical perspective) or emphasize "women's power," disregarding inequalities (whether by employing "cultural relativist" or romantic "feminist" approaches), are equally detrimental, not only because they are not representative of village women in Turkey, but also because they are politically damaging. Neither ignoring anomalies nor dwelling on them will help alleviate gender inequalities.

The image of uneducated, overworked, abused, and powerless village women is supported by some scholarly work: where women are the least educated, their participation in the economy is the highest and their status is the lowest; they are "seen as property" and beaten frequently by their husbands. Yet nowhere in Sakaltutan or Elbaşı, nor among emigrants in cities, have I met any such women. Village women are not necessarily passive recipients in household decision making. During lengthy discussions on pros and cons, some family members participate more, some less, depending on their personalities. And once people are looked at as individuals, like Elif, Gönül, and Güler, with faces, unique life histories, different personalities and tempera-ments, it becomes difficult to generalize *the* village woman. Some women I have come to know have been very forthcoming, talkative, knowledgeable, and friendly, not because they were "urbanized" or "modernized" (and have become more like "us"), and not because they had "peasant wisdom." Some women were quiet and reserved, but not because they were backward or ignorant. Women's participation in the economy is remarkably high, and the labor-intensive nature of women's work in Sakaltutan and Elbaşı conforms with the widespread image of "toilworn village women." Yes, women almost always do all household chores, their days are longer, and they suffer backaches after hours of farm work if they depend on agricultural income.

However, women's work is neither automatically devalued, nor do women have low status as a result of their hard work. Moreover, the implicit assumptions that "illiteracy means ignorance" and "literacy improves gender relations" are both questionable. Wife-beating, though it exists, is not more accepted or more frequent in villages than in cities. There is no reason to believe that the same education system that provides literacy but simultaneously reproduces gender hierarchies, albeit rewiring them, should help raise women's status. Schooling, which comes with its own share of physical violence,[30] does not necessarily reduce abuse and domestic violence. By associating peasant women's low status with several other "factors," none of which "we" educated city women share, we are not only reducing "*the* village woman" into a category, but we are also putting ourselves in the powerful location of identifying "her" problems and suggesting solutions that have no bearing on "our" problems.

If we are dissatisfied with "models" because of the "anomalies" they ignore (or create), what options do we have? Can we abandon models altogether, on the grounds that they are simple and misleading? Here, I want to distinguish between folk models and analytic models, and within each, two further kinds of models: descriptive models and explanatory models. I would argue that, even if we decide to do away with analytic models on the grounds that they are not all-encompassing and do not have any predictive or heuristic value, we as the human species have to have folk models, because that is how we make sense of the world. And even if we do away with analytic explanatory models, we cannot give up descriptive models, because at the *lowest level of abstraction,* whatever we say is a reduction of "reality"; we reduce reality to "numbers" or "words," so unless we stop not only writing, but also philosophizing, thinking, and talking about "reality," we cannot stop model-building. Without models, who can have a "pipeline" to the "reality out there," whatever that might be? If we have to have models, then we can try to have better models that include change, diversity, and the so-called anomalous cases created by the flawed models. How?

We can learn from feminist methodology; namely, the *subjective* analysis of women by women and the "politics of knowledge." If feminist history includes a critique of the silencing of women by men, and if feminist methodology and epistemology encourage women to *subjectively* analyze their own condition, silencing "the village woman" by creating images *for* her cannot be justified in a feminist analysis.[31] Yes, women from villages or living in villages may find themselves in power relations and hierarchies that are different from those who live in cities. However, making "village women" objects and identifying their problems by focusing on their subordination and oppression by their men and "Islam" ignores other sorts of hierarchies, whose "subjects" may include their "urban sisters," whether they be "women in the street" who despise them, "lady doctors" who examine them without respect, "career women" who "matronize" them, or social scientists who make them silent objects in their studies.

Notes

Author's note: An earlier version of this paper was presented at the Social Anthropology Staff-Graduate Seminar, University of Kent at Canterbury, on March 15, 1994.

1. Nazım Hikmet [Ran], 1982 [1941-1945]:133.
2. See Atatürk's speeches. Atatürk, 1959 [1906-1939].
3. Taşkıran, 1976:77.
4. Cowell, 1994:A7.
5. Kazgan, 1981:143-145.
6. Kandiyoti, 1985.
7. Incidentally, the United Nations, the World Bank, and other international development agencies take education as an indicator of modernization and development and automatically equate it with higher status for women.
8. Özbay, 1981.
9. Ş. Tekeli, 1990c:271.
10. G. Lerner, 1986.
11. See for example Marshall, 1985.
12. See for example Ş. Tekeli, 1990c; and Delaney, 1991.
13. See for example Olson, 1982; Hann, 1993; Beller-Hann, 1995.
14. What bits of the complex social "reality," of which we ourselves are a part, do we include in our descriptions? On the one hand, all depictions of reality are incomplete images; on the other, they are all "part real"—unless of course they are complete fabrica-

tions. Whose image is more real? is a question of power; who have the power to pass their images as reality?

15. Although it is common practice in anthropology to use pseudonyms for the communities studied, since Stirling had used the actual village names in his monograph, I will not attempt to change them now. For all individuals, however, I am using pseudonyms and changing certain details in order to make identification difficult.

16. Also see Stirling, 1965, 1974, 1993, and 1995; İncirlioğlu, 1991, 1993, and 1994; Stirling and İncirlioğlu, 1995.

17. I deliberately use the term "nonliterate" in reference to some informants, rather than the more conventional term "illiterate," in order to emphasize the complete lack of literacy.

18. Personal communication with Stirling, 1986.

19. İncirlioğlu, 1993.

20. Stirling, 1965:47, 186, and 112.

21. See for example Morvaridi, 1993:93.

22. See for example Stirling, 1965; Helling, 1960; and personal communication with Olson.

23. In fact, Paul Stirling remembers a man weaving a carpet by himself. Moreover, a middle-aged woman who had migrated to Germany with her Sakaltutan husband later worked as a construction contractor in Antalya, although many Sakaltutan men found it difficult to *call* her a *müteahhit* (contractor).

24. Gailey, 1987:17.

25. An important question to ask here is whether holding the purse strings implies power for poor women or just another burden.

26. *Doğru Yol Partisi* (The True Path Party), to which Minister of Interior İsmet Sezgin belonged, is a continuation of the *Adalet Partisi* (Justice Party), whose emblem prior to its disestablishment in 1981 was a white horse. The voter exercises her choice by putting a stamp on the emblem of the party on the ballot.

27. *Partia Karkaren Kurdistan* (Kurdish Workers Party, or PKK), founded in 1974 in Ankara under Abdullah Öcalan's leadership, was revitalized in 1981, and it declared the Kurdish revolution in 1982. The ongoing war between the Turkish Military and the PKK, since then, has been causing tragic bloodshed.

28. See Göle, 1991.

29. Berktay (Baltalı), 1991: 9; translation mine.

30. Physical abuse of children by teachers and principals is a common occurrence in Turkey, but little research has been done in this area. See Berktay (Baltalı), 1991; Olson, 1981; Tan 1991.
31. Geiger, 1992.

A PROFILE OF TOP WOMEN MANAGERS IN TURKEY

Hayat Kabasakal

WOMEN ARE UNDERREPRESENTED in managerial positions in all countries, regardless of culture, level of economic development, ideology, or religion. Turkey is no exception. Furthermore, women's representation in management positions drops sharply at the upper echelons of the hierarchy. Nevertheless, despite the pervasive barriers, a few women are able to reach the top.[1] What are the characteristics of these few Turkish women who could climb the ladder of success? This study aims to analyze the characteristics common to Turkish women who are top managers—those who are general managers, presidents, or vice-presidents.

STATISTICS ON WOMEN MANAGERS IN TURKEY

There is no comprehensive or conclusive study about the exact number or ratio of women in management positions in Turkey. Women have been encouraged to enter the professional life since the establishment of the Republic, and they have been visible in professional ranks both in the public and private sectors. However, the same level of representation is not observed in managerial posts.

A pioneering study of the manufacturing sector was conducted by Dilber in the 1960s, and it found that women held 4 percent of top management positions.[2] A survey of manufacturing firms around the

İstanbul area in the 1970s showed that women constituted 25 percent of all employees in these firms, while their ratio decreased to 14 percent in middle management and to 4 percent in top management positions.[3] Later in the 1980s, Tabak's study of the 500 largest manufacturing companies showed that in the firms that employed more than 100 people, women constituted 17 percent of all employees and 15 percent of managers, while the ratio dropped to 3 percent among the top managers. In the smaller firms with less than 100 employees, women had "no" representation at top management positions.[4] Another national survey, conducted in the beginning of the 1990s, that included more than 100 industrial firms showed that women made up 4 percent of top managers.[5] Though not comparable, these statistics imply that there has been no increase in the percentage of senior management positions filled by women in the manufacturing sector from the 1960s to the 1990s.

Even in sectors, like banking and insurance, that traditionally employ high numbers of women, percentages of women managers are low. The representation of women in management falls short of their representation in total employment, especially in senior management positions. A 1992 study that included more than half of the banks and insurance companies operating in Turkey showed that women constituted 43 percent of all employees in these firms, yet their representation in middle management was 26 percent, and in top management fell to 4 percent.[6]

Another occupation that is traditionally considered suitable for women is "teaching." Even though women made up approximately 44 percent of the teachers employed by the Ministry of Education in 1990, only 7 percent of school principals were women.[7] The picture has not been much different at the universities. Turkey has been among the countries that have had the highest ratio of women academics in the world, ranking third after the United States and Canada, excluding the formerly called Eastern Block countries.[8] However, in 1989, while 32 percent of full academics were women, their representation in administrative posts was only 16 percent.[9] In 1992, only 11 percent of the deans were women; moreover, from the establishment of the Republic to 1997, only three women have served as university presidents.[10]

Turkish women do have high representation rates in other prestigious professions. In 1990, 60 percent of pharmacists, 19 percent of physicians, 30 percent of dentists, and 34 percent of lawyers were women. However, women professionals had low representations on the boards of the professional chambers: the rate of positions filled by women at chamber boards were 20 percent in pharmacy, 6 percent in medicine, 9 percent in dentistry, and 7 percent in law.[11]

COMMON CHARACTERISTICS OF WOMEN MANAGERS

Why women are able to enter the professional workforce at a high rate but unable to move up and participate in the decision-making process is an important question. Rather than directly addressing this "glass ceiling" phenomenon, however, I will focus on the small population that did manage to reach the top. What are the common characteristics of these women? What factors play a role in shaping these common characteristics? Through a review of survey research, I will attempt to answer these questions and draw a profile of top women managers in Turkey. The overview of the attitudes, values, and backgrounds reported in the literature allows us to identify seven different but interrelated characteristics shared by these women: sustaining low visibility, maintaining a controlled feminine outlook, not being a feminist, having a strong personality, being a high achiever, having a high socioeconomic background, and being married with children.

Low Visibility

In its June 1992 issue, *Ekonomik Panorama* journal presented a list of the 26 "most successful women managers" in Turkey along with short interviews with them.[12] The list was determined through a survey conducted among 220 entrepreneurs and top managers. They were asked to nominate two successful women managers, one from their own sector and one from any field. They were also asked to exclude those women who started their careers in their family firms.[13]

Interviewer M. Sönmez noted that the 26 women were in a way "anonymous" individuals. Even though these women had very important posts, they were not widely known in their business environments or in the sectors in which they operated. In fact, the woman who was chosen as the most successful woman manager pointed out that "women work very hard, they are very successful" but "they are reluctant to be at the forefront."

Another journalist, N. Alpman, published a series of interviews with women managers who were daughters of famous businessmen.[14] Alpman indicated that these women, who were managers in their family firms, were highly reluctant to appear in the press. "It was more difficult to have an interview appointment with these women than to have an interview with an important politician of a foreign country," concluded the journalist. These women wanted to avoid high visibility in the society. In contrast, the sons of famous businessmen take visible posts in voluntary organizations and willingly agree to be interviewed by journalists.

Turkish women managers' desire to maintain low visibility can be better explained as a reflection of the female culture than as a national trait. It is argued that a major difference exists between male and female values, and that the male system emphasizes autonomy and control, while the female system emphasizes connection and relatedness.[15] According to Chodorow, the origin of the differences can be traced back to the fact that universally women are largely responsible for early child care.[16] Since the main caretaker during the early years of life is typically a female, the interpersonal dynamics that boys and girls face during the formation of their gender identities are different. While girls experience themselves as similar to their mothers, boys separate themselves from their mothers by defining themselves as masculine. Because girls are taken care of by the same sex, connectedness becomes a part of femaleness. In contrast, boys experience differentiation and individuation, and these become a part of their sexual identity. Consequently, social significance attached to femaleness becomes connectedness, which excludes individuation.

Turkish women managers seem to be acting according to the female culture, which sustains low visibility. In addition to their efforts to "tactfully" avoid public visibility, they attempt to avoid attracting attention in the workplace by maintaining a controlled femininity.

Controlled Feminine Appearance

The pictures of the twenty-six managers published in *Ekonomik Panorama* showed almost all of the women in "suits." I made the same observation during my professional contact with fifteen top managers in panels or in their organizations in 1993 and 1994. I also noticed that most of them had their hair professionally done at a coiffeur, but in a plain style. They did not have very long nails, nor flashy nail polishes. Neither did they wear big jewelry or accessories. All of them wore light make-up. However, at the same time, they were far from fitting the image of asexual women, with short hair and no make-up, that had been required or promoted in Turkish schools.[17] What I sensed was not an effort toward repressing or highlighting their femininity, but creating a controlled feminine appearance.

Symbolically, a "suit" is associated with masculine values and power.[18] The choice of suits by women symbolizes the fact that organizations are run by male values and that the top women represent these values. While male managers do not drastically change their way of dressing from work life to other public appearances, women managers may switch from suits to more feminine-looking dresses with shorter hemlines, or wear more and larger accessories and heavier make-up. However, they present modest yet feminine attire at work.

If top women in prestigious positions that are dominated by men do not disguise their femininity well enough, they are forced to do so. Otherwise, it is believed that the status of the establishment and the profession would deteriorate with the presence of an improper display of femininity. In *Milliyet,* Kuşçuoğlu reported that in the 1991-1992 legislative year of the Turkish parliament, among the topics that were most discussed were the outfits of two women parliamentarians.[19] Out of an immense number of serious issues on the country's agenda, the Turkish parliament chose to discuss its female members' wardrobe and looks.

Not a Feminist

Another common attribute of women senior executives is that they are reluctant to promote women's rights. In my interviews with thirteen women middle managers who attended a management development seminar at a private bank in 1993, all the women except one declared that they were not feminists. One woman manager said, "It is very dangerous to be a feminist. Men will become our enemies, if we become feminists." Another woman added, "We cannot be managers and feminists at the same time." They agreed on the importance of addressing human rights in general rather than singling out women's rights.

In his interviews with twenty-six top women managers, Sönmez similarly found that all the women except one indicated they were not feminists.[20] Only Duygu Asena, who was the manager of a journal and was famous for her feminist articles and novels, identified herself as a feminist. The woman who was chosen as the most successful woman manager of the year believed that the underrepresentation of women in the business world should be attributed to "women themselves" rather than to "external factors." She believed that even child-rearing responsibilities did not set barriers for women's active involvement in "work life." According to her, "women pose children as excuses."

Similar views on women's problems and opportunities are shared by Turkey's first woman prime minister, Tansu Çiller. In an interview with the *Sabah* newspaper as the new prime minister, Çiller declared that she would not have a special mission geared toward improving women's status in the society.[21] The reason was clear: "Women should only learn to use the rights given to them."

Decision-making bodies in the society or in organizations would seriously question the "credibility" of a woman administrator who advocated women's rights. Kanter argued that only those individuals whom the capital owners can "trust" would be appointed as managers.[22] Furthermore, Üsdiken and Özmucur noted that there are no objective criteria that can measure managerial performance, and it is quite impossible to attribute the performance of a unit or an organization to its leadership.[23] Therefore, when there are uncertainties about the performance of individuals, capital owners and executives would use criteria other than performance in their selection and promotion decisions. They, then, would select only those people whom they could trust for managerial positions, and especially to top management positions in which the significance of the technical expertise becomes minimal. Neither the dominant male coalitions nor the capitalist entrepreneurs would truly trust a woman who believed in and advocated structural changes for the emancipation of women. Thus, only those women who think "like men" are trusted as senior executives, and therefore women managers who reach the top eschew feminism.

Strong Personalities

Although women managers are careful—they avoid being in the forefront or having striking looks or radical ideas—their caution does not necessarily mean that they have weak personalities. In contrast, they have the "active" personality traits that are attributed to men in general, rather than the "passive" traits that societies associate with femininity.

Sunar's study, which compared the Turkish and American cultures with regard to sex-role stereotypes, found that despite wide cultural differences, in both societies women were perceived as dependent, emotional, irrational, passive, not knowledgeable, not straightforward, and weaker than men.[24]

In his study on sex typing, Bem found that the Western culture associated "instrumental" traits with masculinity, and "expressive" traits with femininity.[25] Gürbüz analyzed the pervasive sex-role stereotypes and social desirability of these traits in Turkish society.[26] She found that six socially desirable characteristics—"ambitious," "analytical," "enterprising," "forceful," "insists on one's rights," and "risk taker"—and three socially undesirable characteristics—"dominant," "jealous," and "autonomous"—were identified as masculine. Four socially desirable characteristics—"loves children," "dependent," "elegant," and "thrifty"—and five socially undesirable characteristics—"submissive," "cowardly," "weak," "insecure," and "naive"—were identified as feminine characteristics. This study indicates that femininity in Turkish culture is associated more with negative attributes, as well as with passivity.

Contrary to the pervasive societal values, Turkish women managers are far from perceiving themselves as passive or as carrying only expressive traits. In a study among twenty-five women and twenty-four men who were in middle management at a private Turkish bank, it was found that there were no differences in the self-perceptions of men and women in terms of their personality traits.[27] Similarly, Sönmez labeled the twenty-six top women managers he interviewed as "wolves disguised as lambs."[28]

A study of twenty-five top American women managers conducted by Hennig and Jardim found that these women were either the first child or did not have a brother in the family.[29] All said that they had received "special" attention from their families, especially from their fathers. These women pointed out that their fathers played an important role in the formation of their personalities. Even though their fathers had accepted their sexual identities, they encouraged the girls to engage in activities beyond the traditional feminine roles.

A study conducted in 1993 pointed out that Turkish top women managers were similar to their American counterparts with respect to their birth order.[30] Moreover, while 60 percent of top women managers were the first child in their families, this rate dropped to 20 percent among middle managers. A similar pattern prevailed among Turkish women academics in terms of their birth order.[31]

High Achievement

One would expect to find high achievement characteristics among top managers regardless of their gender. However, what is interesting is that top women managers in general have higher achievement characteristics and aspirations relative to their male counterparts.

Balkır, in her study using international data on university students from forty-three different countries, found that female students at Boğaziçi University scored significantly higher on a "need for achievement" index than the male students.[32] More interestingly, more Boğaziçi University female students indicated a desire to be the director of a large corporation than did male students. According to Balkır's report, among more than forty countries Turkey was the only one where female students had a significantly higher preference for being the director of a large corporation than male students.

This finding can be partly explained by the characteristics of the female students at Boğaziçi University. Receiving an education at a highly prestigious university would be available mostly to female students from the middle and upper socioeconomic groups of the society. Several researchers indicated that in some developing countries middle and upper-class families bring up their girls to have high "achievement needs" and thus women have high aspirations.[33]

Kemalism, which is widely accepted in the urban upper classes of the society, advocates high achievement for Turkish women. Thus, female students at prestigious universities are unusually achievement-oriented, and these females are the prospective candidates for managerial positions. However, these observations should be interpreted with caution. The socialization processes that take place later in life regarding the sex-role attitudes of women and work/family role conflicts may curtail the aspirations of female college students.[34] In order to reach the top, women need to maintain their earlier socialization despite the social barriers.

When I interviewed thirteen women middle managers in 1993, all agreed they had to work harder than their male peers in order to be accepted into management. One woman said, "Women have to do their homework twice as well as men, in order to be considered as successful." Another woman summarized, "Women managers are in general more careful about the details and requirements of the task," and she added, "if you want to pick a manager who is dedicated and willing to work beyond self-interest, a woman is the best choice."

A top woman manager interviewed by Sönmez reflected on her past experiences: "During my years in middle management, I worked at an unbelievable and sometimes inhuman pace." Another woman indicated that until about four years ago she had to work eighteen to nineteen hours a day. Working hard seems to be the accepted norm among top women managers, as indicated by a woman interviewed by Sönmez: "I do technical analysis until two to three AM"[35]

High Socioeconomic Background

Women top managers in Turkey have high socioeconomic origins, reflected in their fathers' prestigious occupations, their elite educational background, and their urban upbringing. In their study comparing female and male managers, Arbak and her colleagues found that fathers' occupations significantly differed for female and male managers.[36] While 53 percent of women managers had fathers who were bureaucrats and 6 percent had fathers who were managers, these rates dropped to 41 percent and 3 percent, respectively, for male managers. On the other hand, while only 2 percent of women managers had fathers who were farmers, this rate was 16 percent for men. Women managers seem to come from families in which the father has a prestigious occupation such as bureaucrat or manager in a large corporation.

The women managers interviewed by Sönmez all received their degrees from highly prestigious high schools or universities. Most went to schools with "Anglo-Saxon" traditions. Some pursued their college education or graduate studies in the United States or the United Kingdom.

While the education policy and ideology of the Turkish Republic have promoted equal opportunity in education, in practice, higher-level education has been possible mainly for boys, or for children of urban, middle, or upper-class families.

The State Planning Institute Report on the problems of university education indicated that university education is basically available for the children of rich bureaucrats. Only 5.7 percent of university students belonged to blue-collar families. Furthermore, 85 percent of this 5.7 percent were boys.[37]

Kazgan noted that the income of a family plays a more significant role in the education of girls; when the income of a family is small, the family does not allocate money to the education of girls, and if there is little money that can be spared for education, it goes to the education of boys.[38]

While it is possible to find male managers with rural or lower socioeconomic origins, women managers come from urban and at least middle-class families. Women managers in Turkey reflect a paradoxical situation: on the one hand, they hold a low status because of their sex; on the other hand they enjoy a high status derived from the position of their families. Male managers at the top consciously or unconsciously attempt to preserve the prestige of their top management team. Thus they are inclined to protect it from the entry of women. However, male managers also hold a distinct class identity and high socioeconomic status.[39] What, then, is the reaction of top male managers and capitalists to the candidacy of women for top management positions? If they have a choice, do these males prefer members of their sex from lower socioeconomic segments, or are they more comfortable with women who share their prestigious backgrounds?

Data from the United States indicate that social class provides a stronger basis of status than sex. Regardless of their sex, managers from families with higher socioeconomic status are promoted more frequently as a result of the mentoring support they receive in their organizations.[40] Moreover, Turban and Jones state that superior-subordinate similarity is positively related to subordinate performance; subordinates who share similar social values and skills with the senior executives receive more informal and formal support, which manifests itself in greater performance.[41]

Given that socioeconomic groups in Turkey have distinct divisions between them, it can be expected that socioeconomic background would play a significant role in the formation of organizational relationships such as mentoring. Most probably because of this reason, almost all top women managers interviewed described "not experiencing any disadvantages of being a woman in moving to the top." Their ascribed characteristic—being born to a family of high status—provided them with the advantage.

A Wife and a Mother

While there is limited data on the demographic characteristics of women managers in general, a few available published studies pointed out that most of the Turkish top women managers were married and had one or two children.[42]

In contrast, Hennig and Jardim's study of twenty-five top women managers in the United States showed that "none" of the women got married before their mid-thirties. Some got married after thirty-five, but no one gave birth to a child.[43] This finding indicates that the women managers had to make a "choice" between their careers and starting a family. Similarly, Alban-Metcalfe and Nicholson's study among British male and female managers in middle and senior management positions indicated that compared with men, women were less likely to be married, almost four times more likely to be divorced, and more likely to be childless.[44]

Given the immense household demands on married women, most women feel the need to make a choice between their careers and household engagements. Wiersma summarized that in the West, role overload creates a need to cycle roles, namely to decide when to start a family relative to one's career progress.[45] Because a child will bring much stress to the lives of working couples, waiting to have children has become more common. Çitçi's study of the Turkish public sector showed that the primary reason for women to leave their jobs was the household demands and child care.[46] For a Turkish woman, leaving her job when she gets married is the accepted norm. Zeytinoğlu pointed out that Turkish legislation encourages this phenomenon.[47]

A 1992 study compared twenty female and twenty male Turkish white-collar workers and found that marriage had an adverse affect on women's careers. In this study, while 50 percent of women indicated that marriage had a negative impact on their careers, not a single man mentioned such an effect. In addition, 75 percent of women indicated that being a mother influenced their careers negatively, while only 5 percent of men pointed to a negative effect of being a father on their work life.[48]

For top women managers in Turkey, the picture is different than for either Western top women managers or other Turkish women employed in unskilled or semi-skilled jobs. Turkish top women managers fulfill their roles as managers, wives, and mothers all at the same time mainly by delegating the housework and child-rearing responsibilities to low-paid maids.[49] Another study conducted in 1992 showed that "all" of the thirty women middle managers included in the sample had a maid working at their house.[50]

Several social scientists note that Turkish society is characterized by its gender hierarchy.[51] While gender hierarchy is present in Western societies as well, it functions differently in the Turkish case. For a woman in the higher socioeconomic strata, having a husband increases the probability of moving to a senior position, rather than serving as a hindrance; it not only adds the extra status needed by a woman to be accepted as a member of the top team, but by holding prestigious positions themselves, husbands facilitate the entry of their wives to the "network" of elite professionals.

Consequently, it can be proposed that the social structure prevalent in Turkish society allows Turkish women to pursue a career at the upper levels of the organizational hierarchy and at the same time continue to be wives and mothers. Thus, the Turkish top women in management do not fit Göle's definition of a recently emerging profile of Western "masculine women" who abdicate their roles as mothers and wives and choose to be successful in their careers.[52]

CONCLUSION

Top management positions are available only to a very restricted group of women in Turkish society. Only those women with a middle or upper socioeconomic background have the opportunity for a high-quality and high-level education. Their families provide them with the necessary education, status, and motivation to achieve that are required and essential for women to be promoted to senior executive positions. These women are also able to marry men from the upper social strata. Consequently, marriage provides them with added status and helps them to move up. Wide income gaps in the society allow them to hire inexpensive "domestic" help. Yet, top women still feel the urge to maintain low visibility, and they avoid public appearances, a "too-feminine" appearance, and controversial ideas. However, despite their low visibility, top women have strong personalities. They have self-perceptions that are beyond the passive role that society expects from women. They seem to be using this strength in a strategy that is not threatening to the male establishment but that helps them to open individual paths to success.

Notes

1. For a discussion on how attitudes influence women's representation in managerial positions, see Kabasakal, 1991.
2. Dilber, 1981.
3. Özbaşar and Aksan, 1976.
4. Tabak, 1989.
5. Arbak, et al., 1995.
6. Kabasakal, Boyacıgiller, and Erden, 1994.
7. "Kadınlar," 1990.
8. Coşar, 1978.
9. Acar, 1991.
10. Şenesen, 1994; "İTÜ 2001 Atılım Projesi," 1997.
11. Koray, 1991.
12. Sönmez, 1992.
13. Although an accepted definition of top management includes the general manager and the vice-presidents, the list rendered by the *Ekonomik Panorama* survey included few department heads, which would be considered as middle-management positions.
14. Alpman, 1992.
15. For discussions on the differences between female and male cultures, see Mumby and Putnam, 1992; Smircich, 1985; Tannen, 1990.

16. Chodorow, 1978.
17. Z. Arat, 1994c. Arat described how the Turkish public schools strictly applied policies that disguised any signs of femininity in their female students.
18. Rafaeli and Pratt pointed out that dress can reflect a variety of organizational dynamics. They argued that dress style may suggest attributes, particularly of status and power. In their description, suits are formal and "male" and indicate traits associated with power. See Rafaeli and Pratt, 1993.
19. Kuşçuoğlu, 1992.
20. Sönmez, 1992.
21. Cerrahoğlu, 1993.
22. Kanter, 1977.
23. Üsdiken and Özmucur, 1994.
24. Sunar, 1982.
25. Bem, 1974.
26. Gürbüz, 1988.
27. Kabasakal, Sunar, and Fişek, 1993.
28. Sönmez, 1992.
29. Hennig and Jardim, 1977.
30. This unpublished research was a 1993 study conducted in the Women in Management course at the Management Department of Boğaziçi University. The study analyzed the demographic characteristics of women top and middle managers.
31. Acar, 1983. Acar's study of Turkish women in academia indicated that they were either the first or last child, and that they received special attention from their families. Furthermore, these women academics pointed out that their fathers had played a special role in helping them to choose their professions.
32. Balkır, 1991.
33. Adler and Izraeli, 1988; Kandiyoti, 1981; Torki, 1985.
34. O'Neil, et al., 1980.
35. Sönmez, 1992.
36. Arbak, et al., (forthcoming).
37. Altındal, 1975.
38. Kazgan, 1979.
39. Several researchers argued that senior managers belong to upper socioeconomic groups and strongly identify with their class. For

discussions on this topic, see Blau and Duncan, 1967; Dilber, 1981; Stinchcombe, 1965.

40. Whitely, Dougherty, and Dreher, 1991.

41. Turban and Jones, 1988.

42. Sönmez, 1992; Tabak, 1989.

43. Hennig and Jardim, 1977.

44. Alban-Metcalfe and Nicholson, 1984.

45. Wiersma, 1994.

46. Çitçi, 1979.

47. Zeytinoğlu, 1994; and Zeytinoğlu in this volume.

48. This was a 1992 study conducted in the Women in Management course at the Management Department of Boğaziçi University. Similar results were obtained in a study conducted by Davidson in the U.K. Davidson found that compared to married male managers, married female managers experienced higher pressures due to career and spouse/partner conflicts, career/home conflicts, and career and marriage/childbearing conflicts. See Davidson, 1989.

49. Öncü, 1979.

50. This was a 1992 study conducted in the Women in Management course at the Management Department of Boğaziçi University.

51. For discussions on gender hierarchy and male supremacy in Turkish society, see Fişek, 1993; Kağıtçıbaşı, 1982; Kandiyoti, 1988b; Kıray, 1976.

52. Göle, 1991.

ELEVEN

ISLAMIST WOMEN IN TURKEY: THEIR IDENTITY AND SELF-IMAGE

Aynur İlyasoğlu

TURKEY HAS BEEN WITNESSING the formation of a distinct Islamic female identity within the last two decades. This process has corresponded to the increase in the public visibility and economic influence of Islamist groups that challenge the foundations of the Republican regime: its hegemonic ideology, assumptions regarding modernity, and concomitant values. Through this new politization of Islam, social groups that used to live at the fringes of society have articulated a comprehensive worldview and endorsed a lifestyle that encompasses the spheres that have not been totally penetrated by the hegemonic Republican ideology. They have done this so successfully that they now appear as a counter-elite in mainstream politics. Islamism, with all its economic, political, and ideological stands, is now an urban-metropolitan phenomenon in Turkey.[1] During this period of growth, Islamism has reinforced its social and political opposition to Republicanism, with significant implications for identity politics. Within the Islamist sphere, while the terms of identity politics have been mainly configured by Islamist men—by defining Islamic "propers" for women, the domain of religion, and policy alternatives, they lead the process that is referred to as the "politicization of Islam"—women have been living the politics of identity, especially gender identity, with all the repercussions.

In this chapter, I will discuss the formative elements of the Islamist female identity and examine the images produced by Islamist women in their own literary writings. I will start with a brief review of the sociohistorical roots of cultural plurality and polarity of identities in Turkey and give an account of the current Islamist manifestations, particularly the new veiling practiced by Islamist women. Then I will try to delineate how Islamist women experience the repercussions of the Islamic faith and its constraints in their lives in terms of their womanhood. For this purpose, I will employ the information gathered through in-depth interviews with twenty-one women who have embraced the Islamist attire and way of life. As another source of self-description by Islamist women, I will discuss the female images in the literary works of Islamist woman writers. I will focus on two issues and propose a redefinition of paradigms for analyzing them: (1) the relationship between the body, self, and identity; and (2) the new veiling of Islamist women as a symbol of the definition/redefinition of transitivity between the public and private spheres.

THE SYMBOLISM OF ATTIRES
AND CULTURAL POLARITY IN TURKEY

The Westernization policy of the Ottoman Empire, also followed by the Turkish Republic, always treated the symbolic value of attire as one of the main criteria in assessing the "dose" of Westernization and the nature of "Westernized Turkish" identity. During the late Ottoman period, this concern evolved around women's attire. The discussion of the issue was centered around two principal concerns: (1) identity, whether it should be based on nationality or religion; and (2) the sexual mores such as virtue and chastity, especially as they applied to women. Starting in the late nineteenth century, Westernization of women's attire and accessories became more and more evident.[2]

The early years of the Republic, essentially the 1920s, can be viewed as a period of transition in many respects, including in women's attire. The earlier styles required covering the head with tulle and the body with capes; typically suits were worn under the capes. Later, overcoats replaced capes, and along with suits they became more and more popular, especially in big cities and among the wives of the bureaucratic elite.[3] In fact, the suit became a symbol of the elite women, the "daughters of the Republic," who were educated, employed in professional occupations, and expected to serve their country. In line with the definition of women's role in the new society, wearing a suit embodied feelings of security and chastity. Moreover, as argued by Ayşe Durakbaşa, this almost gender-neutral outfit served as a "veiling of their sexuality"[4] when women entered the public sphere. Nevertheless, the changes in women's attire and the adaptations of Western styles were gradual and not sanctioned by law; no equivalent of the 1925 Hat Law that banned all headgear but the Western hat for men existed for women's attire.

The successive periods of reforms that have attempted to build a nation-state with a modernist perspective have not been completely successful. The top-down strategy and monolithic approach of the Republican leadership alienated some segments of the society, and the praxis of modernization reinforced differentiations within society and created an ideological center and peripheries. The Islamic reaction to the "secular" center manifested itself in the form of a nativist response that defended authenticity, both in cultural and political terms.

The Islamist radicalism of the last two decades, however, takes a stand different from the Islamic opposition of the past. It does not only react to the modernist project, but it also puts forward a new and well-articulated identity that affects both cultural and political spheres, always involves gender, and stimulates the politics of identity. This more recent form of Islamism, organized in party structures and associations, also differs from the political Islamic stand of the 1960s and 1970s, which was articulated under a general "rightist" banner.

The new veiling of Islamist women in Turkey is a part, and an essential part, of this new Islamism; it is the main instrument of identity politics. While Islamist men may identify the distinct nature of new Islamism in its economic policy alternatives in the public sphere, the identity politics of Islamism, defined in terms of gender roles, have been more essential for women.

As stated earlier, the style of women's attire has always been interpreted as one of the most overt symbolic expressions of the degree of modernity. Thus, within the modern sectors of the Turkish Republic—mainly the major industrial and commercial cities—wearing a headscarf has been treated as the lack of modernity and associated with the peasantry. Although all village women wear some kind of a scarf to cover their head, a headscarf is not a garment used only by rural women. Women who migrate to cities, especially the first generation, continue to cover their hair with a headscarf, albeit a different kind that better fits the city style. For women who live in Anatolian cities and towns, or those of Anatolian origin who have a longer history of settlement in big cities, wearing a scarf is also an essential part of their clothing, especially outside the home. This habitual use of headscarfs is a convention; women do not show a careful effort to hide the hair, and the edges of scarves are not long enough to cover the bosom—thus, they fall short of following the new Islamist dictum. Nevertheless, these women would not go outside and enter the public domain without it. In a symbolical way, the headscarf is an essential part of their identity, relevant to the distance that they have kept from modernism as it has tried to expand. By the same token, as they enter the modern space, mainly as the employees of the urban and upper strata, their head scarves are a sign of their rural origin and hence their low status. Thus, sometimes the new generations of women from these immigrant families break with the tradition by leaving aside the headscarf. All these decisions, as symbolic as they may be, have contributed to the formation of cleavages in terms of cultural and social stratification.

THE NEW VEILING

The new veiling of today's Islamist women is based on the principles of *tesettür,* the Islamic dress code for women as proclaimed by the current Islamist movement and ideology. It requires the complete concealing of the hair, the bosom, the arms, the legs, and the curvatures of the body. The outdoor attire that follows these principles typically includes wearing a loose and long raincoat that is accompanied by a large scarf that tightly frames the face and wraps the hair, shoulders, and the chest. This distinct style is particular to Islamist women, and it expresses that its holder abides with the rules of *tesettür.* Apart from the uniformity of its basic features, variations may be seen in the color and style of the coat and scarf, reflecting a sort of esthetic consideration and a feminine touch.

Esthetic and stylistic concerns are real and most evident in the display of *tesettür* fashions on podiums and the emergence of a specialized ready-wear industry. The headscarfs are sometimes chosen in attractive colors and designs and treated as the main instruments of chicness. Some young women, especially university students, wear pants, sometimes jeans (which are popular among that age group anyway), under their loose raincoats. Thus, even though there is anonymity in covering up the head and hiding the curvatures of the body in loose overcoats, stylistic choices reflect femininity and a limited individuality that circumscribe the level of anonymity. What we see here is not only the convergence of principles that operate at three levels, but also women's attempt to integrate them: the principles based on Islamic precepts on women's attire; the patriarchal codes related to the modesty of women; and the prevailing consumerist code of chicness—all are redefined together in a new, Islamist way.

This new dress code reflects a new female identity that does not fit into previously defined "modern" and "traditional" molds. First of all, the new veiling by the Islamist women alters the social implications of the headscarf. Traditionally, the headscarf has been associated with low status and rural origin. However, the most fervent and militant advocates of new veiling have been the university students in big cities—who organized mass demonstrations in the late 1980s and protested the ban on the "new" Islamic attire at universities. Thus, the preferences and behavior of these educated and active women separate them from the "traditional women."

On the one hand, one of the main premises of the current Islamism centers around the repudiation of assumed wrongs in society (such as moral decay, women becoming instruments of consumerism, pornography, etcetera) that are perceived as the consequences of the "alien/Western influences." On the other hand, the leading advocates of the new Islamist female identity have come forward with a proposal to modify the prevailing "traditional woman image" and to elevate women's status. Even though this female identity is formed within a religious framework, women assert themselves by demanding higher education, employment, career opportunities, etcetera. In this sense, their public stance constitutes a subjective rupture from the roles defined within the boundaries of "traditionalism," and Islamist women situate themselves within the "modern condition." We can argue that, while criticizing modernism and its effects on women in their rhetoric, they nonetheless participate in a process of identity formation that takes place within the space defined by the condition of modernity. In other words, by using the means created by the modernization process, they attempt to revise modernism and develop their own version.

THE ELITE ISLAMIST WOMEN

In an effort to gain insight into how Islamist women experience womanhood and faith, interviews with twenty-one Islamist women, who identified themselves as such, were conducted during the summer of 1990. All the women interviewed hold a degree from a higher education institution, and at the time of the interviews, they were all engaged in gainful employment. All but three were married. The average age in the group was thirty-six, and they had been living in İstanbul for an average of twenty years. Thus, they had been either city-born or highly urbanized.

The mothers of the women in the study were all primary school graduates and none of them was engaged in gainful employment. Therefore, all of the interviewees belong to the first generation of women in their families who acquired higher education degrees and gainful employment. Although this is not unique to this group of women, Islamist women's position is significantly different from that of other first-generation educated women. Secular women have not been short of role models in the modernized and secular section of the society, even if there were none in their own families. The Islamist women, on the other hand, have had to invent a new model by combining mainstream elements of modernity such as higher education and gainful employment with adherence to the Islamic faith. Nevertheless, almost all religious mothers were described as being supportive of their daughter's education and desire to work outside the home; in fact, they had provided help when needed. When the women were asked about the nature of their relationships with their mothers and daughters—eight of them had daughters—however, a considerable difference was observed in their responses. While they mentioned having "a distant relationship based on respect" with their mothers, they described their relationships with their own daughters as "a closer, more tolerant relationship, based on love." This kind of change in intergenerational relationships is in line with the general trend observed in Turkey.[5] Thus, we can argue that this segment of society is not deviant in regard to mother-daughter relationships.

Except one of the respondents, all women in the study grew up in nuclear family households.[6] Moreover, when they were asked about how they met their husband, only a few indicated that their marriages were arranged by their families. Most of the respondents replied that they had met their husbands in circles of friends either during their university years or in their workplaces. It seems that the arranged marriage model, which is usually associated with traditionalism, is not widely observed by the elite Islamist women. However, how the partners had met seems to be related to the spouses' relationship and respective roles in their marriages: while women who had arranged marriages indicated that their husbands did not assume many household responsibilities, other than undertaking some small repairs and paying the bills, women who had chosen their husbands described more egalitarian relationships and shared responsibilities of domestic chores. Although the limited scope of this research does not allow us to make any generalizations about the changes in the Muslim household structures, the findings contradict the common references and cliché statements about the "women's slavery in Islamic marriages" and call for further research.

The husbands of the respondents were also university graduates, and they either occupied well-to-do positions in the private or public sector or were self-employed. Together as partners, such couples compose an elite group in the society that may be evaluated as contributing to the formation of an Islamic elite at the center.

The women themselves were working in various fields as medical doctors (4), teachers (4), lawyers (2), civil-servants (3), clerks (2), pharmacists (1), and preachers at mosques (1); and a few were self-employed (4). With half of them holding professional occupations, they again fit the general employment pattern in Turkey, which has been characterized by a significant representation of women in professional occupations.[7] As noted earlier, what is different for this group of women is their effort to reconcile the role of being a working/professional woman with an Islamic female identity. In fact, the majority of the women in the study were either employed in workplaces that tolerated Islamic attire or they were self-employed. Two of the women who worked as clerks in government offices described in agony how they had been wearing their scarves outside but removing it in the office, since the government had banned the garment for its employees.

When the women in the study were asked to specify their reasons for seeking employment outside the home, they unanimously responded with a reference to the "social significance of *working*." They also listed altruistic reasons such as "helping people," "to be beneficial," and "to serve people." A particularly articulate response by a lawyer expressed the overall sentiment of the group: "To use the advantage that my profession brings to me in the service of my beliefs and to serve people."

The Islamist women's approach to gainful employment took a tone somehow different from the "assertiveness" and "individualism" attributed to the women in the Western context. Their "determination" and "motivation" stemmed from, or was justified by, the "social significance" of working outside the home. The priority they assigned to the "social significance" of their work seems to serve two purposes. On the one hand, it can be used as a point of departure and a negation of the prevailing model of the "modern woman." On the other hand, it attempts to resolve the conflicting identities of "being a working woman" and "being a woman of her home" and to merge them into a new one, especially since the latter has always been kept as the core of their identities. This emphasis on the social contribution of their work ("enlightening," and "serving" people, doing work of "social use," etcetera), however, resembles the position taken by the modernist, enlightened elite women of late nineteenth-century Ottoman society. Those women had also tried to reconcile their demands for a space in the public arena with the principles of Islam.[8]

However, an issue frequently raised by the women in the study—in answering the question "How should the family of a working woman be?"—was "the difficulty of balancing" domestic responsibilities with work life. It seems that the harsh realities and difficulties of being a working woman and the priority assigned "to be a good mother and a housewife" clashed and generated contradictory dynamics within the daily lives of these women. "Ideally speaking," one of them said, "either one shouldn't get married or if married, she and her family should [be willing to] live in poverty like a Hindu *fakir.*"

Some of the interviewees mentioned the setbacks that they had been encountering in their professional lives because of their *tesettür.* One of the lawyers stated that she had to work in the back office and was not allowed to appear in court because of her attire. A physician, a pathologist, indicated that after being expelled from the university hospital where she had been pursuing an academic career, she ended up in a hospital laboratory that was run by Islamists. Another physician, a gynecologist, also sought an academic career upon her graduation from medical school. When she became an assistant at a university hospital, she redesigned the white physician shirt according to the Islamic attire requirements and completed her work outfit by wearing a white turban that covered her hair. Her colleagues and the administration, however, disapproved her attire. Her male colleagues told her that they wanted to see a pleasant woman around and that she had a disturbing appearance. In order to resolve the problem, she consulted the *müftü* of İstanbul (the highest religious authority in the jurisdiction) and pleaded with him to issue a *fetva* (a religious decree) that would have permitted her to wear a wig, instead of a head cover, while working in the hospital. She failed to obtain her request and had to resign from her university post. However, she did not give up, or "vanish" as she put it.

Due to the pressure from her family, this woman agreed to an arranged marriage in her thirties; even though her own plan had been to remain single—a highly unconventional position that undermines both the national and Islamist norms. After getting married, she settled in a district of İstanbul that was largely populated by conservative Islamists, and started to practice medicine as a private practitioner. In her mid-forties at the time of the interview, she was living and working in the same apartment building; she had converted one of the apartments into a doctor's office. Her patients were mostly Islamist women who lived nearby. As the mother of two young children, she had to go back and forth between the two apartments, her home and her office. Among several other women who were struggling to establish this balance between work and home as an Islamist woman, her life seemed to be the most integrated, with all of its components converging rather than pulling her in different directions. The Islamist woman identity that she embraced—faithful to religion yet economically independent—was challenged and negated first by society in the public domain (by excluding her from the university hospital and ending a prospective academic career), then by her family within the private domain (by forcing her to marry). Nevertheless, she managed to work around them; she now lives in this crater-like space, which reinforces her identity, and the society has fewer, if any, means to reach her. It should be noted that although she was forced to leave her university position, her husband was able to work in a state institution and move up the bureaucratic ladder. Their diametrically different work experiences in the public sector imply that while Islamist men are able to blend in or assert themselves, the women who observe *tesettür* are more restricted and have less room for political maneuvers.

Despite their common ideology and similar experiences, the women in the study also showed some differences. When they were asked to explain how they had developed their new religious orientation, they provided responses that seem to vary by age. The older respondents (those who were over forty), referred to the "anxiety," "disturbance," and "isolation" that they had experienced during their university years as factors that had led them to adopt *tesettür* and the Islamic way of life. The younger respondents, those who were university students in the 1980s, mentioned the need to "take a stance" or to "belong to a group" as their reasons for adopting *tesettür*. These two generational clusters seem to correspond to the political changes that occurred in the country during their formative years.

The military regime that followed the military coup of 1980 was determined to "sterilize" the society and eliminate the polarized ideologies of the pre-coup period. Moreover, in an effort to restrain radical (especially leftist) ideologies, the state used religion and employed certain education policies that increased the time and resources spent on religious education at public schools and made such classes mandatory for some grades. The 1980s were also characterized by the liberation of cultural and political identities that had been previously undermined by or subordinated to classical ideologies of the left and right. The Islamist position, once blended into the platform of the right-wing political parties, differentiated itself by pursuing a more autonomous discourse. Thus, these changes in the political and ideological climate of the country established a drastically different set of values and a particular socialization process for the younger generation.

The interviews revealed that, regardless of their age, for this rather elite group of Islamist women, covering and concealing the hair is no longer a sign of low status, but a symbol of a higher religious morality and a strong personality. It also reflects their elevated social position, similar to what Ernest Gellner observes elsewhere:

> Contrary to what outsiders generally suppose, the typical Muslim woman in a Muslim city doesn't wear the veil because her grandmother did so, but because her grandmother did not: her grandmother in her village was far too busy in the fields, and she frequented the shrine without a veil, and left the veil for her betters. The granddaughter is celebrating the fact that she has joined the grandmother's betters, rather than her loyalty to her grandmother.[9]

ISLAMIC WOMANHOOD
AND ITS REPRESENTATION IN WOMEN'S FICTION

The emergence of Islamist women intellectuals has led to the creation of a significant body of literature that is concerned with the problems of contemporary Turkish women. Mostly in the form of novels, the texts not only reflect how Islamist women identify and perceive women's issues, but they also provide a "self-portrait" or a description of the "ideal Islamist woman." Through the female characters' experiences of womanhood, these writings contribute to the process of creating a self-image by Islamist women.

A novella titled *Müslüman Kadının Adı Var* (The Muslim Woman Has a Name), by Şerife Katırcı,[10] narrates the story of a young woman, Dilara. Dilara is from an Anatolian city and moves to a metropolis to study medicine. She joins an Islamist group in the university but pursues a quite independent life. She lives on her own and travels between her Anatolian city and the metropolis. Upon graduation from college, she is employed as a physician. She dedicates herself to her work because of its "social use," and she is particularly proud of serving the pilgrims to Mecca. The story ends with her reaching the decision to marry the man who incited her interest in Islam and with whom she fell in love.

This idealized character—who not only makes the right decisions but is also able to fulfill her dreams by becoming a "socially useful," strong and active Islamist woman—closely resembles the idealized female characters of the late Ottoman and early Republican era, especially Feride, the heroine of Reşat Nuri Güntekin's *Çalıkuşu*.[11] Like Feride, who serves the country by teaching and enlightening backward and poor Anatolian children, Dilara also ventures on a career to serve the public, particularly pious Muslims. Both women not only take an independent stance and undermine prevailing cultural norms, but their stance is taken to serve an ideal and is thus justified. While Feride is the pioneer patriot, Dilara is the faithful Muslim who tries to revive the tradition of socially and politically active Islamist women—women such as Prophet Mohammed's wife Ayşe, who lived during the initial years of Islam and is believed to have been outspoken and active in public life. Although Dilara seems to be following religious figures as role models, we may argue that her dedication to the "social good" is more a reflection of the values promoted and the opportunities created (such as the emphasis on women's education and women's role in modernizing the nation) by the Republican reforms than a continuation of the Islamic rhetoric.

Katırcı's novella ends without telling us anything about Dilara's marriage. However, Cihan Aktaş's two stories in *Üç İhtilâl Çocuğu* (The Child of Three Revolutions)[12] are illustrative of the marriages of young idealist Islamists like Dilara. The middle-aged women presented in these two stories were once radical activists involved in the Islamist movement, and they imagined their marriages would be ideal relationships of "ideological companionship" that would further their service to the Islamic cause. They expected their marriages to be completely different from traditional ones in every way and at every stage. One of the characters explains that she rejected the idea of wearing a wedding gown to break from tradition.

However, their marriages turn out to be quite different from what they expected, and just as traditional as all other marriages. In both stories the Islamist women are characterized as disillusioned by the domestic roles that they had to assume. They complain about the repetitive and boring days, as well as never-ending domestic duties and responsibilities, and are afraid that "they will vanish." Their restricted roles of housewife and mother fail to fulfill the envisioned "Islamic woman" identity. Confined to the routine of domestic life, they become silent and apathetic. The people around them, however, are content with their passivity. Fed up with the situation, the women search for a way out, a way to restore their faith and revive their lives accordingly. Their husbands, however, are involved in their own work and worldly activities; they are interested and engaged in politics and business. Their faith and lives are in harmony, and they do not understand the women's inner conflicts or their struggle to establish a new identity. The women are the ones who problematize the incongruities between being a "housewife" and "the enlightenment" that they acquired during their course of university radicalism.

These stories, which start with women's inner voices, are concluded with episodes in which they speak out, and in their own voices. They recover their voices from the past, from the years of radicalism and university activism. Within that activism, women reformulated their identities and contested the traditions; they were "partners" with men and expected to maintain that camaraderie as husbands and wives. One of the characters contemplates her husband and her marriage:

> This self-indulging man, who is fussy about his looks, work and meals, and cautious in interacting with other people, was once a fearless young man who wouldn't have cared about his life. . . . How could she explain it to him? How could she explain how disconnected their worlds were? Or how the two of them were living the life of one. . . . This was not fusion, not at all. . . . Her husband had a life that excluded his wife. His was a world that was connected to the past, today, everybody and everything. But the woman, in order to be able to stay, she had to live by leaving the past behind.[13]

The women depicted in these stories seem to be living through the antinomies between the existentialist stance that they developed during their radicalization in the Islamist movement and the patriarchal norms and gender regulations that prevail in the country and in its Islamist communities. For women, being an Islamist means a complete restructuring of their lives, while men hardly experience any change. The family life, "the staunch fortress," as it is described in one of the stories, provides men with the support to excel in the public domain, but it confines women within the boundaries of tradition and makes them silent and apathetic. In order to break these boundaries, women cling to their faith, once again, in seeking their voices. After all, it was their faith that once equipped them with a defiant voice. The theme of "women demanding their own voices" is emphasized in the fiction of Islamist woman writers because having a voice proves to be the most vital element in the pursuit of an Islamist vision. It allows them to reformulate an identity and self-image by reassessing the limits of the traditional alternatives.

CURVATURES OF THE BODY
AND CONTOURS OF THE SELF

Islam, as a religion, is quite different from Christianity in its approach to human sexuality. Sexual activity is considered legitimate not only for the purpose of procreation but as a means of psychological satisfaction. It is treated as a pleasure that should be enjoyed within the legitimate union of marriage. Thus, sexual activities are not treated as "sins" as long as they are proper, and improper conduct induces "shame" rather than "sin." Similarly, the body, "the flesh," is also not perceived as "sinful," as it is in the Christian formulation. Islam requires an adherent to attend to his or her own body, continuously and carefully, and offers detailed prescriptions.[14] In addition to keeping the body clean, these prescriptions also include guidelines that apply to the covering of some parts of the body both for men and women. In the case of women, it is suggested that the clothing be closely related to understanding the body as a physical entity, as the flesh that is sensuous to its every cell. Therefore, the curvatures of the body are not neutral in any way; they are sensuous, too, just like *ten*.

The Turkish word *ten* is hardly a synonym of the English word "skin," which denotes mainly a physical, biological area and thus corresponds to *deri*. *Ten*, however, connotes both the "skin" and beyond, the surface of the body that is an arena of interacting forces of sensations, sexual drives, sensualities, and desire. Moreover, the body is more than a physical entity; it embodies both the sense of *self* and the *ten* and serves as a medium of interactions between the two. Therefore, a reconciliation between these two aspects of the body—the body that is the *ten,* and the body that is the self—is needed before the self is allowed to appear at the frontiers of the public and the private. Since the sense of self is closely related to the sense of body, it also dwells around the curvatures of the body; as the sense of self is construed, the body has to be construed, too. Thus, especially at the threshold of the "social" domain, the contours of self redefine the curvatures of the body. More importantly, for women, selfhood becomes the locus of interacting and fragmenting tendencies of gender ideologies and controls, as evident in the contradictory roles dictated by them.

In the case of Islamist women in Turkey, the pale, faded, and impaired contours of selfhood are modified and demarcated through *tesettür.* According to an Islamist woman writer, Cihan Aktaş, "clothing, by preserving the *ten,* achieves social harmony; in this sense, it may be evaluated as the fortress of the body and . . . for a Muslim woman . . . it makes her a social individual."[15] In fact, by employing a metaphoric expression, Aktaş argues that *tesettür* serves as a "home" that enables the woman to be a "social" individual.[16] Thus, *tesettür,* as the demarcating element of an Islamist woman's identity, is the zone of transition from the private to the public.

THE MEDIATION BETWEEN
THE PRIVATE AND THE PUBLIC

The discussions on women's entrance to the public domain, the duality created by the separation of the public from the private, and the various implications of these two issues have been on the agenda of Western feminists since the eighteenth century. These ideas have gained momentum along with the deconstructions of gendered notions in the late twentieth century.[17] As the private domain has begun to be studied for its own sake and history, the dualism perceived in Western cultures has been perpetuated in feminist work and generalized to describe other cultures as well. Although dualities may exist in other societies, they are likely to have different cultural connotations that should be clarified.

A duality in the Islamic culture, that is, a parallel and a functional equivalent of the private and public domains, can be observed in the separation of *mahrem* from *namahrem*. These terms are central to the formulation of the Islamic culture's essential lodging of the sex roles and sexual mores. They sort out the "allowed" from the "forbidden" for both men and women by identifying legitimate partners for marriage, "strangers" with whom one should avoid contact, etcetera. They encircle a lawful domain in which the interactions of men and women are regulated.

Apart from the necessity to understand the specific cultural configurations of public and private, another dimension, the *mediation* between these two spheres and the differential logic of that mediation needs to be addressed. In Turkey, both Islamist and "modern" women, living in a space coded by modernity, experience the differential impacts of the mediation and transitivity between the private and public spheres.

According to the modernization paradigm, the "modern condition" assumes an "automatic" transitivity between the two spheres; as women step into the public domain, it is assumed that the private sphere will have a similar transformation that modernizes sex roles, family structures, and intrafamily relations. However, when Islamist women enter the public domain for education or employment, by observing *tesettür*, they introduce *a definition for this transitivity* since they bring the values and definitions of the private, personal sphere (*mahrem*) into the public one. If *tesettür* is a symbol, it must be the symbol of this definition of the transitivity between the two spheres. These women mediate between the public and the private by diffusing the values of the private—as opposed to the modernization paradigm in which the changes in the public domain are expected to reconstruct the private. Consequently, women in *tesettür* create a space at the intersection of the public and the private that is "neutralized" and out of the subjective "reach" of the manhood. This demarcating strategy seems to be functioning as a strategy of "self-modernization" for Islamist women. They neither comply with the secluded role cast for the traditional woman nor follow the Republican code of modernity. Instead, they carve a space within the "modern space" in order to pursue *their own modernization,* which is secure and distant from *the* "modern condition."

Situated at the intersection between the public and the private, these women, in order to be able to define this transitivity and enable the transition, need a shield to protect the self. That shield is a new identity that is defined both in social and cultural terms. In the formulation of this identity, the close ties among the body, self, and identity become tighter and more visible. The image of a female in *tesettür* denotes protecting the body in the form of an encapsulated existence in the public domain. Moreover, it emphasizes the demarcation between these two domains and the Islamist woman's distinct identity. The demarcation operates simultaneously in three dimensions: between the Islamist and other women; between women and men; and between the "Western-modernist" and the "native-Islamist" perspectives. These overlapping demarcations strengthen cultural identity by establishing a multidimensional yet common ground and alter the duality between the "private self" and the "public self" that is coded by the modernity.

Davidoff argues that understanding the "public sphere(s)" and the slogan of "the personal is political" is central to the analysis of identity formation. According to her, key questions about the creation of *identity* have to be extended beyond family, home, and childhood, and the ragged frontiers between public and private must be recognized as a site where identity is formed (by ethnicity, race, and class, as well as gender).[18]

The current situation of Islamist women in Turkey may be an illustration of Davidoff's point, because their identity is constructed precisely through the mediation of the public and private spheres. If we borrow the words of the Islamist woman intellectual Cihan Aktaş, the process can be described as the "social participation by Muslim women both in family and society" and as "an attempt of re-socialization of an individual who becomes a Muslim, by starting with his or her self entity and expanding toward global *umma* [the community of believers]."[19] According to Aktaş, the crucial point for a woman is achieving an individual identity that demands social participation and allows her to maintain her sexual identity without being exploited sexually.[20] She argues that an independent personality for woman "is guaranteed by the Islamic doctrine."[21] Aktaş also takes a critical stance; she condemns the "patriarchal past" for confining women to the private sphere (presumably as a result of Western influences) and denounces Islamic concepts such as *fitne* and *fesad* (terms used to refer to the ills and chaos caused by uncontrolled female sexuality) that prevented women from participation in public life in the past. She writes,

> . . . the punishment against the possibilities of *fitne* must not reach to the levels of oppressing the condition of humanness of one human sex. The Koran has already defined the guidelines and penalties in order for people to eliminate *fitne* and to restore their *nefs* [the essence of one's soul, spirit, and life]. For women, the Islamic veil has been the guideline for her necessary appearance in public in accordance with her sexual specification. And the existence of the veil already finds its definition together with the existence of women in social life. In other words, veil, as a fact, is already related to *the social* in essence.[22]

What is meant by "veil as a fact" is the new veiling, *tesettür*. It is a demarcating symbol that serves to outline the Islamist gender identity. It is Islamic, as prescribed in Koranic verses, but it also marks the move from the "traditional woman image" to the "enlightened Muslim woman." It reflects the "emancipated" character of the latter, because it enables her to participate in public life through a process of "resocialization." Aktaş describes the enlightened Muslim woman as the one who carries the traits of the strong female characters in history: she is heroic, literate, courageous, honored, virtuous, and productive. The only difference lies in her Islamist character.[23] Aktaş also points out that the enlightened woman is the one who questions her condition by a conscious possession of her identity as a human being and as a woman. She is said to have social sensibility; unlike the traditional woman, she intends to examine and touch the world with her own eyes and with her own hands. She makes every effort to accomplish this and insists on changing the negative conditions surrounding her. Her relationship with men is not a hierarchical one. However, in her effort to assert herself in the light of Islamic correctness, she does not isolate herself from her community and family. She has the choice of getting married. If she chooses to do so, she will be a "good wife." What defines a "good wife," however, is not determined by her husband or marriage, but by the principles of Islam. Marriage is not an oppressive structure that sweeps away her past and remakes her life. It is sacred, just like motherhood. Neither of these, however, is an obstacle for her social involvement. She may do housework and other things such as embroidery, knitting, etcetera, but she does not devote herself to them or expect to be defined by them. She reads, writes, thinks, argues, and narrates. Even though she seeks education, she does not need to hold a university diploma to be considered enlightened; she can educate and remake herself by following in the footsteps of her heroic ancestors such as Kara Fatma, Nene Hatun, and Bombacı Emine.[24] All the ills that one can observe in contemporary marriages, the subordination of women and male supremacy, are attributed to the "traditionalism" that is meant to be dismantled by the enlightened vision of Islamist correctiveness.

Nevertheless, a basic premise of the traditional woman image is kept untouched; the enlightened Muslim woman is expected, or even guaranteed, to make a "good wife." The essence of gendered roles, women as "housewives," prevails, regardless of the "re-socialization of women in the public." This dualism, however, calls for a reconsideration of the basic assumptions underlying the polarity between "traditionalism" and "modernity," which treat the public participation of women as crucial to the process of modernization. Islamist women demand accesses to the public domain within an encapsulated existence construed according to the principles of the Islamic faith. They attempt to update (or revive the undistorted old) Islamic life and reconcile it with the opportunities open to women within the modern setting. What is intended in this process of "self-modernization" that redefines the frontiers of the public and private is the "emancipation" from the boundaries of traditionalism and the creation of a secure arena (through faith).

Deniz Kandiyoti comments on the relationship between subordination and identity formation:

> . . . Islam as an ideological system does provide some unifying concepts that influence women's experiences of subordination. These are vested in the culturally defined modes of control of female sexuality, especially insofar as they influence subjective experiences of womanhood and femininity . . . [and] cultural controls, [and] to the extent that they are intimately related to the construction of oneself as a gendered subject, [they] may engage a deeper level of self-definition, a level that

has to be acknowledged if we are to address the question of feminist consciousness in any meaningful way.[25]

Some analysts negate women's role in the radical Islam by defining the objectives of the ideology as "handing women the norms to live accordingly, as a recipe" and as "attracting them by offering them the task of 'transferring the ideology' as a non-private, leisure time activity."[26] Such an approach may be useful for underlining the still restricted social life of Islamist women, but it misses the clues necessary to understand the dynamics of self-definition, which Kandiyoti rightfully sees as essential to the construction of gendered subjectivity.

Notes

Author's note: This article is largely derived from my book *Örtülü Kimlik* (Veiled Identity), 1994. For an earlier, English version of the text, see my "Islamist Women: Elements in the Formation of an Identity," Ph.D. dissertation, Marmara University, İstanbul, 1993.

1. This phenomenon was emphasized first by Binnaz Toprak and confirmed by recent studies. See B. Toprak, 1981; Göle, 1991; İlyasoğlu, 1993.

2. During the War of Independence (1919-1923), the spokeswomen of the national cause organized and attended rallies with nationalistic fervor and addressed the audience in black *çarşaf* (an overgarment that covers both the head and the body and conceals the figure). Wearing black *çarşaf* was not a common practice in İstanbul at the time. The women's choice of wearing it may be interpreted as a symbol of the solemn conditions encountered by the nation. It might also have served as a tool of ensuring anonymity which also disguised the social inequalities among the women who were committed to the same (nationalist) cause. Finally, it might have been a means of concealing their femininity.

3. Taşcıoğlu, 1958.

4. Durakbaşa, 1987:90-93.

5. Kağıtçıbaşı, 1981, Part 3.

6. This is in line with the conclusion of Akile Gürsoy's survey study of a squatter housing district in İstanbul: living in a nuclear or extended family household is not related to the degree of religiosity. See Gürsoy, 1992.

7. Öncü, 1981.

8. See Demirdirek in this volume.

9. Gellner, 1992.

10. Katırcı, 1989. The title of the book itself is a commentary on a well-known feminist book, *Kadının Adı Yok* (Women Have No Name), by Duygu Asena, and it contrasts the status of Muslim women with that of Westernized "modern" women.

11. In this novel that was first published in 1922, during the War of Independence, Feride is depicted as an upper-class educated woman who escapes from her disappointing fiancé and her home in İstanbul and seeks satisfaction in using her knowledge to benefit the disadvantaged and to contribute to the national development.

12. Aktaş, 1991.

13. Aktaş. "Teşekkürü Hakettiniz Bay Yargıç," in *Üç İhtilâl Çocuğu,* pp. 18-21; translation mine.

14. For a discussion and a comparative analysis of human sexuality in Islam and Christianity, see Boudhiba, 1985.

15. Aktaş, 1988:167.

16. Aktaş, 1988:167.

17. Davidoff, 1995.

18. Davidoff, 1995.

19. Aktaş, 1992:14.

20. Aktaş, 1992:22.

21. Aktaş, 1992:19.

22. Aktaş, 1992:28; translation mine.

23. Aktaş, 1988:81-103.

24. Interestingly, the women listed by Aktaş as the "exemplary women of the past" are the women who are known for their heroic acts during the War of Independence rather than for their Islamist beliefs or dedication.

25. Kandiyoti, 1981:319-320.

26. Üşür, 1989:82, 87.

TWELVE

RESTRUCTURING THE HOUSE, RESTRUCTURING THE SELF: RENEGOTIATING THE MEANINGS OF PLACE IN THE TURKISH SHORT STORY

Carel Bertram

THROUGH RADICAL GESTURES such as escape-holes cut through the walls or furnishings jettisoned to the junk-peddler, Turkish women are in the process of renegotiating the meaning of the Turkish house. These subversive acts that de-fetishize the house and signal a reevaluation of the role of the women perpetrators are literary acts, portrayed in Turkish short stories by Turkish women authors. The self-images of the women in these stories, or the images of these women that are conveyed to the reader, are bound systematically and symbolically to their domestic setting: systematically in that, as keepers of domestic order, Turkish women have been playing out an older concept of *fitne,* in which they were required to contain what was considered their innately seditious, socially dangerous nature; symbolically, because the house was the arena in which women acted out their internalization of this image. But in Turkish stories from the late 1960s through the 1980s, the house has become an arena of rebellion, an arena in which older images are being re-evaluated and destroyed, and where a new image of Turkish women is being created. This new image is still being formed, but these stories, in which women are the ones who protest, question, and offer considered alternatives, show the process of its formation.

In order to elicit the development of these new images and the new meanings that are being assigned to the Turkish house, I will look closely at four stories—"Taşralı," by Füruzan; "Monte Kristo," by Nazlı Eray; "Sessizlik," by Zeynep Karabey; and "Eskici," by Sevgi Soysal—using them as if they were ethnographies or the in-depth personal interviews used by David Canter in his work on the meaning of urban places.[1] The methodology used by the environmental psychologist Canter and other humanistic urban planners and theorists interested in urban or architectural meaning[2] connects place-related actions to the conscious, *intended* meaning of the people who use these places. Thus meaning is inflected by the connection between what one does in a place and what one knows and feels there. These actions and these feelings are bound together by a third variable, and that is how one is trained and thus expected or socially conditioned to both act and feel. Place meanings, then, are influenced by role expectations and role-related rules. For women, the meaning of the home is especially influenced by these role expectations.

In the stories I am analyzing, there is a pervasive reminder that a woman's social role and her "essence" have been conflated, so that how a woman should act and what her essential nature is are considered to be identical. All cultures assume, to some extent, that "role" is "natural," but I will suggest that the knot that binds role and essence in these stories is a specifically Turkish Islamic one that I relate to the concept of *fitne. Fitne* is an idea that implies seditious behavior; when it was applied to women it referred to their sexuality, that is, what was considered to be the "essential self." A woman's unleashed sexuality harbored the potential for disrupting social order, and therefore I argue that the role of women became one of keeping herself and her environment under control.

What is evident in the stories I am discussing, however, is that a female self-image that once was unified by the concept of *fitne* has begun to unravel as women's ideas and *intentional* actions defy or subvert older role expectations. The site of this unraveling of a unified self-consciousness is the home, for it is in the home that the meaning of social order is being contested. The feminist literary critic Elspeth Probyn calls this process of change a "renegotiating of locale," a process by which actions produce new and even unsanctioned meanings.[3] Our "locale," then, is the Turkish house seen not as a physical form but as a social construct, as "domestic space."

A concept of the house that privileges the meaning of women's nuanced emotional and relational activities calls for a methodology that includes deep and extended conversations with the women themselves, as well as an opportunity to observe their actions. Stories and novels offer an entrance into this type of layered information, for not only are the women's activities described, but their social circumstances and inner life is often addressed as well. In the stories I have chosen, the setting is the Turkish house, the protagonists are urban, educated Turkish women, and the house and its contents are deployed strategically to convey women's desire, fantasies, and constraints.

"TAŞRALI"

In her story "Taşralı"[4] ("The Girl from the Provinces," 1968), Füruzan writes of an aging widow whose self-identity was derived from her marriage to a great *Paşa*. She lives an orderly life with her servant in a similarly aging house, which is carefully maintained through devotion to the rituals of cleaning and serving . . . and to keeping up appearances. Into this clean and shiny shrine to tradition comes the niece from "the provinces," the "*taşralı*"[5] girl. She has come to the city hoping to go to college—and hoping for financial assistance in this project from her wealthy aunt. Her aunt, although educated herself, is antagonistic to the idea. "What's the use of it?" she wonders; only finding the right man or the right situation is practical.

The girl, although dreaming of an escape to the garden to read Dostoyevsky, is sent upstairs and ensconced in the "middle room," which has been scoured and prepared for her. Here she notices how stockings, nightgowns, and handkerchiefs have been meticulously folded in the closet, and we feel that her chances for college are slim when she laments that no doubt she, too, will soon "join those addicted to keeping this house tidy."

Thus, what is at issue for the "*taşralı*" girl is not her education at all, but whether or not she will buy into the sex-role stereotypes of the older generation; the issue of her education serves only as a marker of this conflict. In fact, the concept of *fitne* is pertinent to the conflict that Füruzan addresses and updates. But I would argue that *fitne,* with its implications of disorder and chaos, is turned on its head in this story (and the stories that follow) and revised in modern garb as the *valorization of neatness.*

Kandiyoti[6] has pointed out that while *Tanzimat* and Republican progressive elements were arguing for a Western-style education for women, there was a warning from conservative Islam: Westernization had an element of danger because it lead to licentiousness and could unleash the (feminine element) of *fitne,* the chaos resulting when men are tempted from the true path.[7] She points out that in the late Ottoman Turkish novel *fitne* was clearly associated with women's sexual identity and represented the potential for loss of control. This was a particular danger if it entered the home, where it could threaten the traditional Ottoman family system.[8] Certainly this was evident in the classical Ottoman or "Divan" literature of Fuzuli, who wrote that women were the disturbers of peace because their sole interest was in the destruction of their husbands in order to further their own survival.[9] By the time of the early Turkish Republic, a period that championed women's equality, readers are reminded that women's behavior has long held potentially disruptive consequences. A (female) character in Hüseyin Rahmi Gürpınar's novel *Sevda Peşinde* (The Pursuit of Desire) discusses what happens when a women is disloyal, saying, "If any such disloyalty is brought against a man, no action need be taken against him. But is it the same with women? If anything like this is heard about a woman, the world turns upside down."[10]

Women clearly understood that their role was to keep their temperament and thus society under control, which, in daily practice, was translated as keeping everything clean and neat. Gürpınar saw this as "the old way," in which keeping things neat was more important, even, than education. The mother-in-law in his book *Mutallaka* (The Divorced, 1927) shouts at her daughter-in-law scornfully on seeing her reading: "What? At it again? Are you reading a book? Before doing this, you should see the deplorable mess your room is in. No one would believe that room belongs to a woman."[11]

Interestingly, in the novels of the early Republic, men were not always accomplices in this objective. Certainly, they wanted to return to a clean home, but they also wanted a wife who was an intellectual equal. In 1909, the hero of Halide Edib Adıvar's *Seviyye Talip,* says,

> They [Turkish women] are satisfied with little: writing and reading newspapers and that is all. They spend the rest of their time confining themselves to their houses. The most natural thing for them is sewing, sweeping the house, keeping household things clean and in order. . . . While you try to discuss personal ideas with her, her dust-searching eyes concentrate on various parts of furniture. . . .[12]

The aunt in "Taşralı" had been educated to meet these new expectations, but she retained the valorization of neatness that signified an internalized acceptance of women's own nature as the site of chaos in the world; that is, their role, burdened by the potential for *fitne,* was to keep things in order. The home of the aunt is, in fact, a shiny monument to this mission of controlling and countering women's inherent nature, and it publicly attests to her success. Monuments, both physically and symbolically, stand for commonly held values. The fact that neatness is self-weighted as a highly desirable characteristic by women is attested to in studies of intergenerational sex-role standards and stereotypes of Turkish women in İstanbul.[13]

But the "*taşralı*" girl, who fears that she may join in the household's communal feminine *activity,* commits a subversive act in this monument and thus shows that she does not share in its values. As the maid shows her to her room, the girl experiences a moment of defiance: she has brought a scarf as a gift to the maid, but her mother had warned her not to present it herself; "Your aunt doesn't like intimacies with the people she has working for her," the mother says. But she hands it to the maid anyway when they are alone. This conscious act is a key moment in the story because the maid, by saying "Thank you miss," reminds the "*taşralı*" girl that the servant does not even know her name (neither do we), and that she is confined in a house that is emotionally empty. "I should know," she says, "that it isn't necessary to learn names in a house without intimacy."

The "*taşralı*" girl's rebellious actions redefine the house: it is no longer accepted as a monument to a shared way of life, for the "*taşralı*" girl does not share the values. Therefore the house becomes a dysfunctional fetish: along with the "*taşralı*" girl, the reader recognizes that the object (the house and its upkeep) has become more valued than the actions or human relations of which it is only an aspect. In this way, the "*taşralı*" girl is more than just a rebellious presence within the house, she has begun to rupture the paradigm of *fitne* and to suggest an alternative system by which a house and the identity of its women might be endowed with meaning.

"MONTE KRİSTO"

Another attempt to puncture the paradigm of *fitne* is portrayed, albeit differently, in Nazlı Eray's short story "Monte Kristo."[14] Here, Nabile, the "housewife who lived at 51 Orange Blossom Street, Lower Ayrancı," decides to escape from the dreariness of life with her husband and children by slowly digging a hole through the wall of her laundry-room. She had considered running away through the city streets, but the thought of getting lost had frightened her. And where would she go? To her friends who wanted to talk about starching their curtains? Yet whenever she heard the footsteps of the woman who lived on the other side of the laundry-room wall, she imagined high-heeled slippers trimmed with ostrich feathers—that is, a life not committed to endless cleaning and service; not one, like her own, in which her husband began to shout because a button was missing from his shirt and refused to even consider taking her to see foreign movies. And so that other, imagined life became the focus of her longing.

In preparation for her escape, she has her hair and nails done and puts on a black cocktail dress and silver pantyhose. She also sees that everything is in order in her own house—the children's room is neat, the fringes of the rug straightened, and the plants watered. These are to be her final acts in her old role. She then crawls through the hole that she has carefully prepared in the laundry-room wall and conceals it behind her with the laundry basket.

Once on the other side, Nabile finds herself in the private photography darkroom of the husband of the woman next door. It is he who discovers her, and after his initial astonishment he brings her food, and then perfume and fancy clothes, and then birth-control pills, and even flowers. She has completely abandoned her role as keeper of the daily details of the house; now *she* is "kept"; she has become the object, not the subject, and she likes it. Yet very shortly her obsession with the man's wife returns. But this time, she no longer imagines the wife's fancy clothes; rather, she begins to wonder what kind of cooking oil the woman uses, and what brand of laundry detergent. "Selahattin," she says, "I am full of curiosity. What does your wife wash the dishes with? What brand of dish-washing soap does she use? Is it Çiti or Pril? For heaven's sake, tell me, or I shall go mad."

The questions that Nabile asks about her lover's wife are not what the reader expects. And yet they are consistent with an imagination that is curtailed by her self-image: her identity had been defined by an idea of women whose fantasies and desires were confined to those of the keepers of the home. For this reason, the laundry room becomes the obvious site of her breakthrough, for it represents the ultimate female space, reifying the female role as keeper of neatness and cleanliness. Disappearing among the market streets just would not have the same meaning. By cutting through the laundry room, Nabile (hopes to) cut through her role as (for want of another term) "orderly." Furthermore, we understand that this neat home, which she abandons, is empty of emotional connection: her husband and children miss her at first, but after a few weeks she is replaced by, not surprisingly, a housekeeper.

The novelist and literary critic Güneli Gün suggests that the darkroom that Nabile enters is the perfect place in which to "develop."[15] But if we evaluate the darkroom in terms of how our "escapee" *intends* to act there, in the imagined finery of her neighbor, she would appear to have chosen (in an Islamic context) the darker side of femaleness, becoming a "*fitne-i âlem*," or "*fitne* of the world"—that is, a woman who, in classical Ottoman literature, was so beautiful that she could set the whole world in commotion: the ultimate sexual being. Thus, although her escape defines the issues for the reader, we are not at all certain that this is a successful escape for Nabile. Clearly her *anomie* exists at the disjuncture between place and desire, between what her home promises, if kept neat, and her yearnings. Yet although she has cut through the wall, she has not been able to cut through the internalization of her socially defined role, and her rebellious act is a failure. She does not know how to restructure either her own identity or that of the house but is left "in the dark," a prisoner of the paradigm; perhaps, in fact, legitimizing it—because she returns to it as a source of satisfaction.

"SESSİZLİK"

In a story by Zeynep Karabey, "Sessizlik," (Silence, 1980),[16] the protagonist does have a larger vision of her problem, and she actively wrestles with the dichotomy between her role and her essence. But her solution, though less "fabulist" and far less entertaining than Nabile's, is equally unsuccessful.

The story takes place in the apartment of a young couple with two small children. The woman is an author, trying to write her second book at home, at the dining-room table. And her husband is upset. First of all, the place is untidy: he cannot find his newspaper or his pajama tops, his toothbrush bristles are broken, and one of his slippers is missing. Furthermore, his wife has not been available to have sex with him for over a week. This woman is not performing her household duties: she is not holding things together; there is a potential for chaos.

The woman tries to explain to her husband that he has not been replaced by the story she is writing, but that in fact she has a place for everything. "You are just as important . . . and the children too . . . as my writing," she says. "The one thing I wanted was not to replace one thing with another . . ." But her words seem incomprehensible to him, and he does not accept her invitation to a dialogue that explores each other's needs, a dialogue that might lead to real intimacy. Instead, her explanation is followed by "a short silence—and an enormous emptiness." The feminist reader roots for her to rebel against this sex-anchored division of labor (and this reader-incitement may be the implicit message), but the renegotiation of the household that the woman envisions, the full modernist project of urban, educated, child-centered, and, especially, companionate families,[17] cannot be made alone. Her power is just not as large as her vision.

The man, in fact, ends this silence and emptiness (for himself) by leaving the house in the evenings to have an affair. It would appear that by not accepting traditional role-related priorities, the woman has endangered the family's cohesion and allowed *fitne* to be unleashed. In fact, the specter of *fitne* is intensified by the threat posed by an image of "the other woman," a *"fitne-i âlem"* whose perfume now permeates her husband's clothes. What can she do? Like the *"taşralı"* girl, she refuses to accept neatness and service as her prescribed world and thus an end in itself, for the household she values is not one judged on a scale of tidiness versus chaos, but on intimacy versus emotional emptiness. So she chooses to continue her rebellious activity of writing fiction in the evenings at the dining-room table. But by rebelling against her husband's definition of an orderly universe and her role in it, her house is emotionally drained, and she is left alone. One might ask: instead of accepting this silent house, should she have tunneled her way out through the laundry room? Through the *bed*room? Which room might be defined for her as the ultimate female space? The house itself? By staying at home and continuing her rebellious actions, she signals a belief in her own multifaceted identity and a belief in the potential of the home to reflect and nurture it. So she stays at home, finding in her writing the voice to fill the emptiness.

"ESKİCİ"

The woman protagonist in Sevgi Soysal's "Eskici" (The Junk Peddler)[18] does, in fact, leave home. But before she does, she attempts to lighten the burden of an emotionally empty house by tossing everything out. The story begins quite rationally with a woman throwing out the old newspapers that had accumulated in the kitchen, and then some empty bottles. But it soon takes on a frantic momentum as she calls for the junk peddler to come again and again and finally to take the whole lot: her clothes, her furniture, and even the appliances. What she is doing is not only both tragic and comic, it has a ring of validity. "Why do I have ten chairs?" she asks. "Whoever has ten people sitting down at once?" Furthermore, the upkeep of her possessions, their need for dusting and polishing, makes the house into a prison. In fact, she describes them as ugly, meaningless rocks that close off the tunnel to freedom.

She only balks at giving away her bed, because it represents a now-absent intimacy (we suspect a divorce). In fact, at this point she addresses directly the question, How can places or things be carriers of emotional meaning? While vacillating between whether or not to give the bed away, she asks, "How can one establish a connection between a human being and a bed . . . which is just a meaningless flat surface? It's like being attached to clean-sucked chicken bones and not throwing them into the garbage after eating a dinner together—it's the same thing." Nonetheless, she has difficulty letting go of the bed—identifying for us how items of material culture take on emotional charge because they exist at the crossroads of memory, symbolism, and the sacred. But the house is now empty of that intimacy, and therefore the things inside are, to her, as useless and senseless as chicken bones. Therefore, curtains, teapots, towels, and soup bowls, the "homey" items normally arranged and maintained by a wife, are assigned to their "rightful owner": the junk peddler, the person in charge of "burdens, superfluous things, troubles and rags."

Her rebellion is a refusal to continue operating under the role-related rules and expectations assigned to women, and she denies not only that well-dusted teapots are a woman's responsibility, but that they are directly related to a good life. When this good life is defined without emotional content, the dusting of a teapot would become an end in itself, as it had for the "*taşralı*" girl's aunt. But by discarding its contents, the heroine of "The Junk Peddler" refuses to fetishize the house. The emotional intimacy that once gave value to the drama of her life is now gone; why, then, should she waste her time cleaning the props? In fact, it could be argued that she effectively appropriates the tools of an "essentialized" woman, whose role makes her responsible for the house-cum-universe, in order to "renegotiate her locale." By the most thorough of house-cleanings she signals to us how the meaning of the house interacts with what is known and felt there. In the end, her rebellious acts are peculiarly integrating, for she has made her house look exactly the way she feels: empty. In what could be considered a whirlwind of insane activity, she has entirely redefined her role-relationship to the house: the role of the *Paşa's* wife is meaningless to her, and it would be insanity to choose it.

CONCLUSION

Analyzing the protagonists in these four stories by Turkish women authors gives us an insight into the changing ideas of the meaning of the house to the women who live there. I have suggested that the cultural model for these Turkish women was a role influenced by the concept of *fitne,* which imagined them as bearers of potential chaos and required them to counter this inherent failing by assuming responsibility for keeping order in the world. In these stories, this responsibility was often translated into a valorization of neatness, or of clean houses and orderly lives. All the towels were folded.

But the new heroines, who are fabricated by Turkish authors (and readers) of the 1960s to the 1980s, are breaking the paradigm of women as the site of chaos in the universe and the house as its test-site. For these new heroines, the idea that women are a conflation of role and essence, the idea that women have a primary, sex-linked function, is seen as counter-productive to the emerging values of the house as a place for intimacy and personal fulfillment. In fact, what is suggested by the rebellious acts of these heroines is not that rebellion leads to chaos, but that it has the potential to lead to new types of social relations.

Still, a gender-specific understanding of the Turkish household and its contents remains undefined—though as a monument to cleanliness it is certainly "tarnished." Instead, these houses are characterized by rebellious female voices, by women who are throwing everything away or tunneling their way out through the walls. For in these stories women are breaking traditional rules, rejecting traditional roles, and demanding that domestic space become less of a physical and more of a relational concept. Their intentions, therefore, are political and revolutionary, for by redefining their own image they are redefining the operation of social life.

Notes

1. Canter, 1988a:1-14.
2. Canter, 1988b; Gottdiener, 1986.
3. Probyn, 1990:186.
4. Füruzan, 1969:267-72; translation mine.
5. "*Taşralı*" means "provincial."
6. Kandiyoti, 1988a:36-37.
7. *Fitne* (Arabic: *Fitna*) refers to the sedition of the first followers of the prophet Mohammed, who defected from Islam at his death. They were eventually reconquered, but their *fitne,* their infamy, dishonor, and rebellion, was always remembered. Kandiyoti

(1988a), does not mention this root nor discuss in what context the term *fitne* came to be associated over time with women's sexuality.

8. Luce Iragary (1987) suggests that in France, at least, men have objectified women by identifying them as the space that contains order: in the role of mother, she says, women represent a sense of place for a man, his pre-natal home. This definition robs a woman of her own spatiality, but in partial compensation she is bought a house and then shut up in it.

9. Doğramacı,1982:10.

10. As quoted by Doğramacı, 1982:34, from the novel's 1948 reprinted edition; first printing date is unknown.

11. As quoted in Doğramacı, 1982:50.

12. As quoted in Doğramacı, 1982:100.

13. Kandiyoti, 1981:233-258.

14. Eray, 1982:88-92; translation mine. The date of the story is not given.

15. Gün, 1986:279.

16. Karabey, 1983:39-42; translation mine.

17. Kandiyoti, 1993:3.

18. Soysal, 1988:29-37; translated by Nilüfer Mızanoğlu Reedy. The date of the story is not given; however, Sevgi Soysal died in 1978.

THIRTEEN

A SHORT HISTORY OF *KADINCA* MAGAZINE AND ITS FEMINISM

Arzu Öztürkmen

WHEN ON DECEMBER 1978, in the midst of Turkey's most polarized social and political climate, *Kadınca* (Womanly) made its appearance with a rather modest circulation, hardly anyone could guess that the magazine and its editor, Duygu Asena, would grow into popular symbols of feminism in the 1980s. The initial issues included all the characteristics expected of a conventional women's monthly, loaded as they were with pages on cooking, child care, housekeeping, needle work, and clothing patterns offered as free gift. This conventional style, promoted by its first manager, Necla Seyhun, a fashion designer, radically changed after Duygu Asena took control. Under Asena's leadership, *Kadınca* soon developed a discourse of its own using creative techniques and methods. In doing so, it raised its circulation to over ten thousand, a fairly high rate for a women's monthly in Turkey, and received tremendous popular support from middle-class women.[1] In academic circles, however, it evoked more criticism than enthusiasm. The magazine gained some recognition for popularizing fundamental concepts and slogans of the rising women's movement in Turkey during the 1980s. But women scholars involved in this movement were highly critical of *Kadınca*'s concessions to the media market--its consumerist advertisements and its occasional use of sexuality on its covers.[2] Moreover, the image of women promoted by *Kadınca* often contradicted the approaches to womanhood developed by other feminist circles.[3] Yet, despite all the concern about not reducing the newly flourishing feminism to that of *Kadınca*'s, most groups involved in the post-1980s women's movement in Turkey have referred to *Kadınca* one way or another, and thus acknowledged the impact of the 160 issues published between 1978 and 1992 under Asena's editorship as too important a phenomenon to be dismissed. In April 1992, Asena and her team of researchers and reporters trans-ferred to another publishing company to begin the magazine *Kim* (Who; also the initials of *Kadın İçin Magazin,* or A Magazine for Women). Although *Kadınca* continued its publication after their departure, it lost much of its market to *Kim*.

How did *Kadınca* become a popular symbol of feminism? What was the context it grew in and what kinds of tools did the magazine use to establish a communicative mode of its own? This chapter attempts to examine this fragment of the women's movement in Turkey, as it has often been dismissed or shortchanged in the historio-graphic narratives of the rise of feminism during the 1980s.[4] Given Duygu Asena and her team's influential role in formulating the magazine's rhetoric, this chapter focuses on the first thirteen years of *Kadınca*. The development of *Kadınca*'s rhetoric stands as a fascinating example of *form*'s impact over *content:* with its various methods of interview, cover design, and presentation, the magazine gradually created a metacommunicative style of its own.

THE MEETING OF TWO VITAL FORCES: RISING FEMINISM AND NEW FORMS IN THE MEDIA

In the late 1970s, Turkey was in the heyday of political antagonisms and ideological polarization, while feminism was a peripheral issue. "Emancipated women" of the Republic occupied public offices, schools, and banks; housewives probably read their conventional monthlies in their homes; and a large number of young women got involved in political movements. But hardly any of these groups formulated a public expression about the state of their womanhood. A self-contingent women's movement made its rise in Turkey only during the 1980s, which were marked by the military regime that followed the 1980 military coup. Women who identified themselves as "feminists" created new grounds of discussion in literary and academic journals such as *Somut* (Concrete), *Feminist,* and *Kaktüs* (Cactus); initiated campaigns against battering and sexual harassment; founded support organizations and shelters; and organized discussion groups, panels, and conferences.[5]

The period after the 1980 military coup also marked the emergence of entirely new forms of printed media. Widely distributed weekly news magazines and popular monthlies targeted particular consumer groups such as "men," "women," or "professionals" and challenged the domination of dailies in building the everyday public agenda. According to Ahmet Oktay, this change in printed media was a consequence of the 1980 coup, which, by oppressing the freedom of thought and expression, changed the economic structure of news-making in Turkey. Journalists, trying to avoid prison sentencing, were *depoliticized* and gradually became submissive to the rules of the media market that expanded rather quickly with the rise of the liberal economy. Oktay stresses that in the post-1980s the Turkish press was forced to submit to the control of big capital and thus to operate as large conglomerates.[6]

But Nurdan Gürbilek defined the cultural climate of the 1980s as "an explosion of narratives as it was [an] oppression of speech."[7] In the context of the changing political structure under military rule, the rise of liberalism in the 1980s stimulated the advertising industry, which began to both construct and mediate the circulation of new images in its search for new markets. Popular media was now interested more than ever in expressions of "private lives." Gürbilek attributed this upsurge of interest in *the private* to "voluntary narrators who saw a possibility of liberation and self-expression in telling their own stories to the media in search of *news* rather than to an institutional authority chasing for *information*."[8] Most private issues, which were previously hard to discuss publicly, made the front cover of new weeklies and monthlies. One of the most important changes was the new "verbalization of sexuality." Although most accounts of gays, lesbians, bisexuals, or transsexuals reflected the mainstream prejudices of the 1980s, the presentation of private lives was not treated as a subject of extraordinary scandals but as "different life styles."[9]

Kadınca magazine was thus an outcome, a typical outcome, of this changing media market. Its publishing company, *Gelişim Yayınları,* had other target group–oriented magazines as well. *Kadınca* had as its counterpart *Erkekçe* (Manly), a magazine offered to the market as the

"Turkish alternative" to *Playboy. Gelişim's* newsweekly *Nokta* (Period) was among the best-selling news magazines. But *Kadınca's* place in the *Gelişim* family was special. Many called it the "chicken with golden eggs" as its market share, advertisement revenues, and the public charisma of its writers began to stand out. Most of the credit was given to Duygu Asena herself for her ability to do successful business with a completely new product: women's issues! *Kadınca* grew, in a way, parallel with Duygu Asena's public image.

WOMAN AND EDITOR:
WHAT DID DUYGU ASENA STAND FOR?

When, in August 1978, Ercan Arıklı, the head of *Gelişim Yayınları,* called Asena to offer her an editorial job with a new women's magazine, Asena had no experience in magazine editorship and had only a few years' experience writing and reporting for newspapers. But, she was working for *Man Ajans,* a leading advertisement company, and thus was familiar with how the image-making industry operated. In the beginning, Asena was to assist Necla Seyhun, the general editor of the magazine, who had a full-time job in *VAKKO,* a leading fashion company. As Seyhun could contribute to the magazine only during evening hours, Asena prepared the first issues almost by herself.[10] Yet Seyhun's influence dominated the content of the first issues, which had many pages on beauty and fashion. Having more time to work at the office, however, Asena managed to open a space for herself beginning with the very first issue. In an editorial, she openly stated that the magazine did not intend to be like "the others," with gossip columns and romance stories, and that the magazine would challenge the traditional idea that Turkish women do not read "serious stuff." *Kadınca's* readers were thus invited from the beginning issues to pay attention to interviews with successful professional women.[11]

Later, however, Asena would admit that it was not until the third issue that she began to question whether a women's magazine had to be something like the one she was preparing for publication, or, more than that, whether a woman was something like what the magazine perceived her to be.[12] Given Necla Seyhun's reluctance in addressing women's problems, Asena would state,

I [published] our first writing on female sexuality almost secretly. It
[received] such a public response that I [increased] the pages on
sexuality in the following issues without asking anyone's consent. And
finally one month, I [wrote] "Wake up Ayşes and wake Alis up" . . .[13]

Seyhun soon left the magazine, leaving more space and authority
to Asena. Expanding her staff gradually, Asena was now able to
delegate much of the work. For the seventh anniversary, she summarized her own perception of *Kadınca*'s achievements:

. . . What did we want to do almost on our own? We wanted women
not to undermine themselves anymore, [we wanted to] convince them
that they can survive by themselves. We wanted to remind women that
their only aim should not be marriage; we protested our gendermates
who saw marriage as a profession by itself, a source of revenue, a
shelter. We told them "marriage is not absolutely necessary; if there is
no love, do not get married; if there remains no respect, then get
divorced."

We wanted to remind them how wrong was the belief that a
woman's honor depended on her hymen. We protested films that tried
to convince young girls who lost their virginity to believe that they
should commit suicide, that if they don't, they would be prostitutes.
We confronted the issue of battering. We said to women "Leave at the
first slap." We protested those men who consider beating a woman as
a normal behavior and as their right; we judged them as creatures more
brutal than animals. We suggested women to work. We wanted them
to read. We told governments to protect women. . . . We enumerated
those laws of our civil code which are against women. We tried to talk
about feminism whose content remains unknown in our country, and
which haunts people like a ghost.[14]

In the earlier issues of *Kadınca* magazine, Asena worked also as an
active writer and reporter; within ten years, she managed to establish
a sense of solidarity among the team of researchers, writers, designers,
and reporters who joined the magazine. Later, she titled her editorial
corner simply "*İlk Söz*" (Foreword); it covered a wide spectrum of
themes ranging from abortion to war. Among other themes, love came
up consistently in her discourse. She either tried to relieve women

suffering from love pain by saying "Never believe in it" and "Is it worth [it] to feel sad for somebody who does not want you anymore?" or she advised solitude and self-sufficiency and gave hope by saying, "Know that 'he' exists."[15] Asena also entitled essays "Run Toward Love" or "No Need to Be Afraid of Love," through which she did not only call for an ongoing pursuit of excitement and happiness but also mediated a message concerning a misconception that feminism stood against men: "Women in the West reject men in the name of feminism: wrong!" she would state.[16]

Asena's own photo depicting a "young, beautiful, and brave" woman image accompanied her "Foreword." Her regularly renewed poses presented Asena either as a professional woman at her desk or as a meditative woman with her hand placed on her head. Upon the request of Ercan Arıklı, her boss, she posed for *Kadınca's* cover for their tenth anniversary issue. She commented on the promotion of her own visual image:

> . . . KADINCA is known as "Duygu Asena's magazine." In fact, through time a certain team has developed to parallel me in the magazine. Today, what I think is what they think, and what they think is what I think. Even our male colleagues are like that. Also, I am the most visible figure at the forefront--in the outside world, on television, at the panels--and this is why there developed such an image. But this is not bad at all, everything is working fine.[17]

Asena would credit her team also with granting her the time to write her best-selling novel *Kadının Adı Yok* (Woman Has No Name) in 1987.[18] The book achieved its forty-eighth edition within two years, until it was banned by the *Muzır Kurulu,* the Censorial Commission on public morality. Narrating a young woman's experiences from her childhood to maturity, reporting memories of sexual experiences, emotions, regrets, and anger, the book crossed a boundary by reaching out to a large variety of readers, male and female. Şirin Tekeli called the book "Turkey's first original feminist manifesto." "This book," Tekeli stated, "is not simply a woman's story, but a call for women to meet at a minimum level of female consciousness."[19] Nilüfer Göle, on the other hand, related the success of the book to the social climate of the 1980s:

In the post-1980s' Turkey, there formed a sympathetic bridge between the public and the radical movements which focussed on issues previously undermined by leftist movements, such as environmentalism, women's identity and individual freedom. A lot of people were interested in, and thinking about the themes promoted by these movements, without necessarily participating in, or identifying with them.[20]

The popularity of the book and its author evidently added to the popularity of *Kadınca* as well. By the end of the 1980s, *Kadınca* was transformed into an assertive publication, possessing an outlook very different than the timid attitude of its initial years.

THE CONTENT: TOPICS AND MESSAGES

Duygu Asena defined *Kadınca's* approach to feminism as being *egalitarian*, rather than *radical* or *socialist*, feminism.[21] To Asena, egalitarian feminism covered areas such as women's participation in production, liberation from a repressive state and the imposed familial identity, personal achievement, and struggle for obtaining equal opportunities with men.[22] *Kadınca* depicted men as "fellow victims" who suffered as much as women within the male-dominated Turkish society: "Our men are blind with customs and morals. They never raise their heads to see the truth. Once they will get awakened, we will probably be liberated altogether."[23]

Kadınca foregrounded, above all, women's economic independence as the only way to give them happiness in their social and individual lives. "Happiness," "enjoying one's life," "a professional life," "freedom," "equality," and "bad marriage" versus "exciting love"--discussions around these concepts generated precise messages with an implicit "women's ethic." *Kadınca,* for instance, opposed the treatment of marriage as "insurance for women" and urged divorce once love disappeared. It advised mothers to use their maternal authority to teach their sons egalitarian ideology. *Kadınca* protested the sexual division of labor and the separation of domestic work from economic production. It encouraged women to work as wage laborers and urged them to share housework with other members of the family. Slogans like "Men can do it too" and "Who is washing love's dishes?"[24] served to raise consciousness about women's domestic burden. Economic independence was high-lighted as the way to develop an identity independent from the status derived from that of husbands or fathers.[25] With titles like "Beauty at the Office," "Are Working Women More Successful in Married Life?" and "Working Women Be Careful: Fatigue Affects Sex Life," *Kadınca* promoted the image of the career woman.[26] Often backed by Asena's "Forewords," *Kadınca*'s discourse imposed and mediated a female image that was busy but beautiful, married but still attractive and sexy. Ayşe Saktanber elaborately defined *Kadınca*'s genre as follows:

> Kadınca's targeted woman was imagined as a "modern" woman who knows how to manage her husband and/or lover with minimum concession as she learns more about herself and her sexuality, who is in control of her rights, decisive and strong, who respects herself, but at the same time, who can prepare practical modern dinner tables, who takes care of her hair, face and body with cosmetics, diets and exercise, who is updated on today's fashion trends and familiar with home decoration. Economic independence is emphasized, but how women will get it is not one of *Kadınca's* concerns. What is more promoted is to have a career. To be a housewife is not put down but is not shown as a goal either. It advises its reader, or even yells at her, to develop a personality based on the framework stated above.[27]

Kadınca's attitude toward female sexuality can be considered one of *Kadınca*'s weak points, reflecting a double standard or inconsistency. On the one hand, the magazine underlined women's difficulty in expressing their sexuality and criticized social oppression on the issues of virginity and intolerance for women's extramarital affairs.[28] With headlines like "With a Man, Merely for His Body: Why Not?" and "Are We Supposed to Talk about Our Sexual Secrets?" or "First Time with a New Man,"[29] *Kadınca* challenged the traditional boundaries of female sexuality. It opposed beauty pageants for exhibiting female sexuality as a commodity, but nevertheless allowed its advertisements and beauty sections to objectify its readers. Covers depicting sexuality, which had the highest rates of circulation, also fell for the bad old game of using women's bodies to sell more copies.

Advertisements usually targeted urban, middle-class women and promoted a certain way of life: one centered on vacations in touristic resorts, cosmetics, clothing, cars, luxury furniture, entertainment, sports clubs, and household appliances. Professional women especially were shown the means and ways of dealing with domestic burdens while still keeping up their appearance and having fun. In other words, Kadınca's average reader was not perceived anymore as a housewife interested in free clothing patterns, but as a busy woman who had no time for sewing or laundry. Instead, Kadınca's new reader needed massage instruments, dryers, automatic cleaning equipment, and expensive kitchen appliances. In a way, readers were framed as those who knew how to spend their money, how to consume more in order to save time and energy.[30] The increase in advertising was noticed and criticized by readers. Asena answered one such complaint as follows:

> The large number of advertisements shows that this magazine is a very popular one and [with] a high circulation. . . . For the magazine, advertising is also a very important source of income, a device that enables it to survive. Therefore, you should understand from the number of advertisements how widely your magazine is read and appreciated.[31]

On the back pages of the magazine the consumer-career woman image was reinforced with writings teaching the rules--and the tools-- of a modern kitchen, a contemporary house decoration, or in short, a new and modern way of life that differed from the previous generation's saving-oriented "a la Turca" life style. In this respect, Kadınca invited its readers to break the traditional rules not only at the sexual or social level, but also in their consumption pattern. The cooking section, named "Kitchen of the Working Woman," included recipes that could be quickly prepared and elegantly served.

The magazine included pages of self-assessment tests for married life, love, personality, friendship, and so forth. It organized panels on topics such as "Men Discussed the Changing Woman" and "Monogamy or Polygamy?" Every month a page was reserved for a male writer, under the title of "Their Page." Readers were given a special corner to voice emotions of love, deception, anger, and even vengeance, but also observations on public issues that were bothering them. Meanwhile, a separate page was reserved to answer readers' questions about their problems (emotional problems; physical problems such as excessive weight or hair, skin health, abortion; and psychological problems related to the issues of virginity, solitude, jealousy, and divorce). *Kadınca* offered very pragmatic answers for these problems: it gave telephone numbers for doctors who dealt with extramarital abortions or who restored lost virginity for future husbands obsessed with "first night purity." It did not condemn the reader's intent to make her fiancé believe in her virginity, although that contradicted its own messages; instead it provided her with the support and the urgent help she needed.

In the early 1990s, *Kadınca* expanded its content to include women's history. The information on the early female poets,[32] and the late Ottoman feminist movement[33] added an intellectual flavor. Moving from its earlier didactic rhetoric to a discussion of broader public issues, it now provided readers with book reviews and brought Turkey's social and cultural problems into its pages. Asking questions such as "Why Don't Our People Smile?" or "Why Do the Young People Want to Leave Their Country for Abroad?" and exposing issues such as "A Principal Has Beaten a Teacher" or "To Be a Woman under Police Torture," *Kadınca* voiced the everyday life consequences of Turkish society. *Kadınca* of the early 1990s also addressed the question of human rights and protested issues like torture and the death penalty, borrowing from the antistate stance characteristic of the post-1980s women's movement.

The foremost contribution of *Kadınca* to the rising women's movement in Turkey, however, was its voicing and popularization of problems in women's everyday life. According to Şirin Tekeli, Kemalism, by putting women's issues on its nationalist agenda, overshadowed any particular concerns about women's everyday life experiences. Women in the late Ottoman era had already problematized their status in society as well as in private life. The Kemalist rhetoric of "women's rights" was in fact built upon Ottoman feminism, but by officially "granting" rights to women, Kemalism interrupted the original impetus of the Ottoman women's movement, locked it up into a nationalist discourse, and distanced it from the problems of women's private world.[34] With the Civil Code of 1926 placing men at the head of the family, she notes, "the critique of the patriarchal relationships dominating wife-and-husband relations, and their private lives, had been excluded from elite women's agenda."[35]

Kadınca filled in precisely this gap both by publicizing and by politicizing *the private life of women* in Turkey. The well-known slogan "the personal is political" had already been included in the feminist platform of the 1980s. However, due to the limited publicity and the poor circulation of their journals, feminist groups were unable to spread their messages. *Kadınca,* in Tekeli's words, "recognized issues brought up by feminism, and with its circulation reaching 30,000 to 35,000, it played an important role in transferring these issues to circles beyond the reach of the feminist groups."[36] Similarly, Atilla İlhan argued that, compared to other popular women's magazines, *Kadınca*'s greatest distinction was "its interest in the state of womanhood in Turkey, its effort to establish a certain female consciousness"; therefore, "what has publicized the issue of women's rights among the non-politicized women has been *Kadınca*."[37]

Kadınca has thus stood on a boundary line that distinguished it both from the more sophisticated feminist journals and from the conventional women's magazines. Adopting new methods and techniques of interviewing, page-making, and design, *Kadınca* gradually formulated an original, almost militant discourse in publicizing issues of women's everyday life. Digging out intrafamilial relations and narrating true stories on husbands, children, lovers, and mothers-in-law, it filtered through the bedrooms, reporting other women's secrets and personal experiences. The consequence of all this was, of course, the trivialization of many issues dealt with by other feminists in a more multidirectional way. *Kadınca* urged economic independence, but its implications on how women should spend their money contradicted many feminist groups' approach to political economy. It publicized issues regarding women's sexuality, but its approach to the notion of beauty operated within the boundaries of male perspective. In other words, although bravely displaying the themes and concerns of the rising women's movement, *Kadınca* was locked up within the limits of a magazine format, and it failed to go into the in-depth analyses that most feminist journals engaged in. Despite its contradictions, however, with its ability to reach a large number of women, it received most of the public fame and credit on the issue of the resurgence of feminism.

FORM AND STYLE:
NEW TECHNIQUES AND METHODS

The form and style gradually developed by *Kadınca*'s editor and her staff played a major role in the magazine's success. *Kadınca* reporters' interviewing technique, their use of the participant-observer method in doing field research, their discursive technique of role-reversing, as well as *Kadınca*'s dramatic front covers and the use of colorful drawings, were part of *Kadınca*'s signature form and style.

Interviews, which were first conducted in a very shy and modest tone, almost mystifying the female figure presented, soon took an aggressive tone as the magazine's reporters gained self-confidence with *Kadınca*'s rising fame. Initial interviews were mostly devoted to stars or top-ranked female professionals, either the "first" or the "most successful" in their field. These women were exposed as role-models with profiles of their energy, intellectual capacity, and modesty, but also with "scoops" about their decorated houses and perfect relationships with their husbands and children.[38] Later, *Kadınca*'s reporters developed a more arrogant interviewing style. Especially as they developed a sense of solidarity among themselves, they began to visit their interviewees as a group, besieging the person with questions formulated from their perspectives as women. They started to publish critical interviews with a "feminine" if not "feminist" slant. Gradually their focus moved from famous people to ordinary people. Interviews with ordinary figures, especially women, allowed readers closer identification than interviews with "mystified female figures."

Breaking the myths of fame and success, *Kadınca* thus began to take pleasure in evaluating the statements of well-known figures according to the magazine's feminist view. Stars, politicians, or elite bureaucrats and businessmen were classified in a special page as "those to be kissed" versus "those who deserved hot pepper on their lips." Not only that, but one particular figure deserved the "super-pepper" every month. A statement such as "Female dominance over men is as wrong as male dominance is over women" was "kissable," but "Turkish woman is not her home's woman [not a dedicated housewife], but one [who is a follower] of her ambition, egoism, and her lust" deserved pepper.

Another characteristic of *Kadınca* was the "participant-observer" method followed by its reporters. Reporters did not only interview people, but disguised themselves and penetrated the area of investigation. If they reported on gypsy fortune tellers, they disguised themselves as gypsies and even performed as fortune tellers. Sometimes they penetrated male domains; they visited traditional Turkish coffeehouses, strolled at night on some deserted streets notoriously unsafe for women, or attended bars to drink and explore "the male mystique."

Reporters' direct involvement in the situation they investigated consolidated the magazine's credibility in its readers' eyes. Like their editor, Duygu Asena, reporters also posed for their readers, their photos displaying them in action: visiting beauty centers as clients, checking local markets for elegant cloths at lower costs, or taking trips to touristic places as "single female travelers."

Besides living these experiences for their readers, *Kadınca's* staff also displayed a high degree of reflexivity, exposing in their own magazine's pages their group cohesion and solidarity. Every December, their anniversary would be celebrated as a unique event, almost as a victory. They would reserve pages to give their own historical narrative, taking pride in the magazine's progress over the years and stressing their uniqueness among their counterparts. The staff would go to parties together (for example, attend the same New Year's party), narrate how they had entertained each other in great detail, and cite the name of every single member of their staff at any occasion.[39] Such narratives would not only display their close and harmonious relationship at work, but also their intimacy and friendship outside work. Moreover, by caricaturizing themselves with characteristics like "indifferent," "curious," "didactic," "sad," "a megalomaniac," "hurried," "a protester," and "sensitive," they reached the readers as real, fallible figures rather than impersonal writers.[40]

A constructive discursive technique that contributed to *Kadınca's* effectiveness in popularizing issues on *women's private lives* was the illustration of reversed roles. If the common saying told us that "there is a woman behind every successful man," for *Kadınca* there was "[definitely] a man behind every unsuccessful woman." In asking the question, "What if women had moral claims on men's honor?" *Kadınca* would turn men's expectations upside down and make men the objects of role and behavior restrictions.[41] Duygu Asena used the same technique in one of her "Forewords," entitled "Every Home Must Have One." Referring to a wife's services rendered to her husband, she replaced the server with a male figure and the served as a professional woman:

> When you go home in the evening, you see a perfectly cleaned house. A wonderful smell comes from the kitchen. The man has cooked your favorite dishes. . . . You go to your bedroom, change, throw your high heel shoes aside. He collects them. You will wear comfortable jeans and a T-shirt. You ask the man where they are, he immediately rushes and picks them up for you from the second drawer. Both smell wonderful, all cleaned up, ironed. You say: "Hon, my clothes have been all wrinkled today, iron them for tomorrow." . . . While you are sitting in front of your TV, the man gets the dinner ready in the kitchen. . . . But of course you help him after the dinner, by taking a plate or two. Then the man brings your coffee. At night, you say "let's go to bed." The night before, you were too tired, he had wanted to make love, but he did not dare to ask, and you had fallen asleep right away. But tonight, you desire him. You turn to him, hug and kiss. In fact, the man is pretty tired today, but this is also one of his duties, he cannot oppose your will, so he makes love to you the way you want, in any position you request. As you were pretty ready tonight, your orgasm comes very quickly, you kiss your husband softly on his cheek, and say: "good night honey," and you fall asleep. The man suffers. Right at that moment! You pulled yourself back. But what can you do, men do not always need orgasm. Next time. You'll make it up whenever you are not tired.[42]

Kadınca used two other methods to increase its effectiveness: dramatized photos and drawings.[43] On the cover, dramatizations were accompanied by strong statements, ironical questions, slogans, and wishes. One such cover, dramatizing a young woman both at home and in the office, was accompanied by the line, "Despite all the obstacles, women are changing."[44] The front cover of an issue on divorce dramatized a woman with her suitcase without any place to go, and asked "What will happen to the divorced woman?"[45] Similarly, a portrayal of a husband in a comfortable chair bouncing a ball that is, in fact, his wife, was accompanied by the statement, "We don't want a family like this anymore!"[46] Sexual topics were illustrated to make brave statements: "We don't know how to make love," "We can't have orgasms," "There may be good sex in marriage too," or "Very embarrassing! Do women get aroused?"[47]

The use of drawings helped the magazine "lighten up," by offering a colorful and therefore a more spectacular design in pages otherwise deprived of photographs. With the help of dramatic drawings, *Kadınca* transmitted some of its messages visually. Showing a woman either as a puppet whose strings were held by others or as an acrobat who managed loads of housework on her own would illustrate, for instance, women's subordination and exploitation.[48] Nevertheless, the excessive use of drawings may also be taken as a reflection of the belief that women needed visual and colorful stimuli to induce them to read an article.

CONCLUSION

The rise of the magazine *Kadınca* was an outcome of two parallel developments: the women's movement and the changing media market within the cultural climate of the 1980s. Its modest start soon changed as it began to be nourished by the themes of the feminist circles and by the form and style it developed in the economic and cultural liberalism of the post-1980s. But there were doubts about *Kadınca*'s feminism. Although it mediated feminist themes and issues among those who had limited access to urban feminist circles, it was constrained by its magazine format. Moreover, although it identified itself with feminism, the image it promoted did not fully satisfy feminist scholars. According to Duygu Asena, however, the relationship between the academic and activist feminists and *Kadınca*'s "popular feminists" improved through the years. "They soon saw that I do not do anything wrong," she remarked; "I can popularize [feminist themes] so that they can be read more easily." Asena also stated that because *Kadınca* was a commercial publication, it was able to reach a wider audience, an asset other feminist circles had lacked. She saw *Kadınca* as the foremost publication that "disseminated, publicized, and developed feminism in Turkey."[49] In fact, *Kadınca* did contribute to the circulation of news related to other feminist circles' activities, both by publishing their schedules of events on the one hand, and by reporting about their campaigns, meetings, and panels on the other. For those who named her as "the pioneer of feminism in Turkey," Asena replied,

> No, I am not! Perhaps I learned what feminism is from Şirin Tekeli and people around her. But they were not lucky enough to have a publication at their hands. Because I had my own magazine, and because I approached this issue seriously enough, people perceived me as a pioneer. Otherwise, I was not the one who discovered feminism.[50]

Kadınca's and Duygu Asena's popularities grew simultaneously in the public media. Asena had perhaps begun her career in *Kadınca* as an "instinctive voice" without a well-grounded background in feminist theories and methods. Her ground-breaking book was itself probably an outcome of the self-confidence that grew throughout her editorship of *Kadınca*. Nevertheless, the book helped further both *Kadınca's* fame and the publicity of the women's movement. According to Asena, *Kadınca's* most important achievement had been "to convince urban and young women to live by their own, that is, not to marry a man because they had to, to get a divorce if they did not love him anymore, but still, to continue to live on their own and to engage in that struggle."[51]

Kadınca now lives at the hands of another team, and Asena's team works for the *Kim* magazine, which has a somewhat different flavor from the *Kadınca* of the 1980s. However, *Kim's* young, educated, dynamic reader's profile is undoubtedly indebted to the middle-class women who were the silent collaborators in what *Kadınca* achieved in the 1980s.

Notes

Author's note: This paper's original version was presented at the symposium "New Voices in Turkish Women's Studies" organized by the University of Pennsylvania's Middle East Center in Philadelphia, April 27, 1991. The original presentation would be impossible without the resources provided by Ayla Kapan.

1. Publisher's survey of readers showed that about 65 percent of all *Kadınca* readers were either young (20-24), or were single, childless women. 71 percent of readers lived in big cities such as İstanbul, Ankara, and İzmir, and most of them were educated and professional women (Yenigün, 1989).

2. For a discourse analysis of *Kadınca's* advertisements, see Tutal-Küçük, 1994:67-78.

3. To give an example, in her article "'80'lerde Türkiye'de Kadınların Kurtuluşu Hareketinin Gelişmesi," Şirin Tekeli states that discussions in the women's group associated with the YAZKO circle led them "to take *Kadınca,* the most influential women's magazine of the time, as a reference point and to develop a publication out of its criticism" (Ş. Tekeli, 1989:37).

4. Excluding Şirin Tekeli's contribution to *Dünden Bugüne İstanbul Ansiklopedisi* (1994b), most historiographies of feminism in Turkey did not include *Kadınca* among the feminist publications of the post-1980s' women's movement, but named journals such as *Feminist* and *Kaktüs* (Sirman, 1989; Ş. Tekeli, 1989 and 1990b; Y. Arat, 1991; Ovadia, 1994). Scholarly references to the magazine were mostly criticisms brought up in discussions on "media and women." See, for instance, Saktanber, 1990; and Tutal-Küçük, 1994.

5. For a detailed account of the rise of feminism in Turkey during the 1980s, see Ş. Tekeli, 1989, 1990b, and 1994b; Y. Arat, 1991; Sirman, 1989.

6. Oktay, 1987.

7. Gürbilek, 1992.

8. Gürbilek, 1992:18, emphasis added.

9. Gürbilek, 1992.

10. *Kadınca* 12/1988.

11. *Kadınca* 12/1978.

12. *Kadınca* 12/1988.

13. *Kadınca* 12/1988:5; translation mine.

14. *Kadınca* 12/1985:5; translation mine.

15. *Kadınca* 8/1989; 10/1989; 8/1990.

16. *Kadınca* 4/1989; 12/1990; 2/1983.

17. "Söyleşi/Duygu Asena," *Nokta* (11 Aralık 1988):74-75; translation mine.

18. *Kadınca* 12/1988.

19. *Nokta* 4/10/1987:68.
20. *Nokta* 4/10/1987:70; translation mine.
21. However, occasional references to feminist journals such as *Feminist* and the socialist-feminist *Kaktüs* were made. Filiz Koçali, one of *Kadınca's* reporters, also contributed to *Kaktüs,* although in a rather modest way. See *Kaktüs* 12 (September 1990):52-53.
22. *Nokta* 12/1988; Yenigün, 1989.
23. *Kadınca* 7/1983.
24. *Kadınca* 10/1989; 10/1990.
25. Yenigün, 1989.
26. *Kadınca* 9/1982; 7/1989.
27. Saktanber, 1990:203; translation mine.
28. Yenigün, 1989.
29. *Kadınca* 8/1989; 8/1990; 9/1990.
30. For a detailed discourse analysis of *Kadınca's* advertisements, see Tutal-Küçük, 1994; Saktanber, 1990.
31. *Kadınca* 7/1980; translation mine.
32. *Kadınca* 9/1990.
33. *Kadınca* 12/1990.
34. Ş. Tekeli, 1989 and 1990b.
35. Ş. Tekeli, 1990b:21.
36. Ş. Tekeli, 1994b:353; translation mine.
37. *Kadınca* 12/1986:22; translation mine.
38. Duygu Asena's interview with Aysel Öymen is a case in point (*Kadınca* 12/1978:6-9).
39. *Kadınca* 1/1990:20.
40. *Kadınca* 12/1990:8-10.
41. *Kadınca* 3/1991.
42. *Kadınca* 9/1990:5; translation mine.
43. Both methods appeared as a new trend in Turkish printed media of the 1980s, which was described by Ahmet Oktay as a shift of news headlines from an informative state to an imaginative one (Oktay, 1987:108).
44. *Kadınca* 8/1989.
45. *Kadınca* 1/1990.
46. *Kadınca* 1/1991.
47. *Kadınca* 3/1990; 6/1990; 11/1990; 2/1991.
48. *Kadınca* 4/1989; 10/1990.

49. Personal interview with Duygu Asena. İstanbul, September 23, 1992.
50. Personal interview with Duygu Asena. İstanbul, September 23, 1992.
51. Personal interview with Duygu Asena. İstanbul , September 23, 1992.

FOURTEEN

FEMINIST INSTITUTIONS AND DEMOCRATIC ASPIRATIONS: THE CASE OF THE PURPLE ROOF WOMEN'S SHELTER FOUNDATION

Yeşim Arat

SINCE THE FRENCH DECLARATION OF THE RIGHTS OF WOMAN and the Female Citizen in 1791, feminists of all persuasions have contested the prevailing authority structures and their implications for equal participation of men and women in the private as well as the public realm.[1] Feminists who first sought equality through suffrage then demanded the removal of all legal discrimination against women.[2] Disappointed in their experiences with representative democracies, they experimented widely with participatory democracy and attempted to change the prevailing structures of power in the private and public domains.[3] Besides legal equality, they demanded liberation.

Feminists in Turkey also sought equality as well as liberation. As it did in the West, this search translated into a skepticism of hierarchy, professionalism, specialization, and bureaucratization. The controversial issue of feminists functioning without an organization or structure was also debated by Turkish feminists.

This chapter will address the question of how feminists in Turkey struggle with feminist aspirations for democracy as they institutionalize their activities. The Purple Roof Women's Shelter Foundation will be examined as a case study of an attempt to institutionalize feminist activism. Published materials including journals, newspapers, and documents of the foundation will be used as primary sources of information. Intensive interviews carried out in the summer of 1993 with feminists, including members and participants of the Purple Roof Women's Shelter Foundation, will be referred to in discussing the operation of the foundation as well as the feminist experience in Turkey.

FEMINIST ACTIVISM

Feminist activism in Turkey gained momentum in the 1980s in a world of increasing global cultural interrelatedness. Organized in small clusters and representing different versions of feminism, Turkish feminists were influenced by feminist movements abroad; however, personal experiences in the local context prompted activism.[4] The immediate local context in Turkey was defined on the one hand by the transition from military rule to democracy, and on the other by an increasingly vital civil society in a polity that was becoming more integrated to the world.

Although Turkey had prided itself on its cadres of professional women, till the 1980s, when a second and third generation of women came onto the public realm, women's political activism concerning their rights and opportunities was neither visible nor expressed in explicitly feminist terms.[5] The few women who sparked women's consciousness in Turkey by coming together in the early 1980s were mostly professional middle-class women who had profited from the educational opportunities of the Kemalist reforms.

When a group of women came together in 1981 to prepare a series of publications on women for the publishing company YAZKO (Yazarlar ve Çevirmenler Yayın Üretim Kooperatifi—Publication and Production Cooperative of Writers and Translators), they ignited the sparks of feminism in Turkey. In their attempt to prepare the publications, these women prepared a bibliography which included feminist works that had been published in the West.[6] It included studies on women and work, women and family, women and ideology, women and psychology, and the experiences of feminists in various countries.

A much-debated pamphlet that circulated among the feminists who gathered in small circles in the early 1980s was a translated version of Jo Freeman's *The Tyranny of Structurelessness*. Freeman's criticism of feminist consciousness-raising groups, which upheld leaderless, structureless groups as the basic form of organization for the women's liberation movement, led to a controversy among the pioneering group of Turkish feminists as well. These women earnestly discussed Freeman's contention that structureless groups led to a lack of accountability for decisions made within the group by "natural" leaders that emerged under specific circumstances, as well as her claim that feminists had something to learn from modes of organization and decision-making practiced in representative democracies.

Nevertheless, organizing, structuring and institutionalizing were concerns for feminists in Turkey. When the need to go beyond the small friendship networks that functioned as consciousness-raising groups emerged, there was dissent. Despite awareness of the potential dangers of a lack of organization and institutionalization, some of the most earnest feminists were skeptical of the move to institutionalize. Finally, Women's Circle (Kadın Çevresi) was founded in 1987 as a publishing, service, and consultancy company whose mission was to support women's labor, market women's products, improve women's education, and provide consulting services concerning women's health and legal problems. Founding a company, rather than an association, after much debate and dissent, was a solution that aimed to avoid the restrictive state surveillance that existed over other associations at the time. Meanwhile the company would allow women to pursue profits to increase their clout. While members of Women's Circle translated some feminist classics and helped expand the feminist circles in İstanbul, their effectiveness in pursuing their goals was circumscribed. They had neither the resources nor the organization to push feminist goals further.

FEMINIST ORGANIZATIONS AND INSTITUTION-BUILDING

Feminist attempts at institution-building flourished in the early 1990s. On April 20, 1990, the Purple Roof Women's Shelter Foundation was founded in İstanbul by a group of fourteen feminists. A year later, in Ankara, a consulting center was founded in the working-class district of Altındağ (Altındağ Kadın Danışma Merkezi). In 1993 the center opened a women's shelter.[7]

Besides these two institutions, a Women's Library and Information Center run by a group of feminists was established in İstanbul in 1990. The library collects publications on women as well as works written by women. With its conferences, seminars, and exhibitions, it has become a vital center of feminist activism.

These centers instituted by feminist women were accompanied by centers and organizations concerning women founded by the state. The attempt to meet the requirements of the United Nations' Convention on the Elimination of All Forms of Discrimination Against Women (or CEDAW) must have played a role, even if this did not solely account for the establishment of women's institutions by the state. In October 1990, a Directorate General on the Status and Problems of Women was established under the Ministry of Labor and Social Security. The Directorate, which became affiliated with the Prime Ministry a year later, was charged to address women's problems and work toward gender equality.

Women's studies programs or research centers were established at a number of public universities. The first among these was a women's studies center (Kadın Sorunları Araştırma ve Uygulama Merkezi) established in 1990 within İstanbul University. That same year, a women's employment research center (Kadın İşgücü İstihdamı Araştırma ve Uygulama Merkezi) was founded within Marmara University. Later in 1993, a women's studies center (Kadın Sorunları Araştırma ve Uygulama Merkezi) was instituted within Ankara University. More recently, in 1994, Middle East Technical University of Ankara initiated a women's studies program.

At the level of local government, a number of municipalities established units or departments focusing on women's problems, including violence toward women, even though by 1995 most of these were closed due to changes in political leadership.[8] After the feminist campaign against violence and the initiatives taken by the Purple Roof Group, women's shelters were founded in the Bakırköy and Şişli municipalities of İstanbul in 1990.[9] A year later, a women's center was opened in İzmir by the Bornova municipality. In 1992, the Kayseri and Nazilli municipalities opened shelters.[10] Finally, the Directorate General of Social Services and Protection of Children (or SHCEK) opened women's guesthouses in Ankara, Antalya, Bursa, Eskişehir, and İzmir between 1991 and 1992.[11]

DOMESTIC VIOLENCE IN TURKEY

Attempts to organize and build institutions against domestic violence were a central platform of feminist activism and one on which feminist aspirations for egalitarian participation in expanding and protecting women's realms in Turkey were located. The focus on domestic violence was not unfounded.

Domestic violence against women, as in other parts of the world, has been widespread and part of daily life in Turkey. While the research on the subject is scant, and most of the available data severely criticized by feminists who claim that the questions posed and methods of inquiry used to collect data are biased against women, there is evidence that the issue is serious. According to a study conducted in 1988 by Hacettepe Population Studies Institute, about 45 percent of men in Turkey think that a husband has the right to beat his wife if she disobeys him.[12] Another survey, called "Turkish Women in the 1990s," commissioned by the Ministry of State and conducted by the public opinion survey company PIAR, revealed that of a sample of 1,973 people, 18 percent of married women were beaten by their husbands.[13] Finally, a 1991 survey of men and women living in İstanbul conducted by a research group from Boğaziçi University showed that 49 percent of women believed that there could be cases in which a woman deserved to be beaten by her husband. The same survey found that 40 percent of the married women interviewed had been beaten by their husbands; two-thirds of this group claimed that they had been beaten often.[14]

The scant research available shows that domestic violence toward women is not merely commonplace but also widely accepted. The Turkish Criminal Code reflects this prevailing attitude. In cases of domestic violence between a wife and a husband, legal action can only be taken if the violated partner complains.[15] In effect, this means that battered women must go to the police (who often advise women to go back to their husbands), must provide names of witnesses (who are difficult to find because domestic violence usually takes place in the privacy of the home), must insist on being transferred to the coroner's office (when they are already physically and psychologically exhausted), and must persistently pursue their cases (which even for a person in good health is an arduous task because of the inefficient bureaucracy).[16] If the woman succeeds in proving her case, the maximum punishment for engaging in domestic violence is imprisonment for up to thirty months; in reality, prison sentences usually last for only seven days and thus fail to serve as a deterrent for potential aggressors.[17]

On the issue of crimes of sexual aggression, the Criminal Code shows a bias for collective morality and virtue as opposed to personal rights.[18] In cases of rape, loss of virginity is an important condition in determining the nature of punishment. In cases of abduction, if the man who abducts a woman then marries her, his punishment— regardless of the woman's opinion—is lowered.[19]

THE MOVEMENT AGAINST DOMESTIC VIOLENCE

In this context of widespread violence against women and a legal framework that lacked the will and effective means to deter it, the feminist campaign against domestic violence began in February 1987.[20] Some discussion of the significance of this topic had already taken place among feminists. When some women read in a legal journal that a judge had refused a divorce to a woman, a mother of three children and expecting a fourth, who was regularly beaten by her husband, and that the judge had punctuated his decision with the proverb "kadının sırtından sopayı, karnından sıpayı eksik etmemek gerek" (one should not leave a woman's back without a stick, her womb without a foal),[21] they were infuriated. The women who prepared the pamphlet to advocate the Purple Roof Women's Shelter exclaimed that "by not granting a divorce, this male judge, who saw women as deserving of donkeys and beatings, created within the verdict grounds that debased all women!"[22] The judge's fault was not singular; he had not merely refused the divorce, but he had also humiliated women (not one, but all) by equating them with animals and revealing his belief in the legitimacy of domestic violence toward women. Furthermore, he had dared to have his prejudices written into the final verdict.

Feminist women protested to the judge with telegraphs and sent petitions to take the judge to court. The court did not accept the petitions because those who protested were "not considered an interested party in this verdict." One of these feminists, who later initiated the campaign against the beating of women, commented that "while they (feminists) were told that they did not have the right to mind other people's business, unless they themselves were beaten personally, they (feminists) could not refrain themselves from minding other cases thereafter."[23]

Violence was an issue in which women felt themselves potential victims, and they saw violence against any woman as violence against themselves. It was with this spirit that feminists initiated the Campaign Against Beating (Dayağa Karşı Kampanya). Their aim was to delegitimize beating in a society in which the beating of women was accepted as "normal." On May 17, 1987, a protest walk was organized. About 3,000 women, a number much higher than what the organizers had anticipated, participated in the walk. Media attention was positive. On October 4, 1987, a day-long festival was organized to raise money to publish a book on the personal accounts of women who had been beaten or otherwise exposed to violence. That same year, in the TÜYAP bookfair organized in İstanbul, feminist women continued their campaign with a stand named "Solidarity Against Beating" (Dayağa Karşı Dayanışma). By the time the book of personal accounts was published in 1988,[24] the need to found a women's shelter had become tangible. The Purple Roof Women's Shelter Foundation (Mor Çatı Kadın Sığınağı Vakfı) was subsequently founded by fourteen feminists on April 20, 1990.

THE PURPLE ROOF
WOMEN'S SHELTER FOUNDATION

The Purple Roof Women's Shelter Foundation aimed to be different from institutions founded by the state to help women exposed to violence. Feminist ideals and democratic aspirations served as a compass in shaping the activities of the group. Even though the *raison d'etre* of the foundation was the establishment of a shelter, the feminist members refused to have a shelter that they could not operate on principles of feminist solidarity.

The story of the establishment of the foundation reveals this feminist concern.[25] In search of a building that they could use as a shelter, the feminist group first went to the Şişli municipality in İstanbul because the mayor of the Şişli district was a woman, Fatma Girik. When they were told by the mayor that the power to allocate a building was at the discretion of the central city municipality, the members of the group went to Nurettin Sözen, then mayor of İstanbul. The conference and the ensuing exchanges with Mr. Sözen were not fruitful. The feminists felt that the mayor was trying to annex their activities and absorb them into the municipality. They charged the municipality with trying to usurp their project and turn them into mere bureaucrats of the municipality.[26] When asked if it was necessary for women to manage the shelter, Canan Arın, one of the founders of the Purple Roof foundation, explained as follows:

> Look, a woman's shelter is not a prison. It is not a student dorm. It is not at all an association for the protection of animals or for that matter a charitable organization. It is a house the address of which the husband does not know and where the woman who is sick of being beaten can go, and seek shelter. It is a house where women find love and affection from women who have lived through the same incidents, and find feelings of solidarity based on their shared experiences. For that reason, it [the shelter] cannot be put under the jurisdiction of any old authority.[27]

In fact, the city mayor had publicly indicated his skepticism of the amateur spirit with which the feminists approached the issue, compared his experience with theirs, and enumerated the tasks he would like them to assume in the management of the house that he would designate as a shelter.[28] His stance was a mirror image of the feminists' skepticism of professionalism, hierarchy, and authority.

The feminists' concerns were not unfounded. The experience of the women's shelter affiliated with the Bakırköy municipality shows how shelters under the jurisdiction of a political authority are exposed to the vagaries of political power. In Bakırköy, when Mayor Yıldırım Aktuna, who encouraged and allowed for the establishment of a shelter, was replaced by Ali Talip Özdemir, the fortunes of the shelter ebbed. The woman director of the shelter, Uğur İlhan, described the situation:

> The new mayor did not want to allow women whose husbands or fathers sold them as prostitutes to be admitted to the shelter lest they spoil the morality of other "family" women in the shelter; he did not want to admit women to the shelter without the permission of the husband who beat the wife; he severed financial help to the shelter and the employees could not get their wages; he advised the women to practice religion.[29]

Hence, the Purple Roof group sought a long-term solution in establishing its shelter and in the process of talks with the municipality instituted the Purple Roof Women's Shelter Foundation.

The aim of the foundation is stated in their pamphlet as follows: "To provide shelter and opportunity for protection for all women exposed to domestic violence and to help shape new, alternative lives for women in a context of solidarity and mutual help. The foundation also aims to rid women of the guilt that is a result of the widespread perception of beating as legitimate, and to rid women of their fear and sense of inferiority."

Although the primary goal of the foundation was to open a shelter, a number of other services have been provided in the center office of the foundation. Volunteers who are trained in a special course establish solidarity networks to counsel women who are victims of violence and help them in contacting the police, the doctor, or the prosecutor. There are some psychological help services available. The foundation also tries to provide some legal counseling for the victims of violence and helps women find jobs. Workshops and seminars are offered to help build women's self-confidence.

Members of the foundation insist that theirs is not a charity organization. They emphasize that feminist solidarity is the basis of their work. Volunteers of the foundation try to support the priorities and choices of women who come to the center. In the words of Yaprak Zihnioğlu, a volunteer and founder of Purple Roof, their goal is to "develop a relationship with battered women in which feelings of feminist solidarity rather than pity prevail, a relationship that is not one of a senior-junior or a teacher-student."[30]

DEMOCRATIC ASPIRATIONS AND TENSIONS

Purple Roof was instituted as a foundation in order to be able to benefit from opportunities open to foundations. Unlike associations or unions, foundations are allowed by law to pursue trade and run corporations to generate income to be used toward their stated goals.[31] The feminists who founded Purple Roof wanted to be able to raise money to help women exposed to domestic violence.

However, there are other rules that foundations have to follow. It is decreed by law that the founders can remain members of the foundation for life; the law requires that there be a board of directors and specifies its numbers and responsibilities. These requirements can generate a hierarchic framework that fosters seniority and inequality and that the feminists vehemently oppose. However, members of the Purple Roof Foundation preempted these potentially hierarchic rules by disregarding them in practice. Anyone who had been active at the center could participate in decision making regardless of the "status" of their membership. In the spring and summer of 1993, when interviews were carried out with members of the foundation, about twelve people had been attending the Tuesday meetings to make organizational decisions concerning the foundation.

However, bypassing legal requirements that could impose a hierarchy on the institution did not necessarily solve the problem of administering a center on principles of feminist solidarity, equal participation, and consensus. "The iron law of oligarchy"[32] was in operation, and certain members who had the expertise and the time assumed formal as well as de facto leadership positions. While members of the center found themselves pushing certain women to assume leadership positions because they felt that these women could do the job best (and these jobs included responding to TV or journal reporters who wanted interviews, and dealing with the police or the bureaucracy), they also, over time, began resenting the leadership status of these women.[33]

About two years after the foundation was instituted, a conflict over the calendar the foundation offered for sale brought to the surface tensions over issues of leadership, equal participation, and hierarchy. The calender would include four languages, and a group of feminists argued that Kurdish should be one of the languages used. Kurdish was the second-largest spoken language in Turkey and including Kurdish would imply a solidarity with Kurdish women. The issue, however, turned into a controversy and brought the "leadership" into confrontation with the opposition. The incident led to a turnover in "leadership" and a renewed attempt to defy the iron law of oligarchy.

Besides the question of leadership and hierarchy, members found themselves being drawn into imposed consensuses. Women who carried out the daily activities of the center were deeply committed to their mission. Hence their feelings and opinions on how to run the center were strong. When those opinions were suppressed in the process of consensus-building, they became buried frustrations that would erupt on untimely occasions as emotional volcanoes. Suppression of dissent was irreconcilable with egalitarian participation.

Finally, an incident of theft put the idea of feminist solidarity and the prospect of egalitarian participation based on this solidarity to the test. When money that belonged to the center was stolen, some women in the center argued for informing the police, which would mean informing on friends. Many others felt disillusioned. Reporting to the police to solve problems among feminist friends seemed like treason to some. The police were a patriarchal weapon of the patriarchal state. Furthermore, how could the feminists distrust and suspect one another? However, those who felt the need to inform the police raised their voices more loudly and the decision was reached as they willed. When the police resolved the issue, a number of devoted feminists stopped going to the center. There had been no consensus over the problem; the amorphous majority that included those who could speak up loudest had ruled over the dissenting minority.

Moreover, operating on the principles of feminist solidarity and seeking a consensus on every problem was painstakingly slow, if not self-destructive. Some women running the foundation had been successful in raising money to acquire a building that would be used as a shelter. They had also convinced and received money from the minister of state responsible for women's affairs to restore the building. After the money was raised, decisions concerning the restoration would be made collectively. However, with feminist aspirations for participant decision making, urgent resolutions concerning the restoration could not be reached. Meanwhile, opportunities for feasible contracts were missed. In the inflationary context, money was lost.

The enormous demands on the center and the foundation required prompt responses to problems.

Gradually, the number of women who ran the center, as well as the number of volunteers who interacted with the victims who came to the center, dwindled. Problems to address were too many while resources were limited. These feminist women were neither prepared nor equipped to solve the diverse problems of domestic violence in Turkey that their foundation had unearthed. As one member of the foundation put it, they had unwittingly "opened a beehive," and when the bees were out, they did not have the power to control them.

IMPLICATIONS AND CONCLUSIONS

Problems of the Purple Roof Women's Shelter Foundation are large, and how these will be handled to insure the longevity of the institution is an open question. Feminist aspirations for participatory democracy and decision making based on consensus strained the foundation in solving its problems and reaching its goals of protecting women from domestic violence. At times, feminist principles and aspirations faltered when natural leaders emerged or when torturous processes of decision making undermined the goal of sheltering women.

Despite the obvious difficulties in its operation, the foundation is significant in the Turkish context. The members of the foundation exhibit a valiant attempt to practice participatory democracy despite their awareness of the pitfalls and the limitations this brings to the institutionalization of the foundation.

At a macro level, the sustained effort of the feminists to draw attention to domestic violence through the institution of the foundation has helped sketch a more democratic concept of citizenship. The feminist struggle against violence through institution-building is not merely an example of active citizenship. In this case, feminists attempt to *enlarge* the scope of democratic citizenship and to provide a "structure with established, important functions"[34] to make it endure. Women are encouraged to claim their right to citizenship as women with problems peculiar to being women (namely, exposure to violence). If citizenship involves rights and responsibilities between the individual and the state, then in order to be considered citizens, women should have the right to be protected from violence.[35] Unless women have this protection, their equal participation in socio-political life is severely curtailed. Where women's protection from violence is a necessary if not sufficient condition of "substantive" citizenship and democracy, then the attempt to institutionalize the protest against violence becomes all the more critical for democratic citizenship.

Notes

Author's note: I would like to thank the Middle East Research Competition of Ford Foundation for making possible the research on which this paper is based. An earlier version of this article was published in *Boğaziçi Journal* 8:1-2 (1994). I am grateful to the feminists who agreed to be interviewed and especially to Yaprak Zihnioğlu, who allowed me to use her private archive on feminist activities in Turkey.

1. For an extensive and lucid discussion of feminism and various models of democracy, see Phillips, 1991; for compelling criticisms of liberalism, see Eisenstein, 1981; Pateman, 1988; Genovese, 1991.
2. Freeman, 1995.
3. Phillips, 1993.
4. On feminist activities in the 1980s, see Ş. Tekeli, 1989 and 1990b; Sirman, 1989; Y. Arat, 1994a and 1994b; Kadıoğlu, 1993; Ovadia, 1994.
5. For a critical elaboration of Kemalist legal reforms concerning women, see Z. Arat, 1994b. For a critical examination of Kemalist projects and modernity, see Durakbaşa, 1988; Göle, 1991.
6. The nine-page bibliography was included in Yaprak Zihnioğlu's private archive. The bibliography of the "Women's Series" working group (Kadın Dizisi Çalışma Grubu) included classics such as Mary Wollstonecraft's *Vindication of the Rights of Women,* Simone de Beauvoir's *The Second Sex,* John Stuart Mill's *The Subjection of Women,* and works by Bebel and Kollontai, as well as the more contemporary classics such as Betty Friedan's *The*

Feminine Mystique, Kate Millet's *Sexual Politics,* Schulamith Firestone's *The Dialectic of Sex,* and Juliet Mitchell's *Women's Estate.*

7. *The Report Prepared in Accordance with Article 18 of the Convention on the Elimination of All Forms of Discrimination Against Women,* 1993:28.

8. In 1992, the minister of state responsible for women's affairs claimed that women's shelters would open in seventy-two provinces of Turkey (*Cumhuriyet,* 6 May 1992). Within the next three years, the shelters opened by the local municipalities all closed down because conservative groups gained power.

9. On the story of the Bakırköy shelter, see İlhan, 1992; on the Şişli shelter, see Devecioğlu, 1989; and *Kadınca,* October 1990.

10. *The Status of Women in Turkey.* The Turkish National Report to the Fourth World Conference on Women, May 1994, art. 149:36.

11. *The Status of Women,* art. 151:36.

12. *The Combined Second and Third Periodic Country Report Prepared in Accordance with Article 18 of the Convention on the Elimination of All Forms of Discrimination Against Women, Turkey,* 1996:27.

13. *The Combined Second and Third Periodic Country Report,* 1996:27.

14. *Milliyet,* 9 June 1991.

15. Women rarely complain; see A. Parla, 1996. For a case that has received media attention and feminist support, see Düzkan and Koçali, 1995:2-4.

16. *The Status of Women,* 39; Arın, 1996:130-139; Paker, et al., 1988:107-110.

17. *The Status of Women,* 39.

18. *The Status of Women,* 38.

19. *The Status of Women,* 38.

20. *Şimdi Sığınak İçin* (Now for the Shelter), 1989.

21. The judge compares women to donkeys and advises men to beat their wives and to impregnate them.

22. *Şimdi Sığınak İçin,* 7.

23. *Şimdi Sığınak İçin,* 7.

24. Paker, et al., 1988.

25. Koçali, 1990:72-74; Armutçu, 1990.

26. Koçali, 1990:74.

27. Interview with Canan Arın, included in Koçali, 1990:74; translation mine.
28. Koçali, 1990:73.
29. *Cumhuriyet,* 7 February 1992; translation mine. See also *Cumhuriyet,* 9 February 1992; İlhan, 1992.
30. Zihnioğlu, 1993:4; translation mine.
31. On problems of feminism and institution building, see *Dolaşan Mavi Çorap,* February 1994.
32. The term has been coined by Robert Michels to argue that oligarchy is inevitable in any organization as participation is sacrificed to efficiency.
33. The discussion that follows concerning the workings of the Purple Roof Foundation is based on interviews carried out by the members of the foundation.
34. Lawson, 1993:34.
35. For a critical summary of feminist literature on citizenship, see Jones, 1990. On the complexity of the question of women's integration into citizenship, as women, with their "differences," see Pateman, 1992.

References

Abadan-Unat, Nermin. "Educational Reforms on Turkish Women." In *Women in Middle Eastern History: Shifting Boundaries in Sex and Gender,* pp. 177-194. Edited by Nikki R. Keddi and B. Baron. New Haven: Yale University Press, 1991.

———. "Social Change and Turkish Women." In *Women in Turkish Society,* pp. 5-31. Edited by Nermin Abadan-Unat. Leiden, The Netherlands: E. J. Brill, 1981.

———, ed., *Women in Developing World: Evidence from Turkey.* World Affairs Monograph Series. Denver, CO: University of Denver Press, 1986.

Abzug, Robert. *Cosmos Crumbling: American Reform and the Religious Imagination.* New York: Oxford University Press, 1994.

Acar, Feride. "Higher Education in Turkey: A Gold Bracelet for Women." In *The Gender Gap in Higher Education,* pp. 160-170. Edited by Suzanne Stiverlie, Lynda Malik, and Duncan Harris. London: Kogan, 1994.

———. "Women in Academic Science Careers in Turkey." In *Women In Science: Token Women or Gender Equality,* pp. 147-171. Edited by Veronica Stolte-Heiskanen, Feride Acar, Nora Ananieva, Dorothea Gaudart, and Ruza Fürst-Dilic. New York: St. Martin's Press, 1991.

———. "Turkish Women in Academia: Roles and Careers." *METU Studies in Development* 10 (1983):409-446.

Addresses Delivered Before the Sixth International Convention of the Student Volunteer Movement for Foreign Missions, *Students and the Present Missionary Crisis.* New York: Student Volunteer Movement, 1910.

Adıvar, Halide Edip. *Türkiye'de Şark, Garp ve Amerikan Tesirleri* (The Impacts of the East, the West, and America on Turkey). İstanbul: Doğan Kardeş, 1956.

———. *Conflict of East and West in Turkey.* Jamia Millia Extension Lectures. Lahore: S. M. Ashraf, 1935.

———. *Turkey Faces West.* New York: Arno Press, 1930.

Adler, Nancy J. and Izraeli, Dafna N., eds. *Women in Management Worldwide.* Armonk, N.Y.: M. E. Sharpe Inc., 1988.

Ağaoğlu, Adalet. *Karşılaşmalar* (Encounters). İstanbul: Yapı Kredi Yayınları, 1993.

Aït Sabbah, Fatna [Fatima Mernissi]. *La Femme dans l'inconscient musulman*. Paris: Éditions Albin Michel, 1986.

Aktaş, Cihan. *Modernizmin Evsizliği ve Ailenin Gerekliliği* (The Elimination of Home in Modernism and the Necessity of the Family). İstanbul: Beyan Yayınları, 1992.

———. *Üç İhtilâl Çocuğu* (The Child of Three Revolutions). İstanbul: Nehir Yayınları, 1991.

———. *Sistem İçinde Kadın* (Woman Within the System). İstanbul: Beyan Yayınları, 1988.

Alban-Metcalfe, Beverly and Nicholson, N. *The Career Development of British Managers*. London: British Institute of Management Foundation, 1984.

Alpman, Nizam. "Sanayi Prensesleri" (The Princesses of the Industry). *Milliyet* 18 (September 1992):15.

[al-Suyūṭī, Jalālu'd-dīn]. *The Book of Exposition [in the Science of Complete and Perfect Coition] (Kitab al-Izah fi'Ilm al-Nikah b-it-Tamam w-al-Kamal)*. Translated and with a Foreword by an English Bohemian. Paris, London, and New York: Maison d'Éditions Scientifiques [Charles Carrington], 1900.

Altındal, Aytunç. *Türkiye'de Kadın* (Woman in Turkey). İstanbul: Anahtar Kitapları, 1991.

———. *Türkiye'de Kadın* (Woman in Turkey). İstanbul: Süreç, 1975.

Anderson, Benedict. *Imagined Communities: Reflections on the Origin and Spread of Nationalism*. London: Verso, 1983.

Andrew, John A. *Rebuilding the Christian Commonwealth*. Lexington: University Press of Kentucky, 1976.

Annual Report of the American Board of Commissioners for Foreign Missions. Boston: Congregational House, 1902, 1903, 1904, 1910, 1911, 1915, 1916.

Anon. *La Fleur lascive orientale*. n.p.: L'Astrée, 1955.

———. *Les Ruses des femmes (Mikri-zenan), et extraits du Plaisir après la peine (Feredj bad chiddeh)*. Translated by J.-A. [Jean-Adolphe] Decourdemanche. Paris: Ernest Leroux, Éditeur, 1896.

Arat, Necla. "Giriş" (Introduction). In *Kadınlar ve Siyasal Yaşam: Eşit Hak-Eşit Katılım* (Women and Political Life: Equal Rights-Equal Participation), pp. 11-20. Edited by Necla Arat. Çağdaş Yaşamı Destekleme Derneği Yayınları 4, İstanbul: Cem Yayınevi, 1991.

———. *Kadın Sorunu* (The Woman Question). İstanbul: Say Yayınları, 1986.

Arat, Yeşim. "A Women Prime Minister in Turkey: Did It Matter?" *Women and Politics* (forthcoming).

———. "Toward a Democratic Society: The Women's Movement in Turkey in the 1980s." *Women's Studies International Forum* 17:2/3 (1994a):241-248.

———. "Women's Movement of the 1980s in Turkey: Radical Outcome of Liberal Feminism." In *Reconstructing Gender in the Middle East: Power, Identity and Tradition*, pp. 100-112. Edited by Fatma Müge Göçek and Shiva Balaghi. New York: Columbia University Press, 1994b.

———. "1980'ler Türkiyesinde Kadın Hareketi: Liberal Kemalizmin Radikal Uzantısı." (The Women's Movement in Turkey of the 1980s: The Radical Extension of Liberal Kemalism). In *Türkiye'de Kadın Olgusu*, pp.75-95. Edited by Necla Arat. İstanbul: Say Yayınları, 1992.

———. "1980'ler Türkiyesi'nde Kadın Hareketi: Liberal Kemalizm'in Radikal Uzantısı" (The Women's Movement in Turkey of the 1980s: The Radical Extension of Liberal Kemalism). *Toplum ve Bilim* 53 (Bahar 1991):7-19.

———. *The Patriarchal Paradox: Women Politicians in Turkey.* Cranbury, NJ: Associated University Presses, 1989.

Arat, Zehra F. "Kemalism and Turkish Women." *Women and Politics* 14:4 (Fall 1994a):57-80.

———. "Turkish Women and the Republican Reconstruction of Tradition." In *Reconstructing Gender in the Middle East: Power, Identity and Tradition*, pp. 57-78. Edited by Fatma Müge Göçek and Shiva Balaghi. New York: Columbia University Press, 1994b.

———. "Liberation or Indoctrination: Women's Education in Turkey." *Journal of Economics and Administrative Studies* 8:1-2 (1994c):83-105.

———. *Democracy and Human Rights in Developing Countries.* Boulder, CO: Lynne Reinner Publishers, 1991.

Arbak, Yasemin, Kabasakal, Hayat, Katrinli, Alev Ergenç, Özmen, Ömür Timurcanday, and Zeytinoğlu, Işık Urla. "Women Managers in Turkey: The Impact of Personalities and Leadership Styles." *Journal of Management Systems* (forthcoming).

Arın, Canan. "Kadına Yönelik Şiddet Açısından Türk Hukukunun Kadına Yaklaşımı" (The Turkish Law's Approach to Women in Terms of Violence on Women). In *Evdeki Terör* (Terror at Home), pp. 130-139. İstanbul: Mor Çatı Yayınları, 1996.

Armutçu, Emel. "Belediye 'Mor Çatı'ya Sığındı." (The Municipality Has Sought Refuge in 'Purple Roof'). *Güneş*, 1 April 1990.

Atatürk, Mustafa Kemal. *Atatürk'ün Söylev ve Demeçleri* (The Speeches and Statements of Atatürk). Vol. 2: 1906-1939. Ankara: Türk İnkılap Tarihi Enstitüsü, 1959.

Atatürk'ün Söylev ve Demeçleri (The Speeches and Statements of Atatürk). Vol. I-III. Ankara: Türk Tarih Kurumu Basımevi, 1989.

Aziz Haydar. "Kadınlığın Yeni Bir Hatvesi Daha" (Another New Forward Step by the Womankind). *Kadınlar Dünyası* 152 (July 1914/1330):4.

——. "Biraz Dedikodu" (A Little Gossip). *Kadınlar Dünyası* 128 (January 1913/1329):3-4.

Balkır, Bengü. "Gender Differences in Work Related Values of Middle and Upper Class Freshman College Students in Turkey." Master's thesis, Boğaziçi University, 1991.

Barker, J. A. "An Address, Foreign Mission Board, Southern Baptist Convention, Richmond, VA." *The Foreign Missions Journal* 56 (July 1905):25-26.

Bartlett, Samuel C. *Historical Sketches of the Missions of the American Board.* New York: 1862; reprinted, New York: Arno Press, 1972.

Başcı, Pelin. "The Image of Turkey as America's 'Other.'" Paper presented at the annual meeting of the Texas Association of Middle East Scholars. San Antonio, TX, February 1993.

Başgöz, İlhan and Wilson, Howard E. *Educational Problems in Turkey, 1920-1940.* Bloomington: Indiana University Press, 1968.

Baudier (de Languedoc), Michel. *Histoire géneralle du serrail, et de la Cour du Grand Seigneur Empereur des Turcs.* Paris: Claude Cramoisy, 1624.

Baykan, Ayşegül C. "The Turkish Woman: An Adventure in Feminist Historiography." *Gender and History* 6:1 (April 1994): 101-116.

Becker, Gary. *Human Capital.* New York: National Bureau of Economic Research, 1971.

Behar, Cem and Duben, Alan. *İstanbul Households, Marriage, Family and Fertility 1880-1940.* Cambridge University Press, 1992.

Beller-Hann, Ildiko. "Prostitution and its Effects in Northeast Turkey," *European Journal of Women's Studies,* 2 (1995):219-235.

Bem, Sandra L. "The Measurement of Psychological Androgyny." *Journal of Consulting and Clinical Psychology,* 42 (1974):155-162.

Berik, Günseli. "The Social Condition of Women in Turkey in the Eighties and in the Migration Process." *New Perspectives on Turkey* 3:1 (Fall 1989):97-107.

Berkes, Niyazi. *The Development of Secularism in Turkey.* Montreal: McGill University Press, 1964.

———, trans. and ed. *Turkish Nationalism and Western Civilization: Selected Essays of Ziya Gökalp.* New York: Columbia University Press, 1959.

Berktay (Baltalı), Fatmagül. *Kadın Olmak, Yaşamak, Yazmak* (Being a Woman, Living and Writing). İstanbul: Pencere Yayınları, 1991.

———. "Türkiye Solu'nun Kadına Bakışı: Değişen Bir Şey Var mı?" (The Turkish Left's View of Women: Is There Anything New?). In *Kadın Bakış Açısından 1980'ler Türkiye'sinde Kadın,* pp. 289-300. Edited by Şirin Tekeli. İstanbul: İletişim Yayınları, 1990.

Bhabha, Homi K. "The Other Question: Stereotype, Discrimination and the Discourse of Colonialism," pp. 66-84. In *The Location of Culture.* London and New York: Routledge, 1994.

Blau, Peter and Duncan, Otis. *The American Occupational Structure.* New York: Wiley, 1967.

Bon, Ottaviano; Robert Withers [trans.]. *A Description of the Grand Signor's Seraglio, or Turkish Emperours Court.* Edited by John Greaves. London: Jo. Martin and Jo. Ridley, 1650.

Boudhiba, Abdelwahab. *La Sexualité en Islam.* Paris: Presses Universitaires de France, 1975.

Boudhiba, Abdulwahab. *Sexuality in Islam.* London: Routledge, Kegan and Paul, 1985.

Brown, Laura. *Ends of Empire: Women and Ideology in Early Eighteenth-Century English Literature.* Ithaca and London: Cornell University Press, 1993.

Brown, O. E. "The Shadow of Islam." *The Missionary Voice.* 4 (March 1914):179-183.

Brummett, Palmira. "New Woman and Old Nag: Images of Women in the Ottoman Cartoon Space." *Princeton Papers: An Interdisciplinary Journal of Middle Eastern Studies* (forthcoming).

Burton, Richard F., Sir. *A Plain and Literal Translation of the Arabian Nights' Entertainments, now entituled The Book of the Thousand Nights and a Night . . .* 10+7 vols. N.p.: Printed by the Burton Club, n.d. ("The Mecca Edition").

Buzard, James. *The Beaten Track: European Tourism, Literature, and the Ways to Culture, 1800-1918.* Oxford: The Clarendon Press of Oxford University Press, 1993.

Cadaloz. 22 Mart–27 Ağustos 1327/5 April–10 September 1911.

Canter, David C. "Action and Place: An Existential Dialectic." In *Environmental Perspectives: Ethnoscapes: Current Challenges in the Environmental Sciences,* pp. 1-17. Edited by David C. Canter, Martin Krampen, and David Stea. Brookfield, VT: Gower Publishing, 1988a.

——, Krampen, Martin and Stea, David. eds., *Environmental Perspectives: Ethnoscapes: Current Challenges in the Environmental Sciences.* Brookfield, VT: Gower Publishing, 1988b.

Carter, Angela. *The Sadeian Woman and the Ideology of Pornography.* New York: Pantheon Books, 1988.

Cerrahoğlu, Nilgün. "Atatürk İlkelerinin Ürünüyüm" (I am a Product of the Kemalist Principles). *Sabah,* 14 July 1993, p. 30.

Chatterjee, Partha. *The Nation and its Fragments: Colonial and Postcolonial Histories.* Princeton, NJ: Princeton University Press, 1993.

Chodorow, Nancy. *The Reproduction of Mothering: Psychoanalysis and the Sociology of Gender.* Berkeley: University of California Press, 1978.

Clarke, James F. "Americans and the April Uprising." *East European Quarterly.* 11 (Winter 1977):421-428.

Cobb, Stanwood. *The Real Turk.* Boston, New York, and Chicago: The Pilgrim Press, 1914.

The Combined Second and Third Periodic Country Report Prepared in Accordance with Article 18 of the Convention on the Elimination of All Forms of Discrimination Against Women. Turkish Republic Prime Ministry Directorate General on the Status and Problems of Women. Turkey, 1996.

Conant, Martha Pike. *The Oriental Tale in England in the Eighteenth Century.* New York: Columbia University Press, 1908.

Cooper, Anna Julia. *A Voice from the South.* Ohio: Aldine Printing House, 1892.

Coşar, Fatma M. "Women in Turkish Society." In *Women in the Moslem World,* pp. 124-140. Edited by Lois Beck and Nikki Keddie. Cambridge, MA: Harvard University Press, 1978.

Cott, Nancy F. *Bonds of Womanhood: "Woman's Sphere" in New England, 1780-1835.* New Haven: Yale University Press, 1977.

Cowell, Alan. "Career Women Finding Elbowroom in Turkey," *New York Times International,* 2 March 1994, p.A7.

[Craven, Elizabeth, Lady]. *A Journey through the Crimea to Constantinople in a Series of Letters from the Right Honourable Elizabeth Lady Craven, to his Serene Highness the Margrave of Brandebourg, Anspach, and Bareith, Written in the Year 1786.* London: G. G. J. and J. Robinson, 1769.

Croutier, Alev Lytle. *Harem: The World Behind the Veil.* New York: Abbeville Press, 1989.

Crunden, Robert M. *A Brief History of American Culture*. Helsinki: SHS, 1990.

Cumhuriyetin 50. Yılında Milli Eğitimimiz (Our National Education in the 50th Year of the Republic). T.C. Milli Eğitim Bakanlığı Yayını. İstanbul: Milli Eğitim Basımevi, 1973.

Cunbur, Müjgân. "Atatürk'e Göre Türk Kadınıyla İlgili Sorunlar ve Değerlendirmeler" (According to Atatürk the Problems Related to Women and Their Assessments). *Erdem* 4:12 (September 1988):685-732.

Çakır, Serpil. *Osmanlı Kadın Hareketi* (The Ottoman Women's Movement). İstanbul: Metis Yayınları, 1994.

————. "Osmanlı Kadın Dernekleri" (The Ottoman Women's Associations). *Toplum ve Bilim* 53 (Spring 1991):139-159.

————. "Bir Osmanlı Kadın Örgütü: Müdafaa-ı Hukuk-u Nisvan Cemiyeti" (An Ottoman Woman's Organization: Society for the Defense of Women's Rights). *Tarih ve Toplum*. 66 (June 1989):336-341.

Çeviker, Turgut. *Gelişim Sürecinde Türk Karikatürü* (Turkish Cartoons in the Process of Development). İstanbul: Adam Yayınları, 1986-1991.

Çitçi, Oya. "Türk Kamu Yönetiminde Kadın Görevliler" (Women Employees Within the Turkish Public Administration). In *Türk Toplumunda Kadın,* pp. 221-252. Edited by Nermin Abadan-Unat. İstanbul: Araştırma, Eğitim, Ekin Yayınları, 1979.

Dalkavuk. 30 Ağustos–21 Şubat 1324/13 September 1908–7 March 1909.

Danacıoğlu, Esra. "Anadolu'da Amerikan Misyoner Faaliyetleri, 1820-1914" (American Missionary Activities in Anatolia, 1820-1914). Master's thesis, Hacettepe University, 1987.

Daniel, Norman [A.] *Islam and the West: the Making of an Image.* Edinburgh: The University Press, 1960.

Davidoff, Leonore. "Regarding Some 'Old Husband Tales': Public and Private in Feminist History." In *Worlds Between: Historical Perspectives on Gender and Class,* pp. 227-276. Cambridge: Polity Press, 1995.

Davidson, Marilyn J. "Women Managers and Stress: Profiles of Vulnerable Individuals." *Clinical Psychology Forum* 22 (1989):32-34.

Davis, Fanny. *The Ottoman Lady: A Social History from 1718 to 1918.* New York, Westport, CT, and London: Greenwood Press, 1986.

Davis, Grace T. *Neighbors in Christ: Fifty-Eight Years of World Service by the Woman's Board of Missions of the Interior.* Chicago: James Watson & Co., 1926.

Davul. 14 Teşrin-i evvel 1324–14 Nisan 1325/27 October 1908–27 April 1909.

De Certeau, Michel. *The Practice of Everyday Life.* Translated by Steven F. Rendall. Berkeley, Los Angeles, and London: University of California Press, 1984.

De Régla, Paul [Paul André Desjardin], trans. *El Ktab des lois secrètes de l'amour d'après le Khôdja Omer Haleby, Abou Othman.* Paris: Albin Michel, Éditeur, 1906.

Deavereux, Robert, trans. and ed. *The Principles of Turkism by Ziya Gökalp.* Leiden: E. J. Brill, 1968.

Dehoï, Enver F. *L'Érotisme des "Mille et une nuits."* Paris: Jean-Jacques Pauvert, Éditeur, 1963.

Delaney, Carol. *The Seed and the Soil: Gender and Cosmology in Turkish Village Society.* Berkeley: University of California Press, 1991.

Demet (İstanbul). 30 September 1908–11 November 1908.

Demirdirek, Aynur. *Osmanlı Kadınlarının Hayat Hakkı Arayışının Bir Hikayesi* (A Story of the Ottoman Women's Demand for the Right to Life). Ankara: İmge Kitabevi Yayınları, 1993.

Dennis, James S. *Christian Missions and Social Progress.* New York: Fleming H. Revell Company, 1897.

Devecioğlu, Ayşegül. "Şişli'de Bir Mor Karanfil" (A Purple Carnation in Şişli). *Nokta,* 15 October 1989.

Dews, Peter. *Logics of Disintegration: Post-Structuralist Thought and the Claims of Critical Theory.* London: Verso, 1988.

Diderot, Denis. "Les Bijoux indiscrets." In *Œuvres romanesques,* pp. 1–233. Edited by Henri Bénac and reviewed by Lucette Perol. Paris: Éditions Garnier Frères, 1981.

Dilber, Mustafa. *Türk Özel Kesim Endüstrisinde Yönetsel Davranış* (Managerial Behavior in the Turkish Private Manufacturing Sector). İstanbul: Özlem Matbaacılık, 1981.

Dirks, Nicholas B., Eley, Goeff, and Ortner, Sherry B. "Introduction." In *Culture/Power/History: A Reader in Contemporary Social Theory,* pp. 1–45. Princeton, NJ: Princeton University Press, 1994.

Dodge, Bayard. "American Educational and Missionary Efforts in the Nineteenth and Early Twentieth Centuries." *The Annals of the American Academy.* 401 (May 1972):15–22.

Doğramacı, Emel. *Status of Women in Turkey.* Revised and expanded 3rd ed. Ankara: Meteksan Co., Inc., 1989.

———. *Rights of Women in Turkey.* n.p., 1982.

Dolaşan Mavi Çorap. February, 1994.

Douthwaite, Julia V. *Exotic Women: Literary Heroines and Cultural Strategies in Ancien Régime France.* Philadelphia: University of Pennsylvania Press, 1992.

Durakbaşa, Ayşe. "Cumhuriyet Döneminde Kemalist Kadın Kimliğinin Oluşumu" (The Formation of the Kemalist Woman Identity During the Republican Era). *Tarih ve Toplum* (March 1988):39-43.

————. "The Formation of 'Kemalist Female Identity': A Historical-Cultural Perspective." Master's thesis. Boğaziçi University, 1987.

Düzkan, Ayşe and Koçali, Filiz. "Güneş Neler Yaşadı?" (What Did Güneş Live Through ?) *Pazartesi*, no.1, April 1995.

Dyhouse, Carol. *Girls Growing Up in Late Victorian and Edwardian England.* London: Routledge and Kegan Paul, 1981.

Ecevit, Yıldız. "Türkiye'de Kadın İşgücünün Marjinalliği" (The Marginality of Women's Labor Force in Turkey). *Bülten* 11 (April 1992):15-18.

————. "Shop Floor Control: The Ideological Construction of Turkish Women Factory Workers," In *Working Women: International Perspectives on Labor and Gender Ideology,* pp. 56-78. Edited by N. Redclift and T. Sinclair. London: Routledge, 1991.

Ecumenical Missionary Conference. *Report 1900.* New York: American Tract Society, 1900.

Eisenstein, Zillah. *The Radical Future of Liberal Feminism.* New York: Longman, 1981.

Ekonomi, Münir. "Türk Hukukunun Avrupa Topluluğu Hukuku ile Uyumu" (The Consistency of Turkish Law with the Law of European Community). n.p., n.d., pp. 333-346.

Eliade, Mircea. *The Myth of the Eternal Return.* Willard R. Trask, trans. Chicago: University of Chicago Press, 1954.

Ellis, Ellen Deborah and Palmer, Florance. "The Feminist Movement in Turkey." *The Contemporary Review* 105 (January-June 1914):857-864.

Entrikin, J. Nicholas. *The Betweenness of Place: Towards a Geography of Modernity.* Baltimore, MD: Johns Hopkins University Press, 1991.

Eray, Nazlı. "Monte Kristo." In *Contemporary Turkish Literature: Fiction and Poetry,* pp. 88-92. Edited and with an introduction by Talat Sait Halman. Rutherford, NJ: Fairleigh Dickinson University Press, 1982.

Ersanlı, Büşra. "Birinci Türk Tarih Kongresi 1932—Türkçülükten Yurttaşlığa" (The First Turkish History Congress, 1932—

From Turkism to Citizenship). *Toplum ve Bilim* 31/39 (1987):81-104.

Fahri, A. Ziyaeddin. *Ziya Gökalp, sa vie et sa sociologie (Essai sur l'influence de la sociologie francaise en Turquie)*. Paris, 1935.

Falaka. 25 Temmuz–29 Eylül 1327/8 August–12 October 1911.

Fatma Aliye. "Bas Bleulerden İbert Alalım" (Let's Learn a Lesson from the Bas Blues). *Hanımlara Mahsus Gazete* 2 (August 1895/ 1311):2-3.

————. "Meşahir-i Nisvan-i İslamiyeden Biri: Fatma Bint-i Abbas" (A Famous Person from Women of Islamic Community: Fatma Bint-i Abbas). *Hanımlara Mahsus Gazete* 8 (14 September 1895/1311):3-4; and 9 (18 September 1895/1311):2-3.

Fazıl-Bey [Enderunlu Fazıl Hüseyin Bey]. *Le livre des femmes (Zenannameh)*. Translated by J.-A. [Jean-Adolphe] Decourdemanche. Paris: Ernest Leroux, Éditeur, 1879.

Fazy, Edmond and Abdul-Halim Memdouh, eds. *Anthologie de l'amour turc*. Paris: Société du Mercure de France, 1905.

Fındıkoğlu, Ziyaeddin. *Ziya Gökalp: Sa Vie et sa Sociologie*. Paris: Berger-Levrault, 1936.

Finkel, Andrew and Sirman, Nükhet. eds., *State and Politics in Turkey*. London: Routledge, 1989.

Fişek, Güler O. "Paradoxes of Intimacy: An Analysis in Terms of Gender, Culture and Psychotherapeutic Intervention." Working paper, 1993.

Fitzpatrick, William. *Istanbul After Dark*. New York: MacFadden-Bartell, 1970.

Flaubert, Gustave. *The Letters of Gustave Flaubert*. 2 vols. Translated and edited by Francis Steegmuller. Cambridge, MA, and London: The Belknap Press of Harvard University Press, 1980.

————. *Sentimental Education; or, the History of a Young Man*. 2 vols. Akron: St. Dunstan Society, 1904.

Flemming, Leslie A., ed. *Women's Work for Women: Missionaries and Social Change in Asia*. Boulder: Westview Press, 1989.

Foucault, Michel. "Two Lectures." In *Culture/Power/History: A Reader in Contemporary Social Theory*, pp. 200-221. Edited by Nicholas B. Dirks, Goeff Eley, and Sherry B. Ortner. Princeton, NJ: Princeton University Press, 1994.

————. "Technologies of the Self." In *Technologies of the Self: A Seminar with Michel Foucault*, pp. 16-49. Edited by Luther H. Martin, Huck Gutman, and Patrick H. Hutton. Amherst: University of Massachusetts Press, 1988.

————. *History of Sexuality.* Translated by Robert Hurley. Volume I. New York: Pantheon Books, 1978.

Freeman, Jo. "From Suffrage to Women's Liberation: Feminism in Twentieth-Century America." In *Women: A Feminist Perspective,* pp.509-528. Edited by Jo Freeman. California: Mayfield, 1995.

Furüzan. "Taşralı" (The Girl from the Provinces). In *Türk Edebiyatı:1969 Antoloji.* Vol. 4, pp. 267-272. Edited by Mehmet Fuat. İstanbul: De Yayınevi, 1969.

Gailey, Christine Ward. *Kinship to Kingship.* Austin: University of Texas Press, 1987.

Geiger, Susan. "What's So Feminist about Doing Women's Oral History?" In *Expanding the Boundaries of Women's History,* pp. 305-318. Edited by Cheryl Johnson-Odim and Margaret Strobel. Bloomington: Indiana University Press, 1992.

Gellner, Ernest. *Postmodernism, Reason and Religion.* London and New York: Routledge, Kegan and Paul , 1992.

Genovese, Elizabeth Fox. *Feminism Without Illusions.* Chapel Hill: University of North Carolina Press, 1991.

Gilman, Sander L. *Difference and Pathology: Stereotypes of Sexuality, Race, and Madness.* Ithaca and London: Cornell University Press, 1985.

Gobineau, A. [Joseph Arthur] de. *Trois ans en Asie (de 1855 à 1858).* Paris: Librairie de L. Hachette et Cie., 1859.

Gökalp, Ziya. *Türkçülüğün Esasları* (The Principles of Turkism). İstanbul: Kültür Bakanlığı Yayınları, No.7, 1976.

————. *Yeni Hayat* (New Life). İstanbul, 1941.

————. *Türkçülügün Esasları* (Foundations of Turkism). Ankara, 1923.

————. *Küçük Mecmua* (Little Study). Diyarbekir, 1922-1923.

————. *Tükleşmek, İslamlaşmak, Muasırlaşmak* (Turkification, Islamization, Modernization). İstanbul, 1918.

————. *Kızıl Elma* (Red Apple). İstanbul, 1914-1915.

Göle, Nilüfer. *The Forbidden Modern: Civilization and Veiling.* Ann Arbor: University of Michigan Press, 1996.

————. *Modern Mahrem* (The Forbidden in Modern [Society]). İstanbul: Metis Yayınları, 1991.

Gülnar Hanım. "İslam Kadınlarında Hürriyet" (Freedom in Women of Islam). Trans. A. Ulvi. *Kadın* 12 (29 December 1908/1324):2-3; 13 (5 January 1324):5-6; 14 (12 January 1324):10-12; 15 (19 January 1324):5-7.

Gün, Güneli. "The Woman in the Darkroom: Contemporary Women Writers in Turkey." *World Literature Today* 60:2. (Spring 1986):275-279.

Güntekin, Reşat Nuri. *The Autobiography of a Turkish Girl.* Translated by Sir Wyndham Deedes. London: George Allen and Unwin, 1949.

Gürbilek, Nurdan. *Vitrinde Yaşamak: 1980'lerin Kültürel İklimi* (Living in a Shop-window: The Cultural Climate of the 1980s). İstanbul: Metis Yayınları, 1992.

Gürbüz, Emel. "A Measurement of Sex-Trait Stereotypes." Master's thesis. Boğaziçi University, l988.

Gürsoy, Akile. "Islamist Revivalism, the Family and the Popular Literature: A Case Study of Gökçent." Paper presented at the Rockefeller Programme Panel, University of Texas at Austin, April 1992.

Güzel, Şehmus. "Tanzimattan Chumhuriyet'e Toplumsal Değişim ve Kadın" (Social Change and Women from *Tanzimat* to the Republic). *Tanzimat'tan Chumuriyet'e Türkiye Ansiklopedisi,* vol. 3-4, pp. 858-864, vol. 4, pp. 867-874. İstanbul: İletişim Yayınları, 1985.

"Güzellik Ayıp Birşey Değildir" (Beauty Is Not a Disgraceful Thing). *Cumhuriyet,* 13 Kanun-ı sani 1930.

Hall, Charles C. *Christ and the Eastern Soul.* Chicago, IL: University of Chicago Press, 1909.

Hamlin, Cyrus. *My Life and Times.* n.p., n.d.

———. *Among the Turks.* New York: R. Carter & Brothers, 1878.

Hanımlar Âlemi (İstanbul). 9 April 1914–24 October 1918.

Hanımlara Mahsus Gazete (İstanbul). 1 September 1895–25 June 1908.

Hann, Chris. "The Sexual Division of Labour in Lazistan." In *Culture and Economy: Changes in Turkish Villages,* pp. 126-139. Edited by Paul Stirling. Huntingdon: Eothen, 1993.

Harlow, Ralph S. *Student Witnesses for Christ.* New York: Association Press, 1919.

Hatemı, Hüseyın. "Tanzimat ve Meşrutiyet Dönemlerinde Derneklerin Gelişimi" (The Development of Associations During the Periods of *Tanzimat* and Constitutionalism). *Tanzimat'tan Chumuriyet'e Türkiye Ansiklopedisi,* vol.1, pp. 198-204. İstanbul: İletişim Yayınları, 1985.

Helling, Barbara. "Child Rearing Techniques in Turkish Peasant Villages." Master's thesis. University of Minnesota, 1960.

Hennig, Margaret and Jardim, Anne. *The Managerial Woman.* Garden City: Anchor Press, l977.

Hesapçıoğlu, Muhsin. *Türkiye'de İnsan Gücü ve Eğitim Planlaması* (The Human Resource and Education Planning in Turkey). Ankara Üniversitesi Eğitim Bilimleri Fakültesi Yayınları, No. 127. Ankara: Ankara Üniversitesi Basımevi. 1984.

Hessini, Leila. "Wearing the Hijab in Contemporary Morocco: Choice and Identity." In *Reconstructing Gender in the Middle East: Tradition, Identity and Power,* pp. 40-56. Edited by Müge Göçek and Shiva Balaghi. New York: Columbia University Press, 1994.

Heyd, Uriel. *Foundations of Turkish Nationalism: The Life and Teachings of Ziya Gökalp.* London: The Harvill Press, 1950.

Hill, Patricia R. *The World Their Household.* Ann Arbor: University of Michigan Press, 1985.

Hutchison, William R. *Errand to the World.* Chicago, IL: University of Chicago Press, 1987.

Iragary, Luce. "Sexual Difference." In *French Feminist Thought, A Reader,* pp. 118-130. Edited by Toril Moi. New York: Basil Blackwell, 1987.

Işın, Ekrem. "Tanzimat, Kadın ve Gündelik Hayat" (*Tanzimat,* Women, and Daily Life). *Tarih ve Toplum.* 51 (March 1988):150-155.

İlhan, Uğur. *Kadın Evi* (Women's Shelter). İstanbul: Cep Kitapları, 1992.

İlyasoğlu, Aynur. *Örtülü Kimlik* (Veiled Identity). İstanbul: Metis Yayınları, 1994.

İnan, Afet. *Medeni Bilgiler ve M. Kemal Atatürk'ün Elyazıları* (Civic Instructions and the Handwritten Notes of M. Kemal Atatürk). Ankara: Türk Tarih Kurumu Basımevi, 1969.

———. *Atatürk ve Türk Kadın Haklarının Kazanılması: Tarih Boyunca Türk Kadınının Hak ve Görevleri* (Atatürk and Gaining Turkish Women's Rights: The Rights and Duties of the Turkish Woman Through History). İstanbul: Milli Eğitim Basımevi, 1968.

İncili Çavuş. 12:4, 16 Eylül 1324/29 September 1908.

İncirlioğlu, Emine Onaran. "Negotiating Ethnographic Reality: Team-Fieldwork in Turkey." In *When History Accelerates: Essays on Rapid Social Change, Complexity and Creativity,* pp. 255-275. Edited by Chris M. Hann. London: Athlone Press, 1994.

———. "Marriage, Gender Relations and Rural Transformation in Central Anatolia." In *Culture and Economy: Changes in Turkish Villages,* pp. 115-125. Edited by Paul Stirling. Huntingdon: Eothen, 1993.

————. "Gender Relations and Rural Transformation: Two Central Anatolian Villages." Ph.D. dissertation, University of Florida, 1991.

"İTÜ 2001 Atılım Projesi " (2001 Progress Project of İstanbul Technical University). *Hürriyet.* 31 March 1997, p. 22.

"İzmir'de Balo" (Ball in İzmir). *Cumhuriyet,* Kanun-ı sani, 1930.

JanMohamed, Abdul R. "The Economy of Manichean Allegory: the Function of Racial Difference in Colonialist Literature," in *"Race," Writing, and Difference,* pp. 78-106. Edited by Henry Louis Gates, Jr. Chicago and London: The University of Chicago Press, 1986.

Jayawardena, Kumari. *Feminism and Nationalism in the Third World.* London: Zed Press, 1988.

Jelin, Elizabeth. "Introduction." In *Women and Social Change in Latin America,* pp. 1-11. Translated by J. Ann Zammit and Marilyn Thomson. London: Zed Books, 1990.

Jones, Kathleen. "Citizenship in a Woman Friendly Polity." *Signs: Journal of Women in Culture and Society* 15:4 (1990):781-812.

Jowkar, Forouz. "Honor and Shame: A Feminist View from Within." *Feminist Issues* (Spring 1988):45-65.

Kabasakal, Hayat E. "Kadınlar, Örgütler ve Güç Dağılımı" (Women, Organizations, and the Distribution of Power). *Toplum ve Bilim* 53 (Spring 1991a):55-62.

————. "Yöneticilik, Kadınlar ve Toplumsal Tutumlar" (Management, Women, and Social Attitudes). *Ekonomi ve İdari Bilimler Dergisi* 5:1 (winter l991):25-35.

————, Boyacıgiller, Nakiye A., and Erden, Deniz. "Organizational Characteristics as Correlates of Women in Middle and Top Management." *Boğaziçi Journal: A Review of Social, Economic and Administrative Studies* 8 (1994):45-62.

————, Sunar, Diane G., and Fişek, Güler O. "Kadın Yöneticilere İlişkin Tutumlar, Cinsiyet ve Cinsiyete Bağlı Roller" (Attitudes Related to Women Mangers, Sex, and Sex Related Roles). Paper presented at the conference on Turkish Management. Silivri, İstanbul, l993.

Kadın (İstanbul). 24 August 1911–18 July 1912.

Kadın (Selanik). 26 October 1908–7 June 1909.

"Kadın ve Hürriyet-i Şahsiyye" (Women and Personal Freedom). *Kadınlar Dünyası* 135 (March 1914/1330):2.

Kadın Eserleri Kütüphanesi Bibliyografya Oluşturma Komisyonu. *İstanbul Kütüphanelerinde Eski Harfli Türkçe Kadın Dergileri Bibliyografyası* (The Bibliography of the Turkish Women's Journals in Old Script in İstanbul Libraries). İstanbul, Kadın

Eserleri Kütüphanesi ve Bilgi Merkezi Vakfı, Metis Yayınları, 1993.

Kadınca. 12/1978; 7/1980; 9/1982; 7/1983; 12/1985; 12/1986; 12/1988; 4/1989; 7/1989; 8/1989; 10/1989; 1/1990; 3/1990; 6/1990; 8/1990; 9/1990; 10/1990; 11/1990; 12/1990; 1/1991; 2/1991; 3/1991.

"Kadınlar" (Women). *Cumhuriyet*. 15 September 1990, p.7.

Kadınlar Dünyası (İstanbul). 17 April 1913–21 May 1921.

"Kadınlarımız ve Spor" (Our Women and Sports). *Akşam Spor* 20 (April 1938):9.

Kadınlık (İstanbul). 21 March 1914–16 July 1914.

Kadıoğlu, Ayşe. "(Alaturkalık ile İffetsizlik Arasında) Birey Olarak Kadın" (A Woman as an Individual). *Görüş*, (May 1993):58-62.

Kağıtçıbaşı, Çiğdem. *Value of Children in Turkey*, East-West Center, Honolulu, Hawaii: Current Studies on the Value of Children, 1982.

———. *Çocuğun Değeri: Türkiye'de Değerler ve Doğurganlık* (The Value of Children: Values and Fertility in Turkey). İstanbul: Boğaziçi Universitesi Yayınları, 1981.

Kalem. 21 Ağustos 1324–16 Haziran 1327/4 September 1908–29 June 1911.

Kandiyoti, Deniz. "Strategies for Feminist Scholarship in the Middle East." Paper presented at the 27th annual meeting of the Middle East Studies Association, November 11-14, 1993.

———."Introduction." In *Women, Islam and the State*, pp. 1-21. Philadelphia: Temple University Press, 1991b.

———."The End of Empire: Islam, Nationalism and Women in Turkey." In *Women, Islam and the State*, pp.22-47. Philadelphia: Temple University Press, 1991c.

———. "Ataerkil Örüntüler: Türk Toplumunda Erkek Egemenliğinin Çözümlenmesine Yönelik Notlar." In *Kadın Bakış Açısından 1980'ler Türkiye'sinde Kadınlar*, pp.341-357. Edited by Şirin Tekeli. İstanbul: İletişim, 1990.

———. "Slave Girls, Temptresses, and Comrades: Images of Women in the Turkish Novel," *Feminist Issues* (Spring, 1988a):35-50.

———."Bargaining with Patriarchy." *Gender and Society* 2 (1988b):274-290.

———. "Emancipated but Unliberated? Reflections on the Turkish Case." *Feminist Studies* 13 (Summer 1987):317-338.

———. *Women in Rural Production Systems*. Paris: UNESCO, 1985.

———. "Dimensions of Psycho-Social Change in Women: An Inter-generational Comparison." In *Women in Turkish Society*, pp.

233-258. Edited by Nermin Abadan-Unat, in collaboration with Deniz Kandiyoti and Mübeccel B. Kıray. Leiden: E. J. Brill, 1981.

———, ed., *Women, Islam and the State*. Philadelphia: Temple University Press, 1991a.

Kanter, Rosabeth M. *Men and Women of the Corporation*. New York: Basic Books Inc., 1977.

Karabey, Zeynep A. "Sessizlik" (Silence). In *Kötü Bir Yaratık* (A Worthless Creature), pp. 39-42. İstanbul: Yazko, 1983.

Karal, Enver Ziya. *Atatürk'ten Düşünceler* (Thoughts from Atatürk). Ankara: Türk Tarih Kurumu Basımevi, 1956.

Katırcı, Şerife. *Müslüman Kadının Adı Var* (The Muslim Woman Has a Name). 3rd ed. İstanbul: Seha Neşriyat, 1989.

Katrinli, Alev Ergenç and Özmen, Ömür Timurcanday. "Attitudes Toward Women As Managers: A Case of Turkey." 7. Ulusal Psikoloji Kongresi, Hacettepe University, Ankara, Fall 1992. Mimeo.

———. "Women in Management." Paper presented at the Conference on Women in Management Learning: An Holistic Approach. Lancaster, England, Fall 1991. Mimeo.

Kazgan, Gülten. "Labor-Force Participation, Occupational Distribution, Educational Attainment and Socio-Economic Status of Women in the Turkish Economy." In *Women in Turkish Society*, pp.131-159. Edited by Nermin Abadan-Unat. Leiden: E. J. Brill, 1981.

———. "Türk Ekonomisinde Kadınların İşgücüne Katılması, Mesleki Dağılımı, Eğitim Düzeyi ve Sosyo-Ekonomik Statüsü." In *Türk Toplumunda Kadın* (Women in the Turkish Society), pp. 137-170. Edited by Nermin Abadan-Unat. İstanbul: Araştırma, Eğitim, Ekin Yayınları, 1979.

[Kemâl Paşa Zâde Şemseddin Ahmed bin Süleyman (a.k.a. İbn-i Kemâl Paşa), possibly translated from Tifâshî]. *The Old Man Young Again, or Age-Rejuvenescence in the Power of Concupiscence (Kitab Ruju'a as-Shaykh ila Sabah Fi-l-Kuwwat 'ala-l-Bah)*. Translated, annotated, and with a Foreword by an English "Bohemian." Paris: Charles Carrington, 1898.

Kıray, Mübeccel. "Changing Roles of Mothers: Changing Intra-family Relations in a Turkish Town." In *Mediterranean Family Structures*, pp. 261-271. Edited by J. G. Peristiany. London: Cambri― ― University Press, 1976.

Kızıltan, M ―cel. "Türk Kadın Hakları Mücadele Tarihinde Fatma A ― Hanım'ın Yeri" (The Place of Fatma Aliye *Hanım* within the History of the Struggle for Turkish Women's Rights). *Kurum* 1 (January1993):83-93.

Knibiehler, Yvonne and Goutalier, Régine. *La femme au temps des colonies* Paris: Éditions Stock, 1985.

Kocabaşoğlu, Uygur. *Anadolu'daki Amerika* (The America in Anatolia). 2nd ed. İstanbul: Arba Yayınları, 1991.

———. "Amerikan Okulları" (American Schools). *Tanzimat'tan Cumhuriyet'e Türkiye Ansiklopedisi.* n.d., s.v.

Koçak, Cemil. "Tanzimat'tan Sonra Özel ve Yabancı Okullar" (The Private and Foreign Schools after *Tanzimat*). *Tanzimat'tan Cumhuriyet'e Türkiye Ansiklopedisi.* n.d., s.v.

Koçali, Filiz. "Kadın Evi Tartışması" (Controversy on Women's Shelter). *Kadınca* (8 June 1990):72-74.

Koray, Meryem. "Günümüzdeki Yaklaşımlar Işığında Kadın ve Siyaset" (Women and Politics in the Light of Current Approaches). Türkiye Sosyal Ekonomik Araştırmalar Vakfı, l99l.

Köker, Eser. "Feminizim Muzir Cereyan mı? Türk Kadını, Nezihe Muhittin" (Is Feminism a Harmful Current? The Turkish Woman Nezihe Muhittin). *Tarih ve Toplum* 44 (August 1987):127-128.

Köksal, Duygu. "Nationalist Theory in the Writings of Halide Edib." *The Turkish Studies Association Bulletin* 17 (Fall 1993):80-91.

Kuşçuoğlu, Cengiz. "Bir Yasama Yılı Böyle Geçti" (A Legislative Year Passed this Way). *Milliyet*, 20 July l992, p. l2.

La France: Images of Woman and Ideas of Nation 1789-1989. Exhibition at the Hayward Gallery, London and the Walker Art Gallery, Liverpool. London: South Bank Centre, 1989.

Lak Lak. 1323-1325/1907-1909.

Lawrence, Margarette W. *Light on the Dark River or Memorials of Mrs. Henrietta A. L. Hamlin, Missionary in Turkey.* 3rd ed. Boston: Ticknor, Reed, and Fields, 1853.

Lawson, Kay. *The Human Polity.* Boston: Houghton Mifflin Co., 1992.

Le Rouge, Gustave. *Turquie: mariage, adultère, prostitution, psychologie de l'eunuchisme. Anthologie.* Paris: H. Daragon Libraire-Éditeur, 1912.

Lerner, Daniel. *The Passing of Traditional Society.* New York: Free Press, 1958.

Lerner, Gerda. *The Creation of Patriarchy.* New York and Oxford: Oxford University Press, 1986.

Lewis, Bernard. *Christians and Jews in the Ottoman Empire.* New York: Holmes & Meier Publishers, 1982.

———. *The Emergence of Modern Turkey.* London: Oxford University Press Paperbacks, 1968.

Lowe, Lisa. *Critical Terrains: French and British Orientalisms.* Ithaca and London: Cornell University Press, 1991.

Maarif Sergisi Rehberi (The Guide for the Education Exhibition). İstanbul: Devlet Matbaasi, 1933.

Malti-Douglas, Fedwa. *Woman's Body, Woman's Word: Gender and Discourse in Arabo-Islamic Writing.* Princeton: Princeton University Press, 1991.

Mardin, Şerif. "Religion and Secularism in Turkey." In *Atatürk: Founder of a Modern State,* pp. 119-219. Edited by Ali Kazancıgil and Ergun Özbudun. London: C. Hurst and Co., 1981.

————. *Continuity and Change in the Ideas of the Young Turks.* İstanbul: Robert College, 1969.

————. "The Mind of the Turkish Reformer." *Humanities Review* 15 (1960):413-436.

Marshall, Susan E. "Development, Dependence, and Gender Inequality in the Third World." *International Studies Quarterly* 29 (1985):217-240.

Martin, Edwin W. *The Hubbards of Sivas: A Chronicle of Love and Faith.* Santa Barbara: Fithian Press, 1991.

Martino, Pierre. *L'Orient dans la littérature française au XVIIe et au XVIIIe siècle.* Paris: Hachette, 1906.

Masemann, V. L. "The Hidden Curriculum of a West African Girls' Boarding School." *Canadian Journal of African Studies* 8 (1974):479-94.

Mathers, E. Powys, ed. and trans. *Eastern Love.* 3 vols. New York: Horace Liveright; London: J. Rodker, 1930.

Mazumdar, Sucheta. "Moving Away from a Secular Vision? Women, Nation, and the Cultural Construction of Hindu India." In *Identity Politics and Women: Cultural Reassertions and Feminisms in International Perspective,* pp. 243-273. Edited by Valentine Moghadam. Boulder: Westview Press, 1994.

Mehâsin (İstanbul). September 1908–November 1909.

Melman, Billie. *Women's Orients: English Women and the Middle East, 1718-1918; Sexuality, Religion, and Work.* Ann Arbor: University of Michigan Press, 1992.

Micklewright, Nancy. "Woman's Dress in 19th Century İstanbul: Mirror of a Changing Society." Ph.D. dissertation, University of Pennsylvania, 1986.

Missionary Herald (Boston), January 1901–July 1901.

Mohanty, Chandra Talpade. "Under Western Eyes: Feminist Scholarship and Colonial Discourses." In *Third World Women and the Politics of Feminism,* pp. 51-80. Edited by Chandra Talpade

Mohanty, Ann Ruso, and Lourdes Torres. Bloomington, IN: Indiana University Press, 1991.

[Montagu, Mary Wortley, Lady]. *Letters of the Right Honourable Lady M—y W—y M——e: Written during her Travels in Europe, Asia and Africa, to Persons of Distinction, Men of Letters, &c. in different Parts of Europe. Which Contains, among other curious Relations, Accounts of the Policy and Manners of the Turks; Drawn from Sources that have been inaccessible to other Travellers.* 3 vols. London: T. Becket and P.A. De Hondt, 1763.

Montesquieu [Charles-Louis de Secondat, Baron de la Brède et de Montesquieu]. *The Persian Letters.* Translated and with an introduction by George R. Healy. Indianapolis and New York: The Bobbs-Merrill Company, Inc., 1964.

Morvaridi, Behrooz. "Gender and Household Resource Management in Agriculture: Cash Crops in Kars." In *Culture and Economy: Changes in Turkish Villages,* pp. 80-94. Edited by Paul Stirling. Huntingdon: Eothen, 1993.

Mumby, Dennis K., and Putnam, Linda L. "The Politics of Emotion: A Feminist Reading of Bounded Rationality." *Academy of Management Review* 17 (1992):465-486.

Musavver Kadın (İstanbul). 16 April 1911–3 July 1911.

Musavver Papağan. 6 Eylül 1324–30 Temmuz 1325/19 September 1908–13 August 1909.

Mükerrem Belkıs. "İnsanlığın İki Kanadı." (Two Wings of Humanity). *Kadınlar Dünyası* 169 (April 1918):3-4.

Naak, Munise. "Mor Çatı Kadın Sığınağı Vakfı" (Purple Roof Women's Shelter Foundation) *İktisat Dergisi* (March-April 1991):11-12.

Nabokov, Vladimir. "On a Book Entitled *Lolita.*" In *The Annotated Lolita.* Edited and annotated by Alfred Appel, Jr. New York and Toronto: McGraw-Hill Book Company, 1970:313-319.

Najmabadi, Afsaneh. "Beloved and Mother: The Erotic Vatan [Homeland]: To Love, to Hold, and to Protect." Paper delivered at the Social Science Research Council Conference, Cairo, May 1993.

Navaro, Yael. "Using the Mind at Home: The Rationalization of Housewifeing in Early Republican Turkey, 1928-1940." Unpublished Bachelor's thesis, University of Brandeis, 1991.

Nekregu ile Pişekar. 18 Ağustos 1324–29 Temmuz 1325/1 September 1908–12 August 1909.

Nicolaidès [Nicolaïdes], Jean, ed. *Contes licencieux de Constantinople et de l'Asie Mineure.* With introductory essays by C. de W. and G.

Froidure d'Aubigné. Paris: Gustave Ficker; Kleinbronn: Jacob Martin, 1906.

Nimet Cemil. "Yine Feminizm, Daima Feminizm!" (Feminism Again, Feminism Always!). *Kadınlar Dünyası* 194-8 (February 1921) 2.

Nisvân (Bağçesaray). 24 March 1906.

Oktay, Ahmet. *Toplumsal Değişme ve Basın* (Social Change and the Press). İstanbul: Bilim/Felsefe/Sanat Yayınları, 1987.

Olson, Emelie A. "Duofocal Family Structure and an Alternative Model of Husband-Wife Relationship." In *Sex Roles, Family and Community in Turkey,* pp. 33-72. Edited by Çiğdem Kağıtçıbaşı. Bloomington: Indiana University, Turkish Studies, 1982.

———. "Socioeconomic and Psycho-Cultural Contexts of Child Abuse and Neglect in Turkey." In *Child Abuse and Neglect: Cross-Cultural Perspectives,* pp. 96-119. Edited by Jill Korbin. Berkeley: University of California Press, 1981.

O'Neil, James M., Ohlde, Carroll, Tollefson, Nona, Barke, Charles, Piggott, Tonya, and Watts, Deborah. "Factors, Correlates and Problem Areas Affecting Career Decision-Making of a Cross-Sectional Sample of Students." *Journal of Counseling Psychology* 27 (1980):571-580.

Ortaylı, İlber. "Osmanlı İmparatorluğunda Amerikan Okulları Üzerine Bazı Gözlemler" (Some Observations Concerning American Schools in the Ottoman Empire). *TODAIE* 14 (September 1981):87-97.

Ovadia, Stella. "Çok İmzalı ve Çok Öznel bir Kronoloji Denemesi" (A Multi-Signature and Very Subjective Chronology Essay). *Birikim* 59 (March 1994):55- 57.

———. "Kadınların Kurtuluşu Hareketinin Zorlukları" (The Difficulties of the Women's Emancipation Movement). *İktisat* (Kasım-Aralık 1991):51-56.

Öncü, Ayşe. "Turkish Women in the Professions: Why So Many?" In *Women in Turkish Society,* pp. 180-193. Edited by Nermin Abadan-Unat. Leiden, The Netherlands: E. J. Brill, 1981.

———. "Uzman Mesleklerde Türk Kadını" (Turkish Women in Professional Occupations). In *Türk Toplumunda Kadın,* pp. 253-267. Edited by Nermin Abadan-Unat. İstanbul: Araştırma, Eğitim, Ekin Yayınları, 1979.

Özbaşar, Serra, and Aksan, Zeki. "İşletmelerimizde Beşeri Kaynakların Özellikleri ve Yönetimi" (Human Resource Characteristics and Management in Our Organizations). *Yönetim* 2 (1976):97-116.

Özbay, Ferhunde, ed., *Women, Family and Social Change in Turkey*. Bangkok: UNESCO, 1990.

——. "The Impact of Education on Women in Rural and Urban Turkey." In *Women in Turkish Society*, pp.160-180. Edited by Nermin Abadan-Unat. Leiden, The Netherlands: E. J. Brill, 1981.

Özbilgen, Füsun. *Sana Tütün ve Tesbih Yolluyorum. Semiha Berksoy'un Anıları* (I am Sending You Tobacco and Praying Beads: The Memoirs of Semiha Berksoy). İstanbul: Broy Yayınları, 1985.

Özen, Hatice. *Tarihsel Süreç İçinde Türk Gazete ve Kadın Dergileri (1868-1990)* (Turkish Newspapers and Women's Journals Within a Historical Process, 1868-1990). İstanbul: Graphis Ltd., 1994.

P. B. "Beyaz Konferans 9" (The White Conference 9). *Kadın* 9 (July 1912/1328):2-7.

——. "Beyaz Konferans 1" (The White Conference 1). *Kadın* 14 (November 1911/1327):2-7.

Paker, Banu, et al. "Bağır Herkes Duysun" (Shout, Let Everyone Hear). İstanbul: Kadın Çevresi Yayını, 1988.

Parla, Ayşe. "Anlatılar, Duvarlar ve Direniş Sesleri; Aykırı bir Mekan Olarak Mor Çatı (Narratives, Walls, and Voices of Resistance: Purple Roof as an Incongruous Site). In *Evdeki Terör* (Terror at Home), pp. 53-65. İstanbul: Mor Çatı Yayınları, 1996.

Parla, Taha. *The Social and Political Thought of Ziya Gökalp 1876-1924*. Leiden: E. J. Brill, 1985.

Pateman, Carol. "Equality, Difference, Subordination: The Politics of Motherhood and Women's Citizenship." In *Beyond Equality and Difference*, pp. 17-31. Edited by Gisela Bock and Susan James. London: Routledge, 1992.

——. *The Sexual Contract*. Cambridge: Polity Press, 1988.

Patrick, Mary Mills. *Under Five Sultans*. New York: The Century Co., 1929.

Peirce, Leslie. *The Imperial Harem: Women and Sovereignty in the Ottoman Empire*. Oxford: Oxford University Press, 1993.

Phillips, Anne. "Must Feminists Give Up on Liberal Democracy?" In *Prospects for Democracy*, pp. 93-111. Edited by David Held. Stanford, CA: Stanford University Press, 1993.

——. *Engendering Democracy*. Cambridge: Polity Press, 1991.

Phillips, Clifton Jackson. *Protestant America and the Pagan World*. Cambridge, MA: Harvard University East Asian Research Center, 1969.

Pinhas ben Nahum [pseud.]. *The Turkish Art of Love*. New York: Panurge Press, 1933.

Porter, Roy. "Mixed Feelings: The Enlightenment and Sexuality in Eighteenth-Century Britain." In *Sexuality in Eighteenth-Century Britain,* pp. 1-27. Edited by Paul-Gabriel Boucé. Manchester: Manchester University Press; Totowa, NJ: Barnes & Noble Books, 1982.

Powell, Kirsten, and Childs, Elizabeth C. *Femmes d'esprit: Women in Daumier's Caricature.* Christian A. Johnson Memorial Gallery and Middlebury College Exhibition. Hanover and London: University Press of New England, 1986.

Pratt, Mary Louise. *Imperial Eyes: Travel Writing and Transculturation.* London and New York: Routledge, 1992.

Probyn, Elspeth. "Travels in the Postmodern: Making Sense of the Local." In *Feminism/Postmodernism,* pp. 176-189. Edited by Linda J. Nicholson. New York: Routledge, 1990.

Public Instruction in the Republic of Turkey. Ankara: The Press Department of the Ministry of the Interior, 1936.

Rafaeli, Anat and Pratt, Michael G. "Tailored Meanings: On the Meaning and Impact of Organizational Dress." *Academy of Management Review* 18 (1993):32-55.

Rajan, Rajeswari Sunder. *Real and Imagined Women: Gender, Culture, and Postcolonialism.* London: Routledge, 1993.

[Ran], Nazım Hikmet. *Human Landscapes.* Translated by Randy Blasing and Mutlu Konuk. New York: Persea Books, 1982 (1941-1945).

The Report Prepared In Accordance With Article 18 of the Convention on the Elimination of All Forms of Discrimination Against Women. Turkish Republic Prime Ministry Undersecreteriat for Women's Affairs and Social Services Directorate General on the Status and Problems of Women. Ankara: Ankara University Printing House, 1994.

Ribeiro, Aileen. *Dress and Morality.* New York: Holmes and Meier Publishers, 1986.

Richter, Julius. *A History of Protestant Missions in the Near East.* n.p.:1910; reprint ed., New York: AMS Press, 1970.

Riggs, Charles T. "What the Missionaries Are Doing in Turkey." *The Missionary Review of the World* 32 (March 1909):167-180.

Riza Bey. *Darkest Orient.* London: Arco Publications Ltd., 1937.

Rodin Pucci, Suzanne. "Letters from the Harem: Veiled Figures of Writing in Montesquieu's *Lettres persanes.*" In *Writing the Female Voice: Essays on Epistolary Literature,* pp. 114-134. Edited by Elizabeth C. Goldsmith. Boston: Northeastern University Press, 1989.

Said, Edward W. *Orientalism.* New York: Vintage Books, 1979.

————. *Orientalism*. New York: Pantheon Books, 1978.

Sakaoğlu, Necdet. *Cumhuriyet Dönemi Eğitim ve Tarih*. Cep Yayınları. İstanbul: İletişim Yayınları, Nisan 1992.

Saktanber, Ayşe. "Türkiye'de Medyada Kadın: Serbest, Müsait Kadın veya İyi Eş, Fedakar Anne" (Women in the Media in Turkey: A Free, Available Woman or A Good Wife, Devoted Mother). In *Kadın Bakış Açısından 1980'ler Türkiye'sinde Kadın*, pp. 195-215. Edited by Şirin Tekeli. İstanbul: İletişim Yayınları, 1990.

Sandys, George. *A Relation of a Journey begun An. Dom. 1610: Foure Bookes. Containing a Description of the Turkish Empire, of Aegypt, of the Holy Land, of the Remote Parts of Italy, and Islands Adjoyning*. London: W. Barrett, 1621.

Sarafian, Kevork A. *History of Education in Armenia*. Los Angeles: C. C. Crawford, 1930.

Schumpeter, Joseph. *Capitalism, Socialism and Democracy*. New York: Harper and Row, 1975 (original publication in 1942).

Scott, Catherine V. *Gender and Development: Rethinking Modernization and Dependency Theory*. Boulder, CO: Lynne Rienner Publishers, 1995.

Seventy-Second Annual Report of A.B.C.F.M.. By the Board. Cambridge: Riverside Press, 1882.

Sevinç, Necdet. *Ajan Okulları* (Spy Schools). İstanbul: Oymak Yayınları, n.d.

Sharpe, Jenny. *Allegories of Empire: The Figure of Woman in the Colonial Text*. Minneapolis: University of Minnesota, 1993.

Shields, Rob. *Places on the Margin: Alternative Geographies of Modernity*. London and New York: Routledge, 1991.

SIS (State Institute of Statistics). *Household Labor Force Survey Results, April 1993*. Ankara: State Institute of Statistics, 1994.

SIS (State Institute of Statistics). *Statistical Yearbook of Turkey, 1996*. Ankara: State Institute of Statistics, February 1997.

Sıyanet (İstanbul). 4 June 1914–9 July 1914.

Sibley, David. "Outsiders in Society and Space." In *Inventing Places: Studies in Cultural Geography*, pp. 107-122. Edited by Kay Anderson and Fay Gale. Melbourne: Longman Cheshire; n.p.: Halstead Press, John Wiley & Sons, Inc., 1992:107-22.

Sirman, Nükhet. "Feminism in Turkey: A Short History." *New Perspectives on Turkey* 3:1 (Fall 1989):1-34.

Smircich, Linda. "Toward a Women Centered Organization Theory." Symposium of Women and Social Change, co-sponsored by the Women in Management and Social Issues in Management Divisions of the Academy of Management. San Diego, CA, 1985.

Sonnini [de Manoncourt], C[harles Nicholas] S[igisbert]. *Travels in Upper and Lower Egypt, Undertaken by Order of the Old Government of France.* London: J. Debrett, 1800.

Soysal, Sevgi. "The Junk Peddler" (Eskici). Translated by Nilüfer Mizanoglu Reddy. In *Twenty Stories by Turkish Women Writers,* pp. 29-37. Indiana: Indiana University Press, Turkish Studies 8, 1988.

Sönmez, Mehmet. "En Başarılı Kadın Yöneticiler" (The Most Successful Women Managers). *Ekonomik Panorama* 4:21 (June l992): l4-27.

Spivak, Gayatri C. "A Literary Representative of the Subaltern: A Women's Text from the Third World." In *In Other Worlds: Essays in Cultural Politics,* pp. 241-268. New York: Routledge, 1988.

Stallybrass, Peter and White, Allon. *The Politics and Poetics of Transgression.* London: Methuen, 1986.

Statements in Regard to Colleges in Unevangelized Lands. n.p., 1864.

The Status of Women in Turkey. The Turkish National Report to the Fourth World Conference on Women. Turkish Republic State Ministry for Women's Affairs and Social Services Directorate General on the Status and Problems of Women. Ankara: Bizim Büro, 1994.

Stern, Bernhard. *Medizin, Aberglaube und Geschlechtsleben in der Türkei: mit Berücksichtigung der moslemischen Nachbarländer und der ehemaligen Vasallenstaaten.* 2 vols. Berlin: Verlag von H. Barsdorf, 1903. Second volume published in English translation as *The Scented Garden: Anthropology of the Sex Life in the Levant.* Translated by David Berger. New York: American Ethnological Press, 1934.

Stinchcombe, Arthur. "Social Structure and Organization." In *Handbook of Organizations,* pp. l42-l93. Edited by J. March. Chicago: Rand McNally, 1965.

Stirling, Paul. "Labour Migration in Turkey: Thirty-Five Years of Changes." In *Humana: Bozkurt Güvenç'e Armağan,* pp.413-441. Edited by N. Serpil Altuntek, Suavi Aydın, and İsmail H. Demirdöven. Ankara: Kültür Bakanlığı, 1995.

———. "Growth and Changes: Speed, Scale, Complexity." In *Culture and Economy: Changes in Turkish Villages,* pp.1-16. Edited by Paul Stirling. Huntingdon: Eothen, 1993.

———. "Cause, Knowledge and Change: Turkish Village Revisited." In *Choice and Change,* pp. 191-229. Edited by J. Davis. London: Athlone Press, 1974.

———. *Turkish Village.* London: Weidenfeld and Nicolson, 1965.

————, and İncirlioğlu, Emine Onaran. "Choosing Spouses: Villagers, Migrants, Kinship and Time." In *Turkish Families in Transition*. Edited by Gabriele Rasuly-Palaczek. Vienna, Austria: Wiener Universitätsverlag, forthcoming.

Stone, Frank A. *Academies for Anatolia*. Lanham, MD: University Press of America, 1984.

————. "The American Middle West in the Ottoman Middle East: Anatolia College, Turkey, 1886-1921." *Duquesne University History Forum*. (October 1980):1-26.

Sunar, Diane G. "Female Stereotypes in the United States and Turkey." *Journal of Cross-Cultural Psychology* 13 (1982):445-460.

Şenesen, Gülay G. "Female Participation in the Turkish University Administration: Econometric and Survey Findings, 1992." *Boğaziçi Journal: Review of Social, Economic and Administrative Studies* 8 (1994):63-81.

Şeni, Nora. "19. Yüzyıl Sonunda Mizah Basınında Moda ve Kadın Kıyafetleri" (The Fashion and Women's Attire in the Humor Press at the End of the 19th Century). In *Kadın Bakış Açısından 1980'ler Türkiye'sinde Kadınlar*, pp. 43-67. Edited by Şirin Tekeli. İstanbul: İletişim Yayıncılık, 1990.

Şimdi Sığınak İçin (Now for the Shelter). İstanbul: Ayhan Basımevi, 1989.

Şükufezar (İstanbul). 1886.

Tabak, Filiz. "Women Top Managers in Different Types and Sizes of Industry in Turkey." Master's thesis, Boğaziçi University, 1989.

Tan, Mine. "Eğitimde Bedensel Ceza" (Physical Punishment in Education). *Ankara Üniversitesi Eğitim Bilimleri Fakültesi Dergisi*, 23:2 (1991):545-556.

————. "Atatürk'çü Düşünüş ve Karma Eğitim" (Atatürkist Thinking and Coeducation). In Proceedings of the International Conference on Atatürk. Paper no. 61, Vol. 3, Boğaziçi University, November 9-13, Bebek, İstanbul: Boğaziçi Üniversitesi Matbaası, 1981.

————. *Kadın: Ekonomik Yaşamı ve Eğitimi* (Woman: Her Economic Life and Education). Türkiye İş Bankası Kültür Yayınları. Ankara: TISA Matbaası, 1979.

Tannen, Deborah. *You Just Don't Understand: Women and Men in Conversation*. New York: William Morrow and Company, 1990.

Taş, Ayşe Karaduman, Dikbayır, Gülfer, Aydus, Banu, and Tokman, Bahadır. *Temel Kadın Göstergeleri, 1978-1993* (Basic Indicators About Women, 1978-1993). DIE (State Institute of Statistics), Toplumsal Yapı ve Kadın İstatistikleri Şubesi, IV.

Kadın Dünya Konferansı, Ulusal Hazırlık Komitesi Toplantısı, Ankara, 16-18 April, 1994.

Taşcıoğlu, Muhadere. *Osmanlı Cemiyetinde Kadının Sosyal Durumu ve Kadın Kıyafetleri* (Women's Social Status and Women's Attire in Ottoman Society). Ankara: Kadının Sosyal Hayatını Tetkik Kurumu Yayınları, 1958.

Taşkıran, Tezer. *Women in Turkey.* Translated by Anna G. Edmonds. İstanbul: Redhouse Yayınları, 1976.

———. *Cumhuriyetin 50. Yılında Türk Kadın Hakları* (The Rights of Turkish Women in the 50th Anniversary of the Republic). Ankara: Başbakanlık Basımevi, 1973.

Tavakoli-Targhi, Mohamad. "Women of the West Imagined: the *Farangi* Other and the Emergence of the Woman Question in Iran." In *Identity Politics and Women: Cultural Reassertions and Feminisms in International Perspective,* pp. 98-122. Edited by Valentine Moghadam. Boulder: Westview Press, 1994.

Tavernier, J.-B. [Jean-Baptiste]. *Nouvelle relation de l'intérieur du Serrail du Grand Seigneur. Contenant plusieurs singularitez qui jusqu'icy n'ont point esté mises en lumière.* Paris: Olivier de Varennes, 1675.

Tekeli, İlhan. *Toplumsal Dönüşüm ve Eğitim Tarihi Üzerine Konuşmalar* (Lectures on Social Change and the History of Education). Ankara: Mimarlar Odası Yayını, 1980.

———, İlhan and İlkin, Selim. *Osmanlı İmparatorluğunda Eğitim ve Bilgi Üretim Sisteminin Oluşumu ve Değişimi* (Foundation and Transformation of the System of Knowledge and Education Production in the Ottoman Empire). Ankara: Türk Tarih Kurumu Yayınları , 1993.

Tekeli, Şirin. "Kadın Hareketi" (The Women's Movement). *Dünden Bugüne İstanbul Ansiklopedisi* 33 (Haziran 1994b):349-354.

———. "1980'ler Türkiye'sinde Kadınlar" (Women in the Turkey of the 1980s). In *Kadın Bakış Açısından 1980'ler Türkiye'sinde Kadınlar,* pp. 7-40. Edited by Şirin Tekeli. İstanbul: İletişim, 1990b.

———. "Women in the Changing Political Associations of the 1980s." In *Turkish State, Turkish Society,* pp. 259-289. Edited by A. Finkel and N. Sirman. SOAS Centre of Near and Middle Eastern Studies, London and New York: Routledge, 1990c.

———. "80'lerde Türkiye'de Kadınların Kurtuluşu Hareketinin Gelişmesi" (The Development of the Women's Emancipation Movement in Turkey in the 1980s). *Birikim* (July 1989):34-41.

———. *Kadınlar İçin* (For Women). İstanbul: Alan Yayıncılık, 1988.

———. "The Meaning and Limits of Feminist Ideology in Turkey." In *Development of Studies on Women in Turkey*. Unpublished Report prepared by Ferhunde Özbay. Unesco and Turkish Social Science Association, 1986a.

———. "Emergence of the New Feminist Movement in Turkey." In *The New Women's Movement*, pp. 179-199. Edited by Drude Dahlerup. London: Sage Publications, 1986b.

———. *Kadınlar ve Siyasal Tomplumsal Hayat* (Women and Socio-political Life). Ankara: Birikim Yayınları, 1982.

———, ed. *Women in Modern Turkish Society*. London: Zed Books, 1994a.

———, ed. *Kadın Bakış Açısından 1980'ler Türkiye'sinde Kadın* (Women from a Woman's Perspective in the Turkey of the 1980s). İstanbul: İletişim Yayınları, 1990a.

Terakki (İstanbul). 28 June 1869–2 September 1870.

Toplum ve Bilim. 53 Special Issue [on women]. Spring 1991.

Toprak, Binnaz. "Religion and Turkish Women." In *Woman in Turkish Society*, pp. 281-292. Edited by Nermin Abadan-Unat. Leiden: E. J. Brill, 1981.

Toprak, Zafer. "1909 Cemiyetler Kanunu" (The 1909 Law of Associations). *Tanzimat'tan Chumuriyet'e Türkiye Ansiklopedisi*, vol. 1, pp. 205-208. İstanbul: İletişim Yayınları, 1985.

———. "Halk Fırkası'ndan Önce Kurulan Parti, Kadınlar Halk Fırkası" (The Party that Was Founded Before the People's Party: The People's Party of Women). *Tarih ve Toplum* (March 1988):158-159.

———. "1935 Uluslararası 'Feminizim Kongresi' ve Barış" (The 1935 International 'Congress on Feminism' and Peace). *Düşün* (March 1986):24-29.

Torki, M. A. "Achievement Motivation in College Women in an Arab Culture." *Psychological Reports* 56 (1985):267-271.

Tucker, Ruth A. *Guardians of the Great Commission*. Michigan: Academie Books, 1988.

Tunaya, Tarık Zafer. *Türkiye'de Siyasal Partiler* (Political Parties in Turkey). vol. 1. İstanbul:Hürriyet Vakfı Yayınları, 1988.

Tunçay, Mete. "Osmanlı Devleti'nde Sol Akımlar ve Partiler" (The Left Wing Currents and Parties in the Ottoman State). *Tanzimat'tan Chumuriyet'e Türkiye Ansiklopedisi*, vol.6, pp. 1445-1450. İstanbul: İletişim Yayınları, 1985.

Turban, Danial and Jones, Allen P. "Supervisor-Subordinate Similarity: Types, Effects, and Mechanisms." *Journal of Applied Psychology* 73 (1988):228-234.

Turkey: Women in Development. Country Studies Series. Washington, D.C.: World Bank, 1993.

Tutal-Küçük, Nilgün. "İdeolojik Bir Örtü: Geleneksel ve Modern Kadın İkiliği" (An Ideological Wrap: The Dichotomy of the Traditional and Modern Women). *Birikim* 59 (March 1994):58-78.

Uchard, Mario. *French and Oriental Love in a Harem.* New York: Falstaff Press, n.d. [ca. 1935].

Üsdiken, Behlül and Özmucur, Süleyman. "Genel Müdür Değişikliğinin Strateji ve Performans Üzerindeki Etkisi" (The Impact of Changing the Chief Executive on Strategy and Performance). Paper presented at the Conference on Turkish Management, Kuşadası, İzmir, 1994.

Üşür, Serpil. "Radikal İslamcı İdeoloji ve Kadının Kimliği Sorunu" (The Radical Islamist Ideology and the Problem of Women's Identity). *Onbirinci Tez* 9 (1989):82-87.

Van Den Abbeele, Georges. *Travel as Metaphor: From Montaigne to Rousseau.* Minneapolis and Oxford: University of Minnesota Press, 1992.

Velidedeoğlu, Hıfzı V. *Türk Medeni Kanunu* (The Turkish Civil Law). Ankara: Türk Dil Kurumu, 1970.

Voilquin, Suzanne. *Souvenirs d'une fille du peuple; ou la Saint-Simonienne en Egypte.* Paris: François Maspero, 1978.

Welter, Barbara. "She Hath Done What She Could: Protestant Women's Missionary Careers in Nineteenth-Century America." *American Quarterly* 30 (Winter 1978):624-638.

White, Jenny B. *Money Makes Us Relatives: Women's Labor in Urban Turkey.* Austin, TX: University of Texas Press, 1994.

Whitely, Williams, Dougherty, Thomas W., and Dreher, George F. "Relationship of Career Mentoring and Socio Economic Origin to Managers' and Professionals' Early Career Progress." *Academy of Management Journal* 34 (1991):331-351.

Wiersma, Uco J. "A Taxonomy of Behavioral Strategies for Coping with Work-Home Role Conflict." *Human Relations* 47 (1994):211-221.

Wintle, W. J. *Florance Nightingale and Frances E. Willard.* London: 1923.

Yaraman-Başbuğu, Ayşegül. *Elinin Hamuruyla Özgürlük* (Freedom with Her Apron). İstanbul, Milliyet Yayınları, 1992.

Yeğenoğlu, Meyda. "Supplementing the Orientalist Lack: European Ladies in the Harem." *Inscriptions* 6 (1992):45-80.

Yenigün, Candan. *Feminist Themes After 1980 in Turkey: A Study of Two Magazines.* Master's thesis, Boğaziçi University, 1989.

Yörükoğlu, Atalay. "Türkiye'de Kadının Kimliği" (Women's Identity in Turkey). *Bülten* 11 (April 1992):35-36.

Yücel, Hasan Ali. *Türkiye'de Orta Öğretim* (Secondary Education in Turkey). İstanbul: Devlet Basımevi, 1938.

Yuval-Davis, N. and Anthias, F., eds. *Woman-Nation-State,* London: Macmillan, 1989.

Zeytinoğlu, Işık Urla. "Employment of Women and Labour Laws in Turkey" *Comparative Labor Law Journal* 15:2 (Winter 1994):177-205.

Zihnioğlu, Yaprak. "Mor Çatı Kadın Sığınağı Vakfı: Aile İçi Şiddete Karşı Bir Merkez" (The Purple Roof Women's Shelter Foundation: A Center Against Domestic Violence). *Kadın Eserleri Kütüphanesi ve Bilgi Merkezi Haberler* 6 (January 1993):4.

Contributors

Yeşim Arat is Professor at the Department of Political Science and International Relations at Boğaziçi University, in İstanbul, and currently serving as the department head. Her main area of research is women in politics, and her publications include *Patriarchal Paradox: Women Politicians in Turkey* (Fairleigh Dickinson University Press, 1989). She is currently working on contemporary feminist activism in Turkey.

Zehra Arat is Professor of Political Science and the Coordinator of the Women's Studies Program at Purchase College of the State University of New York. In addition to *Democracy and Human Rights in Developing Countries* (Lynne Rienner, 1991), her writings include journal and book articles on democracy, human rights, women's rights, and women in development. Currently she is working on a manuscript on "The Role of the Bourgeoisie in the Making of European Democracies."

K. Pelin Başcı is Assistant Professor of Turkish Studies at Portland State University. She was a Fulbright scholar in American Studies at the University of Texas-Austin where she completed her doctoral studies. Her publications include research articles, literary criticisms, book reviews, as well as translations for Turkish journals.

Carel Bertram is an architectural historian completing her doctoral studies in Art History at the University of California at Los Angeles. Her dissertation traces the pictorial and literary images of the Ottoman Turkish house in İstanbul, Amasya, and Sarajevo and includes an investigation of the uses of literary narrative as a source in Art History. Her publications include articles on the uses of urban space in Ottoman and formerly Ottoman lands as well as in other areas of the Islamic world.

Palmira Brummett is Associate Professor of History at the University of Tennessee and a member of the sisterhood of Bunting Institute Fellows. She is the author of *Ottoman Seapower and Levantine Diplomacy in the Age of Discovery* (SUNY Press, 1994). She is currently working on *Image and Imperialism in the Ottoman Revolutionary Press,* a study of Ottoman revolutionary satire and the critique of imperialism.

Aynur Demirdirek has been teaching Turkish language and literature at a secondary school in Ankara. Her study on the Ottoman women's movement was published as *Osmanlı Kadınlarının Hayat Hakkı Arayışının Bir Hikayesi* (İmge Kitabevi Yayınları, 1993). More recently, she participated in the compilation of *Kadın Dergileri Bibliografyasi,* a project sponsored by the Women's Library and Information Center in İstanbul. Her current research focuses on the women's movements during the "years of truce" and the early Republican era.

Ayşe Durakbaşa is Assistant Professor of Sociology at Mimar Sinan University in İstanbul. Interested in interdisciplinary work, she undertakes research on feminist cultural studies. Her publications include articles on Halide Edib Adıvar and Turkish female identity in the early Republican era.

K. E. Fleming is Lecturer at the History Department of the University of California, Los Angeles. Her research interests include the Balkans, Modern Greece, the emergence of modern Turkey, and the nature and role of ethnic and religious pluralism in the Ottoman Empire. She is the author of a forthcoming book on the late eighteenth-century Ottoman governor Ali Pasha of Ioannina (Princeton University Press).

Aynur İlyasoğlu is Lecturer in Sociology at the Department of Economics at Marmara University in İstanbul. In addition to her book *Örtülü Kimlik* (Metis, 1994), she authored several articles on women, Islam, women's history, and sociology in Turkey. Currently she participates in a team project at the Women's Library and Information Center, in İstanbul, where she also works on the "Women's Oral History Project" that involves the development of an audio-visual oral history archive of the experiences of the first generation of Republican women.

Emine Onaran İncirlioğlu is Visiting Assistant Professor of Architecture and Anthropology at the Department of Landscape Architecture and Urban Design at Bilkent University in Ankara. She writes on various topics in urban anthropology, urban sociology, sociological problems of economic development, and village life and gender relations in Turkey.

Hayat Kabasakal is Professor of Management at the Management Department at Boğaziçi University. Interested in the study of organizational culture, women in management, and gender equality in management, she authored numerous articles and contributed to several co-authored publications in those areas.

Arzu Öztürkmen is Assistant Professor of History and Folklore at Boğaziçi University in İstanbul. She received her Ph.D. in Folklore and Folklife from the University of Pennsylvania and published articles on Turkish folklore and history, national day celebration, and dance history. In addition to participating in the "Women's Oral History Pilot Project" sponsored by the Women's Library and Information Center, she conducts her own oral history research on Black Sea Women.

İrvin Cemil Schick received his Ph.D. in Applied Mathematics from the Massachusetts Institute of Technology. He currently teaches at Harvard University, in addition to working in the computer communication industry. He is the co-editor of *Turkey in Transition: New Perspectives* (Oxford University Press, 1987) and the author of *The Erotic Margin: Sexuality and Spatiality in Alteritist Discourse* (forthcoming).

Işık Urla Zeytinoğlu is Professor of Industrial Relations at the MGD School of Business and an advisor for the Women's Studies Programme at McMaster University. She is the principle investigator of the McMaster Research Center for the Promotion of Women's Health. She is the author of articles on various topics that include women and paid/unpaid work, women's health, part-time and other non-standard workers, and international labor standards.